PARTIES AND

'ERSITY OF
'ESTER

Don't Believe The Lies!

God is not angry with you, He loves you more than you know. In this book, Pat Schatzline introduces you to a God who accepts you, transforms you, and gives you a future filled with abundant blessing and opportunity.

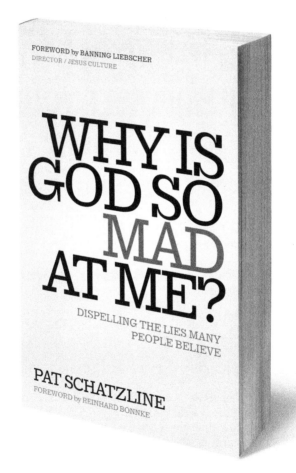

FOREWORD by BANNING LIEBSCHER
DIRECTOR / JESUS CULTURE

WHY IS GOD SO MAD AT ME?

DISPELLING THE LIES MANY PEOPLE BELIEVE

PAT SCHATZLINE
FOREWORD by REINHARD BONNKE

Order today!
Available at local bookstores, online, and in e-book
www.charismahouse.com   www.facebook.com/charismahouse

CHARISMA
HOUSE
12289

Parties and People

England 1914–1951

ROSS MCKIBBIN

The Ford Lectures delivered in the
University of Oxford in Hilary Term 2008

OXFORD

UNIVERSITY PRESS

OXFORD

UNIVERSITY PRESS

Great Clarendon Street, Oxford OX2 6DP

Oxford University Press is a department of the University of Oxford.
It furthers the University's objective of excellence in research, scholarship,
and education by publishing worldwide in

Oxford New York

Auckland Cape Town Dar es Salaam Hong Kong Karachi
Kuala Lumpur Madrid Melbourne Mexico City Nairobi
New Delhi Shanghai Taipei Toronto

With offices in

Argentina Austria Brazil Chile Czech Republic France Greece
Guatemala Hungary Italy Japan Poland Portugal Singapore
South Korea Switzerland Thailand Turkey Ukraine Vietnam

Oxford is a registered trade mark of Oxford University Press
in the UK and in certain other countries

Published in the United States
by Oxford University Press Inc., New York

© Ross McKibbin 2010

The moral rights of the author have been asserted
Database right Oxford University Press (maker)

First published 2010
First published in paperback 2011

British Library Cataloguing in Publication Data

Data available

Library of Congress Control Number: 2009942565

Typeset by Laserwords Private Limited, Chennai, India
Printed in Great Britain
on acid-free paper by
MPG Biddles Ltd., King's Lynn, Norfolk

ISBN 978–0–19–958469–7 (Hbk.)
ISBN 978–0–19–960517–0 (Pbk.)

2 4 6 8 10 9 7 5 3 1

Preface

This book has a somewhat complicated history. It is the published version of the Ford Lectures in British History which I gave in the University of Oxford in 2008. The lectures themselves arose from my book *Classes and Cultures: England 1918–1951* (1998) which was originally commissioned by the Oxford University Press as a volume in the *New Oxford History of England*. In this instance the author exercised insufficient discipline and the volume got out of hand. As a result I suggested to the Oxford Press that the single volume become two—one primarily social and the other primarily political. The Press understandably rejected this suggestion but generously agreed to publish the predominantly social volume as *Classes and Cultures*. It was, however, not entirely 'social'. A significant part of the book, particularly the chapters on the social classes, was in the broadest sense 'political'. That was deliberate; without it the book lacked a conceptual spine. But there was undoubtedly an awkward element in this. When I was asked to give the Ford Lectures I decided to deliver them as the unwritten second volume. As a result, there is inevitably some overlap between *Parties and People* and *Classes and Cultures*, especially in the second chapter. Where this occurs I have noted it in the footnotes. But even where there is overlap the argument is not necessarily the same. The explanation, for instance, I gave in *Classes and Cultures* for the radicalization of opinion during the Second World War, a fairly conventional one, missed the only explanation that can be drawn from the evidence. The treatment of the Second World War here differs both in argument and length from its treatment of *Classes and Cultures*. This book also 'begins' earlier. I thought it necessary to have a chapter on the nature of the Edwardian political system and the effect of the First World War on it. Otherwise what happens after 1918 makes little sense.

Parties and People is a study of England. It comes from what was to be a history of England, but that is not the only reason why it is confined to England. It concentrates on England not from any insensitivity to the plurality of the United Kingdom, nor simply because England's size made its political system the most important in that idiosyncratic Kingdom, but because in this period English politics were to a quite unusual degree in step with the politics of Scotland, and Wales, if not so in step with Northern Ireland. It is also a study of the political culture of a democratic society. After 1918, nearly everyone thought of England as a democracy and almost all were agreed that a parliamentary system based upon a wide (and after 1928 universal) franchise, together with free and apparently class-neutral political and judicial institutions, was both democratic and desirable. Even in the darkest days of war and depression few thought that this system could or should be undermined. There was, however, less agreement as to whether democracy meant more than this. How far, for example, was it to be 'social'? How far was the state to be an instrument of democratization? How far were the political parties themselves to be democratic, to be 'open' rather than 'closed' institutions? How far should they encourage democratic behaviour among the electorate? And how far was there to be a democratic relationship between the electorate and political and social elites? To what extent, in other words, did the electorate make up its own mind on politics or allow others to do it for them? What kind of democracy did emerge and what other forms might have done so? As well as being a study of England's political culture this is, therefore, a history of the sociology of the English electorate in this period and the forces that shaped its political opinion and behaviour. These are questions not unique to this book. David Marquand has recently tried to answer them in *Britain Since 1918* (2008), but the treatment of them here is significantly, indeed almost completely different, both as to method and answer.

The second theme of the book is what we might call structure and contingency. There was in this period a party-political transformation which happened in three stages. The first was the disappearance of the Liberal Party as England's major 'progressive' party after the First World War and the simultaneous emergence of Labour in that role. The second occurred in 1931 when the failure and then collapse of the 1929 Labour government made possible a huge regrouping of the 'anti-socialist' electorate in a 'National' government Conservative in almost all but name. The third was the unexpected overthrow in 1940 of the Conservative predominance established in 1931—something formally recognized by the voters in 1945 when Labour won its first outright victory. How we explain this transformation largely depends on what kind of balance we draw between 'structure', what seems likely given underlying social and economic evolution, and 'contingency', those unpredicted and unpredictable historical accidents that can still have profound consequences: one of which was to determine not only the fate of the parties themselves but the type of democracy England was to be. If, for example, the Liberal Party had survived or the political–military crisis of 1940 had not undone Conservative predominance, England could easily have developed different constitutional forms and a different kind of democracy.

There were six lectures in the series and each lecture has become a chapter in this book. Although each chapter is longer than its original, the structure of the lectures has been preserved. The first chapter I have described. The second chapter has two main foci: the reasons for the failure of Lloyd George's coalition to transform itself into an anti-socialist party embracing all anti-Labour forces, which seemed within the logic of English politics at the end of the war; and the inability of the political system to adjust to post-war social change. The third chapter considers the apparent failure of the second Labour government (1929–31), why that happened and why the 1931 crisis re-founded a stable political system based upon a moderate constitutional Conservatism whose electoral hegemony seemed permanent. That hegemony did come to an end, however, and the fourth chapter considers what part the Second World War played in this. The fifth chapter is concerned primarily with the policies of the Attlee government, their ideological origins, their results and the way the electorate (and the Conservative Party) did or did not react to them. The sixth chapter sums up the argument of the whole book: the development of class as the principal (but by no means perfect) determinant of political behaviour, the relation of 'events' to structures, and the emergence of a hybrid democracy, neither individualist nor social, whose institutions and values were allowed to survive more for the stability they promised than for the democracy they promoted.

This is not a text book. It does not pretend to be a political history of England, 1914–51. It is, rather, an interpretation of what happened; an argument within which England's political history as a whole can be contained.

Note on usage: For much of this period the Conservative Party was known as the Unionist Party—that is the party of the Union of Great Britain and Ireland—or officially as the Conservative and Unionist Party. Usage was informal and formal, however, and both names 'Conservative' and 'Unionist' tended to be interchangeable. The word Unionist was widely used in the interwar period. In the 1935 election, for instance, Tories stood as Unionists, but in 1945 they stood as Conservatives. This can be confusing and I have therefore adopted the word Conservative throughout unless the name Unionist was technically necessary.

Acknowledgements

Many people, in one way or another, have contributed to this book, particularly my colleagues in the Oxford history faculty, and I must thank them. I should also thank by name Joanna Innes, Nick Owen, and John Welshman, who were especially helpful in the rewriting of the Lectures and, at the Oxford University Press, Rupert Cousens, Seth Cayley, and Christopher Wheeler. Above all, I should thank Martin Ceadel, Janet Howarth, and the Oxford University Press's anonymous readers whose meticulous, scholarly, and pointed comments significantly delayed the book's completion.

There is one other person, the late Colin Matthew, who had, both directly and indirectly, much influence on the development of *Parties and People* but who never heard the Lectures or read the book, and it is to his memory that it is dedicated.

Contents

1

Edwardian Equipoise and the First World War

Those English who reached adulthood before 1914 and were still alive in 1945, of whom there were very many, saw a party-political transformation possibly unique in modern English history: namely, the effective destruction of the Liberal Party as one of England's two governing parties, and with it the marginalization of an important element of the country's political elite. Unless they threw in their lot with the Conservative or Labour Parties, or were world-historical figures like J. M. Keynes, the younger members of that elite, like the Mastermans or the Pringles, or even younger ones like the junior Asquiths, who in 1914 could have expected to remain part of a governing class, never governed again. Furthermore, many of those marginalized were representatives of a form of social Liberalism which could claim to have dominated Edwardian politics both intellectually and politically. In 1914 few would have predicted this outcome and there is little agreement among historians as to why it happened. Nor how it happened; how far, especially, it was the result of the First World War. We could argue that it was bound to happen and that the war merely accelerated an inevitable development. Or that the political system was stable in 1914 but buckled under the remorseless pressure of war. I once argued the first proposition[1] but now think that it inadequately represents the reality of Edwardian politics. I no longer see the Edwardian system as already disintegrating. Rather,

---

[1] In R. McKibbin, *The Evolution of the Labour Party* (Oxford, 1975).

I would see it as based upon an equipoise in balance in 1914 but one delicate enough for it to be severely unbalanced by events which began with the outbreak of the First World War.

If the Edwardian system was not disintegrating in 1914 on what then was its stability based? Edwardian politics were dominated by a 'progressive alliance', a radical grouping which combined the Liberal Party, the Labour Party, and, from time to time, the Irish Nationalists. It was led by the Liberal Party and sustained the Liberals in office even after they had lost their independent parliamentary majority in the January 1910 elections. It was ideologically grounded on free trade, free collective bargaining, an active social policy and constitutional reform. Even though the Liberal Party's attack on the House of Lords and its renewed attempt at Irish Home Rule after 1910 were rather forced on it, the Lords and Home Rule as issues held the alliance together when it might have frayed, and both were supported by a majority of the electorate. Furthermore, the electorate was so structured as to be democratic enough to give working men and their institutions significant political influence but not yet so democratic, despite some fears,[2] as to excite the kind of hostility to the working class which was characteristic of the 1920s. Nor were the Tories plausibly able to present themselves as the party of the constitution or sound finance (as they did in the 1920s) given their behaviour over Irish Home Rule and the House of Lords between 1911 and 1914 and their official or unofficial commitment to the heterodoxy of tariff reform. Finally, the Liberal Party was animated by a still viable nonconformist culture which united elements of the progressive middle class with many of the leaders of the labour movement. In 1914, as a result, this progressive free-trade political system was not immediately threatened and few were confident enough to predict its likely demise. Nonetheless, its equipoise was very finely balanced. In observing it the historian has an unavoidable sense of impermanence.

[2] See below, 8–9.

There are, broadly speaking, two reasons for this.[3] The dynamic of Edwardian politics, as I have suggested, was provided by that tacit alliance of the Liberal and Labour Parties which upheld the Liberal governments throughout the crises of Edwardian politics. While it was, however, by far the senior partner in this alliance the Liberal Party, after its great victory in 1906,[4] could neither win an election nor govern on its own. It could govern only with the support of the Labour Party and the Irish Nationalists. Were the Southern Irish to withdraw from the House of Commons, as they eventually did, that left only the Labour Party. But the alliance between the Liberal and Labour Parties was based not upon a long-term programmatic affinity but fundamentally on what proved to be the unfinished business of nineteenth-century politics. The Liberal Party's revival after 1900 and its electoral victories in 1906 and 1910 were not primarily due to new forms of social politics but to the re-emergence of issues which most people thought had been settled. What drove the Liberal and Labour Parties together

[3] There is now a very large literature on Edwardian politics. On the Liberal Party and Liberalism see P. F. Clarke, *Lancashire and the New Liberalism* (Cambridge, 1971), H. V. Emy, *Liberals, Radicals and Social Politics, 1892–1914* (London, 1973), G. Bernstein, *Liberalism and Liberal Politics in Edwardian England* (Boston and London, 1986), M. Freeden, *The New Liberalism: An Ideology of Social Reform* (Oxford, 1978), B. K. Murray, *The People's Budget, 1909–1910* (Oxford, 1980), P. Weiler, *The New Liberalism: Liberal Social Theory in Great Britain* (London, 1982); on the Conservative Party: A. Sykes, *Tariff Reform in British Politics* (Oxford, 1979), E. H. H. Green, *The Crisis of Conservatism 1880–1914* (Cambridge, 1995), J. Ramsden, *The Age of Balfour and Baldwin 1902–1940* (London and New York, 1978), G. Phillips, *The Diehards* (London, 1979), N. Blewett, *The Peers, the Parties and the People* (London, 1972); on Labour: K. D. Brown (ed.), *The First Labour Party 1906–1914* (London, 1985), D. Tanner, *Political Change and the Labour Party 1900–1918* (Cambridge, 1990), P. Thompson, *Socialists, Liberals and Labour: The Struggle for London, 1885–1914* (London and Toronto, 1967), D. Marquand, *Ramsay MacDonald* (London, 1977), H. Pelling, *Popular Politics and Society in Late Victorian England* (London, 1968); on the welfare state: B. B. Gilbert, *The Evolution of National Insurance in Great Britain: The Origins of the Welfare State* (London, 1966), D. Fraser, *The Evolution of the Welfare State* (London, 1984 edn), J. Harris, *Unemployment and Politics: A Study in English Social Policy 1886–1914* (Oxford, 1972).

[4] The Liberals won a majority of 129 over all other parties. They never won an independent majority again.

after 1900 was an unexpected attack on the basic foundations of late-nineteenth-century politics: free trade and the neutrality of the law within industrial relations. In the 1860s and 1870s most believed these were ideological fixtures: things that could not and should not be questioned. The stability of the state was thought to be anchored to them. Labour's relationship with the Liberal Party in this period (as we shall see) was by no means consistently antagonistic, which was to complicate life for both of them, but the tendency in the late nineteenth century was for them to drift apart—largely because both assumed that those basic foundations of late-nineteenth-century politics were no longer seriously in contention. It was, in other words, safe to drift apart. That the Conservative Party should abandon its adherence to free trade and that the courts, in a series of rulings culminating in the Taff Vale Judgement, should overthrow an industrial relations regime which had been put in place by general agreement therefore upset the political calculations of those in the labour movement who looked to 'independent' labour politics. The Labour Party's determination to defend free trade and the Liberal Party's willingness to repeal the Taff Vale Judgement by legislation forced the two together; and the evolution of Edwardian politics kept them together. Furthermore, that unfinished business of nineteenth-century politics—particularly the status of Ireland and the constitutional position of the House of Lords—were all issues about which the Labour Party felt as one with the Liberals. Equally, the social programme of the Liberal government—though incomplete from Labour's point of view—was better than nothing and difficult to oppose simply because it was incomplete.

Nonetheless, had the Conservative Party not decided to oppose the Liberal government *à outrance*—education, the 1909 budget, Ireland, the constitution and all—the progressive alliance might have collapsed sooner than it did, since what held it together did not constitute a common progressive programme for the long-haul. Even more, had Balfour's Conservative government itself decided to overturn the Taff Vale decision by legislation the progressive alliance might never have happened at all.[5] By 1918, as unifying issues all of them, even the New Liberal social programme, had disappeared or been superseded.

A second source of impermanence was the sociology of the Edwardian electorate. It also was delicately poised: in this case, between religion and class, whose boundaries moved unpredictably. Although it was not the only variable, so far as we can tell religion probably determined the way enfranchised Edwardians voted more than anything else.[6] As Barry Doyle has argued of Edwardian Norwich, the 'most complex and enduring influence' on political preference was religion.[7] Anglicans were Conservatives and nonconformists Liberals; which is how contemporaries understood it. Both major political parties had strong religious ties which they openly exploited and for which they were prepared to take great risks. The Conservatives, for example, carried the 1902 Education Act in the knowledge that it would outrage nonconformist opinion with almost certainly dire electoral consequences.[8] For their part, under strong nonconformist pressure, the Liberals persisted with pub-licensing legislation though they knew it to be unpopular and that in part it had already cost them at least one general election (1895).[9] The young Labour Party,

[5] That this was a possibility was widely canvassed in the Conservative Party, and the failure to do so was regretted by some Conservatives, including Stanley Baldwin. Given the reluctance of many unions to become involved in the Labour Representation Committee before the Taff Vale decision drove them to affiliate with it, the decision of the Balfour government to leave the Judgement in place was a godsend for the Liberals. For the politics of the Taff Vale Judgement see H. Clegg, A. Fox, and A. F. Thompson, *A History of British Trade Unions since 1889* (Oxford, 1964), I, 313–25.

[6] For the best exposition of this view, see K. D. Wald, *Crosses on the Ballot: Patterns of British Voter Alignment since 1885* (Princeton, 1983).

[7] Barry M. Doyle, 'Urban Liberalism and the "Lost Generation": Politics and Middle Class Culture in Norwich, 1900–1935', *Historical Journal* 38, 3 (Sept. 1995), 626.

[8] For the details and evolution of the 1902 Act, see S. J. Curtis, *History of Education in Great Britain* (London, 1968), 312–21. For the Anglican character of the Conservative Party in parliament, see J. Ramsden, *The Age of Balfour and Baldwin, 1902–1940* (London and New York, 1978), 99–100. Ramsden notes that at least 90 per cent of Conservative MPs were Anglican and that many were politically active defenders of the Church of England.

[9] For this, see H. Pelling, *Social Geography of British Elections, 1885–1910* (London and New York, 1967), 18. See also A. L. Lowell's contemporary comments: 'The

however, was more secular. Secular not in belief—it was neither anti-clerical nor unbelieving, a number of its leaders were well known for their religious activities, and many of its adherents saw socialism as a kind of practical Christianity—but increasingly secular in its organizational and social roots. Its local networks, especially the trade unions, were neither formally nor even informally tied to specific religious institutions and slowly this detachment from religion grew wider. The Party also became increasingly reluctant to become involved in 'political' religion (like temperance) because there was no agreement within the Party as to what political religion should be. In this sense, it is as much a secular as a socialist party that Labour should be understood. The survival of the Edwardian political system, therefore, to a considerable extent depended on how long religion continued to shape political allegiances.

It also depended on the structure of the Edwardian electorate. The degree to which it was limited was and is widely known. About 40 per cent of the male population at any one time was unenfranchised while 100 per cent of the female population was always unenfranchised.[10] There were many who wished that the life of this electorate could be perpetuated but virtually all knew it could not. The electoral system established in 1884, by the so-called Third Reform Act, had a reasonably long life but was undermined, one the one hand, by the pressure for women's suffrage in some form, which no longer could be waved away even by those who opposed it, and, on the other, by the conflict between an increasingly democratic conception of politics and the reality of a highly undemocratic electorate. There was, however, little agreement as to who should be included in a reformed electorate. Some wanted only universal manhood suffrage; some only manhood suffrage with a limited enfranchisement for women; some only limited franchise for both men and women; and

Conservatives tend strongly to favour the claims of the Church of England, of the landowners and now of the publicans, while the Liberals are highly sensitive to the appeals of the Nonconformist conscience'. (*The Government of England* (New York, 1910), II, 120.)

[10] Though many women had the vote in local elections.

some—the Labour Party's position—wanted the 'adult' suffrage: full enfranchisement of men and women on an equal basis. Which of these was preferred was usually decided by a combination of political principle and political calculation (though not always a well-informed calculation). Much was to hang (as we shall see) on the outcome of this debate.

The Edwardian political system was thus in many ways highly provisional and all three English parties found themselves in territory over which they had only loose control.[11] Of the three, the Liberals probably had the most fragile social base. Historically, the Liberal Party was an alliance of a nonconformist and disproportionately middle-class social network and a working-class network which had a nonconformist presence. Nonconformity was the common element. But the process of political secularization, the waning influence of political religion, however slow or fast, was remorselessly rendering this alliance increasingly anomalous, something of which many Liberals were aware. In these circumstances there were two strategies open to them. One was simply to widen the electorate by its extension either to unenfranchised men or to both unenfranchised men and to women (all or some). The House of Commons had already voted in favour of women's enfranchisement as early as 1897 (a private member's bill) and was to do so again in 1911. In 1912 the Liberals introduced a bill which they thought would probably be in their interest: it would have enfranchised the majority of men hitherto excluded (largely by altering the registration rules) and gave the House of Commons the opportunity to insert a clause extending the vote to women if it wished. This bill was killed in January 1913 by the 'speaker's bombshell': a 'dubious and politically slanted ruling' that a women's franchise clause could not be 'tacked on' to the bill, which was then withdrawn by the government.[12] There has been much debate among historians as to the possible consequences

---

[11] This is to exclude the Irish Nationalists, though they did actually hold one English seat: T. P. O'Connor's constituency of Liverpool Scotland.

[12] For the details of this imbroglio see M. Pugh, *Electoral Reform in War and Peace 1906–18* (London, 1978), 40–3.

of a mass franchise to the Edwardian political system.[13] What one concludes of this debate is probably as much dependent on historical guess-work and intuition as anything else. My own intuition is that the enfranchisement of four million younger men—and the old system unquestionably discriminated strongly against younger working-class men[14]—and twelve million women would almost certainly benefit the Conservative and Labour Parties but would be of less certain benefit to the Liberals. Nor was the Liberal Party much disadvantaged by the existing Edwardian electorate; the abolition of the plural vote would probably have satisfied it. A redistribution of constituencies, however, would not necessarily have favoured it, even though a redistribution was long overdue: a result of the inherent electoral strength of the Conservatives.[15]

The Liberals did consider some reforms of the voting system, and, given the problems it had with the Labour Party after 1906 (especially 'three-cornered contests'),[16] there was a case for this. But proportional representation had little support. It was thought the realm of the cranks and faddists of whom (it was believed) the Liberals already had too many. The alternative vote was a more serious possibility. This, so long as the Liberal and Labour Parties agreed to exchange preferences, could have rescued the Liberals from the morass of three-cornered contests and increasingly difficult negotiations with Labour. But it would have eliminated one of the most effective restraints on Labour's growth: the threat that Labour candidatures would simply despatch seats to the Tories. Furthermore, the Liberals felt reasonably confident that they had contained Labour by 1914; that the threat of three-cornered contests had now been minimized. A system which 'squeezed' rather than accommodated

[13] For the literature, see R. McKibbin, *The Ideologies of Class: Social Relations in Britain, 1880–1950* (Oxford, 1990), 66–7 n.

[14] This now seems to have been established beyond reasonable doubt. See M. Childs, 'Labour Grows Up: the Electoral System, Political Generations and British Politics, 1890–1920', *Twentieth Century British History* 2, 6 (1995), 126–31.

[15] See below, 14.

[16] These occurred in constituencies where the intervention of Labour candidates was responsible for the defeat of the Liberals—often in apparently safe Liberal seats. The reverse was rarer and Labour intervention did not often damage the Conservatives.

the Labour vote, they had concluded, was thus in their interest:[17] a conclusion which probably did suit their short-term interests but which they later deeply regretted.

The second strategy open to the Liberals was to widen their electoral base not by widening the electorate but by mobilizing a larger proportion of the existing electorate via an essentially secular social programme. In that mixture of policies usually called the New Liberalism the Liberals could claim to have such a strategy. Although New Liberalism was probably more ambitious in theory than in practice, it was intellectually coherent and certainly competitive with its rivals' intellectual systems—for example, the Labour Party's socialism or the protectionist-imperialism which was the nearest thing to a formal intellectual system the Conservative Party possessed. And as legislation—especially after the 1909 budget pointed the government in a new political direction—it had the effect of giving the Liberals the initiative. The other parties had to run hard to keep up. It also tied Labour to the Liberals in an area, social policy, where, other things being equal, conflict between the two was most likely. But its success as an electoral strategy was not inevitable. To begin, there was an unresolved confusion at its heart. It was designed to appeal to the industrial working class (and, after 1911, to the agricultural working class) *and* to be classless. The point of New Liberalism, after all, was to prevent politics being determined by class allegiance. But it also had an explicit and implicit redistributionary aim which was not class-neutral. Furthermore, it was unclear where the middle class fitted into all this. We tend to think that the success of New Liberalism depended on the extent to which it won working-class support; the extent to which, in other words, it held off the Labour Party. We might equally argue, however, that its success depended upon the degree to which it converted the middle classes. C. F. G. Masterman, Liberal MP and cabinet minister (intermittently)[18] and one of the most influential popularizers of

---

[17] Pugh, *Electoral Reform*, 16–17.
[18] Masterman, it is worth noting, was a conspicuous victim of the voting system. As a minister he was defeated (in Bethnal Green) by the intervention of an independent

New Liberalism, certainly thought so. In his widely read book *The Condition of England* (1909) Masterman argued that progressive politics in England were blighted by a middle class which, for all its virtues, drew its values from a moneyed upper class and a plutocratic press.[19] Its willingness to ape the aristocracy or 'Society' was reinforced, he argued, by an increasingly heartfelt dislike of the working classes and their politics. The victory of the Moderates (very much a ratepayers' anti-socialist party) at the 1907 London County Council elections symbolized the absorption of the middle class into a social order dominated by the Conservative Party. Until the middle class, whose expertise was crucial to both state and empire, developed its own self-confident and democratic culture, social solidarity and with it a successful progressive politics would founder. Masterman, certainly, might well have overargued his case. *The Condition of England* was written just before the Liberal government got its second wind,[20] and the heavily financial-commercial middle class he was describing in London was not representative of the English middle class as a whole. Nevertheless, it is clear what he meant, and much of what he meant was true. The political culture of the Conservative Party and anti-socialism (as we shall see) was extraordinarily resilient and, as an active political nonconformity decayed, actually strengthened its hold on the middle class.[21]

Also electorally problematic was the highly selective character of the government's social policies. Under the Old Age Pensions Act (1908) only a small proportion of the population was likely to reach pensionable age (seventy) and of these, the majority (women) did not have the vote. National Insurance was more inclusive but still excluded the majority of the population. Furthermore, the compulsory deduction of a National Insurance contribution from

---

socialist, Jack Scurr, who was opposed to the contributory clauses of the National Insurance legislation. Scurr did not poll well but enough to rob Masterman of victory. Had the alternative vote operated Masterman would almost certainly have been elected.

[19] C. F. G. Masterman, *The Condition of England* (London, 1909), 79–82.

[20] The book was published, indeed, almost simultaneously with the delivery of the 1909 budget.

[21] See below, 91–2.

workers' wages was, at least initially, very unpopular with parts of the working class. Because no one was obliged to use them the labour exchanges, a centrepiece of the government's employment policies, played little part in working-class life. Most people found their jobs in the old way. How electorally successful the 'land campaign' would have been we do not know.

By linking agricultural wages—and possibly industrial wages—into a major programme of housing and development Lloyd George had unquestionably conceived an ambitious way of sustaining a radical Liberalism.[22] There is some evidence that the rural campaign was having an effect and it undoubtedly worried the Conservatives. But the evidence is nonetheless thin and the inadequately prepared urban campaign almost died at birth.[23] Had the First World War and its consequences not seriously undermined a radical land politics directed at the landlord and agricultural and urban poverty[24] the land campaigns could, of course, have served as a vehicle for a renewed Liberalism, but a scepticism about their chances is advisable. Furthermore, the policies themselves were insufficiently controversial to be of long-term political utility. The Conservatives in principle supported the government's social policies, and though they conducted an opportunist campaign against the National Insurance Act,[25] they prudently made plain they would leave it in place. There was thus probably little fear in the electorate that social legislation would be repealed if the Conservatives returned to office. Lloyd George hoped (and expected) that the land campaign would be profoundly divisive,

[22] For the land campaign, see I. Packer, *Lloyd George, Liberalism and the Land: the Land Issue and Party Politics in England, 1906–1914* (Royal Historical Society, Woodbridge, 2001); A. Offer, *Property and Politics 1870–1914* (Cambridge, 1981), 363–400.

[23] For the evidence, see Packer, *Lloyd George, Liberalism and the Land Issue*, 132–41. Packer argues that the positive effect of the rural campaign together with the abolition of plural voting meant that the Liberals could 'look forward to gains rather than losses in the English rural seats' (137). But such a conclusion is dependent upon the result of one by-election (Wycombe in February 1914) and on the efficacy of legislation on plural voting which was never in fact enacted.

[24] See below, 24.

[25] For this campaign, see Bentley B. Gilbert, *The Evolution of National Insurance in Great Britain* (London, 1973), 371–3, 394–9.

but whether it would have been we have, as I have suggested, no way of knowing.[26] Evident after the First World War was the absence of working-class gratitude for the Liberal government's pre-war social programme. On the contrary, the war and post-war exposed its limitations. Furthermore, although the government was careful to protect the broad middle class fiscally—you had to be very well off to suffer from the tax increases of the 1909 and 1914 budgets—it is questionable how much the Liberals benefited. The middle classes were by means testing excluded from both pensions and national health insurance, and the latter, particularly, rankled. Their exclusion encouraged not only class grievance but class hostility. Even allowing for the financial demands of naval rearmament, the government, therefore, might have chanced its arm on a more expensive social programme that did in some way include the middle class. In the long term it possibly got the worst of both worlds: it did too little for the working class to earn their support but too much for them to win the middle class.

Yet in 1914 the standing of the Conservative Party seemed hardly more firm than that of the Liberals. A casual observer in 1914 could reasonably have predicted a bleak future for the Conservatives. They had lost three successive general elections, had been forced, at least publicly, effectively to abandon 'the full programme' of tariff reform,[27] as much as the Union itself was now the Party's *raison d'être*, and had stoked up the fires in Ireland to the point of sedition.[28] The Conservatives, however, were not offended by the

[26] Lloyd George wrote to his wife that there was 'a glorious row last night [in the House of Commons] . . . Our fellows were delighted. They rose & cheered as I left the House. But it has definitely raised the Land Question & it gave the House a glimpse of the savage passions that will be raised by the campaign when it is well on. Home Rule & all else will be swept aside.' (Lloyd George to Margaret Lloyd George, 16 Oct. 1912 in K. O. Morgan (ed.), *Lloyd George: Family Letters, 1885–1936* (Cardiff and London, 1973), 164.)

[27] That is, the so-called 'food taxes'—duties on imported grain and other food-stuffs—had been abandoned, but protection for manufacturing remained in place.

[28] For the official abandonment of tariff reform, see Sykes, *Tariff Reform in British Politics*, 236–94; E. H. H. Green, *The Crisis of Conservatism: The Politics, Economics and Ideology of the British Conservative Party, 1880–1914* (London and New York, 1995), 267–306. It is easy, however, to exaggerate the extent to which the Party had retreated,

heightened and often extreme political rhetoric of the Edwardian period—something they had, in fact, done much to encourage ever since the House of Lords rejected the 1909 budget. Lloyd George and Churchill were themselves no slouches at inflammatory rhetoric, but the historian cannot escape the conclusion that the Conservatives were more comfortable on the edge of the abyss than anyone else. The Conservatives also had advantages in England they did not have in Great Britain as a whole. The English social order and its related ideology disproportionately favoured the Conservatives. In 1967 Frank Parkin argued that in England (if not necessarily in Britain as a whole) to vote Tory was 'natural' since the Tories represented England's predominant values and institutions: the monarchy, the aristocracy, the Church of England, the ancient universities, the public schools, the City.[29] But that was true also of the Edwardian years and the Tories had to work hard to make it unnatural to vote Conservative. Even in 1906, A. L. Lowell wrote, the Conservatives 'still comprise by far the greater part of the people of title, wealth, fashion, or leisure; nearly all of the clergy of the Established Church; and a large majority of the university graduates, of the members of the bar, and of the richer merchants and manufacturers'. He noted that 'clerks . . . and other employees, who live upon small fixed incomes and are by nature the most unchangeable of men, belong in the main to the Conservative Party' (something Masterman had, of course, noted), and pointed out that as working men became enfranchised, 'to the surprise of the Liberals' they 'divided between the parties not very unequally'.[30] Despite the damage done to the Conservatives by the 1902 Education Act their religious affiliations were still on balance advantageous. They had a double tie to Anglicanism. One was to real religion based upon belief and practice; the other to a semi-secular religion based upon the low-level Anglican Protestant,

except tactically, on tariff reform. For Ireland, see P. Jalland, *The Liberals and Ireland: the Ulster Question in British Politics to 1914* (Brighton, 1980); R. Blake, *The Unknown Prime Minister* (London, 1955), 119–218.

[29] F. Parkin, 'Working-Class Conservatives: A Theory of Political Deviance', *British Journal of Sociology* 18 (1967), 278–89. See also McKibbin, *The Ideologies of Class*, 262.

[30] Lowell, *The Government of England*, II, 124–5.

anti-Irish-Catholic (particularly in Lancashire), anti-nonconformist and (in London) anti-Jewish sentiments of their working-class electorate.[31] Their final card was 'anti-socialism'. Were 'socialism' to become politically central to English politics, which even in 1914 an observer would have conceded possible, the Unionists were more convincing as an anti-socialist party than anyone else; indeed, had done much to fashion themselves as such a party since the end of the nineteenth century.[32]

But the Conservatives were also the national party of England. They were, of course, the Unionist Party in Scotland and Ireland, but their Unionism, their Britishness, was subsumed within the idea of England. Robert Blake, Conservative historian of the Conservative Party, in his biography of Andrew Bonar Law, entitled the twenty-ninth chapter 'Prime Minister of England' even though Bonar Law was of Canadian birth, Scots-Free Presbyterian origin and MP for Glasgow Central when he became prime minister. Their status as the party of the dominant social order of England and as the party of the English nation meant that even in the 1910 elections the Conservatives won a majority of the English seats and, probably, a majority of the votes cast.[33] In addition a redistribution of seats was likely to favour them in England. Although they held a significant number of small agricultural seats they also held many large suburban seats in Greater London and the home counties which were likely to yield them big electoral dividends—and after 1918 did.

Like the Liberals the Conservatives faced the prospect of almost inevitable electoral reform. They were nervous of reform. As the

---

[31] Pelling, *Social Geography of British Elections*, 42–6, 247–60; P. J. Waller, *Democracy and Sectarianism: A Political and Social History of Liverpool, 1868–1939* (Liverpool, 1981), 166–266. Whether the Party was actually anti-Jewish in London has been doubted. See below, 190–1.

[32] Green, *Crisis of Conservatism*, 250–3.

[33] In January 1910 the Conservatives won 234 seats in England, the anti-Conservatives 222. In December 1910 they won 235 seats in England, the anti-Conservatives 221. Calculating votes is very difficult. The Conservatives were certainly the main beneficiaries of plural voting which exaggerated the number of actual individuals who voted Conservative. The majority of unopposed returns, however, in both elections (especially December 1910 when 54 Conservatives were returned unopposed) were in Conservative seats and those returns necessarily deflated the total Conservative vote.

Liberals really wanted the abolition of the plural vote and not much more, so the Conservatives really wanted a reduction of Irish representation in the House of Commons and not much more. How they would have coped with a mass electorate must be a guess. They coped very well after the First World War, though in circumstances made highly favourable by the war itself. But for the war circumstances would have been less favourable. Yet Conservatism was always likely to benefit disproportionately from women's enfranchisement—at least in such circumstances as women were likely to be enfranchised in Britain—and, given the reasons why so many working-class men *already* voted Tory, they were unlikely to suffer too much from full manhood suffrage.

That the Conservatives had problems before 1914 is undeniable. Their weakness in Scotland made them overdependent on England (as the Liberals were overdependent on Scotland and Wales) and despite their winning a majority of England's parliamentary seats in 1910 that was not enough to give them victory overall. They were also divided politically and found it difficult, as Ewen Green has argued, to find issues that could unify the whole party.[34] He, however, probably exaggerates the Party's electoral difficulties in England. There is little evidence that it faced (in his words) 'disintegration'. Its social-sociological bedrock in England, its domination of England's official status order and its consistently large working-class vote, gave it an electoral cushion largely unavailable to the other parties.

If the futures of the Liberal and Conservative Parties were problematic, no less problematic was the future of the newest and smallest of England's parties, the Labour Party. And yet, paradoxically, it was the fate of the Labour Party which was to determine the development of English politics; it was within the Labour Party that the issues of a secularized politics—whether, for instance, the schools should promote not religion but social mobility—and the secular shaping of political allegiances was most explicitly debated. The labour movement, as we have seen, was deeply influenced by religious and

34 Green, *Crisis of Conservatism*, 267–306.

political nonconformity. Much of that early generation of Lib-Lab MPs were products of nonconformity and an associated political Radicalism, and many continued to sit in the 1906 parliament.[35] The same was true of a significant proportion of the leadership of the Labour Representation Committee, which became the Labour Party in 1906. These were the men Ben Tillett abused in his polemic *Is the Parliamentary Labour Party a Failure?* (1908),[36] and who were unpopular with those in the Party's 'Tory' tradition, a tradition strong in London, the West Midlands, parts of Lancashire and among its drinking and betting voters more generally.[37] They were men who were either active nonconformists or professed an ethical Christianity or ethical socialism which had much in common with nonconformity. These were men in whose breasts the war between nonconformist radicalism and an areligious redistributionary economics was fought.

However, in that same generation were those who believed or hoped that the apparent failure of the 1892 Liberal government and the Liberal defeats in the 1895 and 1900 elections had created a vacuum in the left which only a secular socialist politics could fill. Those two famous calls-to-arms of the 1890s Sidney Webb's and G. B. Shaw's *To Your Tents Oh Israel* (1893)[38] and Ramsay MacDonald's and Keir Hardie's *The Programme of the Independent Labour Party* (1899)[39] both assumed that the Liberal Party had done its work and had its day. Indeed, *The Programme of the Independent*

[35] Especially was that true of the 23 Lib-Lab MPs who were not elected as candidates of the Labour Representation Committee.

[36] For this see McKibbin, 'Arthur Henderson as Labour Leader', in *Ideologies of Class*, 48; J. H. Stewart Reid, *The Origins of the British Labour Party* (Minneapolis, 1955), 199–200; J. Schneer, *Ben Tillett: Portrait of a Labour Leader* (London, 1982), 135–8.

[37] For this, see M. Pugh, 'The Rise of Labour and the Political Culture of Conservatism, 1890–1945', *History*, 87 (2002), 514–37. It would be wrong, however, to argue as Pugh does, that the dominant political culture of Birmingham and the West Midlands was aristocratic and Tory. Its dominant tradition was Liberal Unionist not Tory. The two were not identical.

[38] For this, see A. M. McBriar, *Fabianism and English Politics, 1884–1918* (Cambridge, 1962), 249–51.

[39] The article appeared in *The Nineteenth Century*. See D. Howell, *British Workers and the Independent Labour Party, 1888–1906* (Manchester, 1983), 367.

Labour Party was written on the specific premise that the Liberal Party had 'collapsed'.[40] In the circumstances—the resignation of William Harcourt as leader of the Liberal Party and its deep divisions over imperial policy—this was a reasonable assumption and upon it the Labour Representation Committee was founded in 1900. We know, of course, that the assumption was wrong. The spectacular re-emergence of those apparently settled issues—education, the fiscal system and legally unfettered collective bargaining—and with them the unexpected revival of the Liberal Party obliged MacDonald to make the kind of arrangement with the Liberals (1903)[41] which *The Programme of the Independent Labour Party* had effectively repudiated.

Even as the ILP programme was being written, however, even as its authors argued that the Liberal Party was on its last legs, the labour movement's position was less straightforward. The fact is that the conditions necessary for the establishment of a mass working-class party in England at the turn of the century, though not absent, were comparatively few. Pre-1914 was not altogether a bad time to found a labour party; but it was not obviously good either. In the late nineteenth century working-class MPs (mostly miners) had been elected as Liberals or with Liberal forbearance. Keir Hardie had been elected as an independent 'labour' MP in 1892 without Liberal opposition, while the 'labour' vote, such as it was, tended to rise and fall with the Liberal vote. Furthermore, Labour's attachment to free trade, which makes a number of appearances in this story, looks as instinctive and ideological as the Liberal Party's. Free trade admittedly had a quasi-distributionary element: the 'cheap loaf' was self-evidently cheaper than the 'dear loaf'. To that extent the working-class family benefited financially. Free trade was also central to a liberal political system which was peculiarly favourable to the

[40] The full title of the article was *The Liberal Collapse: The Programme of the Independent Labour Party.*

[41] The so-called MacDonald-Gladstone Pact (or Entente), for which see F. Bealey and H. Pelling, *Labour and Politics, 1900–1906: A History of the Labour Representation Committee* (London, 1958), 125–59.

labour movement.[42] Frank Trentmann has interestingly argued that
the labour movement's attachment to free trade developed within
a specific socialist critique of capitalism, 'an important tradition
in its own right', and was not simply 'free food'.[43] His argument
certainly gives a rationale to behaviour which is otherwise almost
inexplicable. There was, however, an instinctive, unreflective support
for free trade within the Labour Party which almost lifted it beyond
conventional debate. It also meant that even for MacDonald and
Hardie Labour's relation to Liberalism was less one of hostility than
of apostolic succession. Furthermore, as we shall see, the Labour Party
persisted in its adherence to free trade—until 1931 in fact—long
beyond the moment when that was readily defensible. Adherence
to free trade was one reason for the labour movement's ambivalent
relationship to the political system; the trades unions's insistence
on the inviolability of free collective bargaining was the other.
Before 1914 there were, generally speaking, two models of industrial
relations which the unions could have adopted. There was the
British, the one adopted, which embodied free collective bargaining
between employers and unions within the regime established by the
1875 legislation: a regime which gave the unions even more than
they had hoped for and more than the employers had feared.[44]
The state was not entirely excluded from this system. It could,
for example, have a conciliating role and, as in the case of the
miners or the 'sweated trades', could even legislate for hours worked
and wage minima.[45] But the miners and the sweated trades were
an exception and it was understood that the state's function as
arbitrator was not to be supported by legal sanctions. The unions,

---

[42] I have argued this elsewhere. McKibbin, *Ideologies of Class*, 31–2.

[43] F. Trentmann, 'Wealth versus Welfare: The British Left between Free Trade and
National Political Economy before the First World War', *Historical Research* 70 (1997),
70–98.

[44] A. Fox, *History and Heritage: The Social Origins of the British Industrial Relations
System* (London, 1985), 153–60; M. Curthoys, *Governments, Labour and the Law in
Mid-Victorian Britain* (Oxford, 2004), 189–243.

[45] H. A. Clegg, *A History of British Trade Unions Since 1889*, II (Oxford, 1985),
97–105.

perhaps not surprisingly in the era of the Taff Vale and Osborne Judgements, above all wished to keep industrial relations out of the courts.

The other model was the Australian one: a system of industrial relations dependent upon compulsory arbitration and judicially established wage minima for both skilled and unskilled workers within a protected economy. Its rock was the famous Sunshine Harvester Case (1907) when Mr Justice Higgins in the Conciliation and Arbitration Court imposed a 'basic' wage on the manufacturers of the Sunshine harvesters.[46] That was not a subsistence but a 'living' wage of the kind that the British unions never actually got. This was the bargain of Australian tariffs: employers got protected markets and employees got protected wages. It was the kind of system that might have emerged from Joseph Chamberlain's campaign for tariffs had he a clearer and more limited idea of what he wanted; had he not tried to bundle up in one policy proposals both to save the Empire and provide guaranteed employment for British workers—proposals either of which could have worked separately but not together.[47] Support for compulsory arbitration was not entirely absent from the labour movement. Ben Tillett of the Dockers, who after his first visit to Australia (1893–4) had been converted to compulsory arbitration,[48] repeatedly tried to persuade the TUC to support it, but always failed, as did Arthur Henderson in 1911. Tillet's rather wayward and uningratiating personality might not have helped his case; but the same cannot be said of Henderson. The determination of the unions to exclude the state from such an important area of political and economic life, other than in exceptional circumstances, was fateful and was to undermine both interwar Labour governments,

[46] The High Court of Australia actually ruled that the Harvester Judgment was unconstitutional but it remained the basis of the Australian system of wage determination for nearly a century. Higgins based his judgement upon 'the normal needs of the average employee as a human being [with a wife and three children] in a civilized community'. (G. Greenwood (ed.), *Australia: A Social and Political History* (Sydney, 1960), 218.)

[47] R. Jay, *Joseph Chamberlain: A Political Study* (Oxford, 1981), 285–91.

[48] Schneer, *Tillett*, 115–16.

particularly the second, with disastrous results.[49] As part of the bargain struck with the Labour Representation Committee in 1903 the Liberal Party agreed to restore by legislation legally unfettered bargaining (including sympathetic strikes) that had been struck down by the Taff Vale and earlier decisions. The 1906 Trades Disputes Act gave the unions what they wanted, as it should have since they wrote it, but at the price of further entangling the Labour Party with Liberalism.

The future of the Labour Party in 1914 was therefore obscure. The subordinate relationship to the Liberal Party was seemingly inevitable but at the same time much disliked by many in the Party—as MacDonald's increasingly beleaguered leadership suggests. Even something as elementary as electoral reform could not overcome this hurdle. Philip Snowden, who was of Labour MPs probably the most hostile to the Liberal government, wanted proportional representation, since that really would have liberated the Labour Party. MacDonald and most members of the parliamentary Labour Party, however, wanted the alternative vote since that would favour Labour (it was believed) while not wrecking the party of progress or the ability of the Labour leadership largely to determine the pace of Labour's expansion. In the end the 1914 Conference of the Party, almost inevitably, rejected both PR and the alternative vote.[50] The Labour Party was not unique in having complicated relations with 'bourgeois' parties. Those between French socialism and radical republicanism or between German social democracy and left liberalism were also complicated. But neither had quite so much in common with 'bourgeois' parties as did Labour nor did they exist in political cultures quite so favourable to the working class. And they worked within electoral systems—either forms of proportional representation or the second ballot—which gave them more freedom of manoeuvre.

[49] See below, 73–9.

[50] For the Labour debate over electoral reform, see L. Barrow and I. Bullock, *Democratic Ideas and the British Labour Movement, 1880–1914* (Cambridge, 1996), 276–83.

What would have happened to the relative standing of the parties without the intervention of the war we do not know. What is said here is speculation. We cannot know for certain how far the Liberal welfare system would have developed without the intervention of the war. We cannot know whether Lloyd George's attempt to drive social Liberalism forward through instruments such as the land campaign would have succeeded. We can only guess at how an enlarged electorate would have voted and whether Labour would have disproportionately benefited by it. Nor do we know what would have happened in Ireland had not the Home Rule Act been suspended at the outbreak of war. What does seem certain, however, is that the progressive alliance could hold together only so long as the Labour Party both stayed within it and stayed subordinate within it. Many people would vote 'progressive' while the progressive alliance was dominated by the Liberal Party but would not do so if it were dominated by Labour. If Labour ceased to be the subordinate partner, the party of progress would probably fly apart. Which is exactly what happened in the 1920s.

Even if some of these eventualities were vaguely in the minds of the political elite in 1914, what actually happened, and so fast, was not. Most striking to the historian about Britain's behaviour in July and August 1914 is the insousiance with which she went to war. Even if we accept that Britain could probably do little else, the absence of real doubt and the easy assumption that it would be 'business as usual' (Churchill's phrase) is nonetheless remarkable in a country which more than any other depended on the world not going to war. We should remember that Britain's political system was obliged to cope not just with war but war against Germany, the most formidable opponent imaginable. It was thus not any war which put such pressure on that system and the political party unlucky enough to be in charge of it. That party was the Liberal Party and the war began its almost immediate fragmentation. Why did this happen? A. J. P. Taylor argued that the Liberals were disqualified as a war party because of a commitment to 'free trade', 'free enterprise', and '*laissez-faire*', whereas war demanded state intervention on a huge scale.[51] But that argument cannot be right, at least as Taylor expressed it. Whether the Liberals were ever *laissez-faire* is doubtful. Certainly the Edwardian Liberal Party was not. Furthermore, the Conservatives were no more *étatiste* in this sense than the Liberals. Nor were they a more competent party of war: something the Boer War had established beyond doubt. Nonetheless, the war presented many Liberals with fundamental ideological problems. All wars have posed problems for the Liberals, especially their radical wing. Taylor's own Ford Lectures, *The Trouble Makers*, were a brilliant analysis of those who not only made trouble but were troubled by war.[52] Many, for example, who cheerfully supported the state as an actor in social policy were opposed to military conscription and saw no conflict between supporting the one and opposing the other. Some members of the radical wing of the Party began drifting towards the Union of Democratic Control and the Independent Labour Party very early indeed.[53] In their case it was not so much state intervention as such they disliked as the purposes for which state intervention was being put. Furthermore, the formation of both wartime coalitions (May 1915 and December 1916) demanded concessions that many Liberals found deeply distasteful—the inclusion of Sir Edward Carson, the foghorn of Ulster Unionism, for instance, or the exclusion of R. B. Haldane at the behest of the Tory press.[54] Most Liberals, including Asquith, supported the war in some way, but the Party's demoralization, the widespread feeling among many that this was not what the Liberal Party was supposed to do however much one might want to win the war, is unmistakable. Furthermore, wanting

---

[51] A. J. P. Taylor, *English History, 1914–1945* (Oxford, 1965), 1–70 *passim*. This argument is anticipated, sometimes word for word, in Taylor's Raleigh Lecture of 1959, reprinted in Taylor, *Politics in Wartime* (London, 1964), 11–44.

[52] A. J. P. Taylor, *The Trouble Makers: Dissent Over Foreign Policy, 1792–1939* (London, 1957), 132–66.

[53] For the Union of Democratic Control, see M. Ceadel, *Thinking about Peace and War* (Oxford, 1987), 118–19; M. Swartz, *The Union of Democratic Control in British Politics during the First World War* (Oxford, 1971).

[54] Haldane was the victim of anti-Germanism. His education in Germany and his admiration for many aspects of German life, it was alleged, made him unfit for office. Asquith made no attempt to defend him.

to win the war was very different from liking it.[55] One result of all this was the rapid decay of the Party's organization in the country: never very strong at the best of times but in 1914 actually stronger than it usually was.[56] The split in the Party in December 1916, when Asquith and his supporters left the government,[57] was not inevitable but by then not surprising. Personality and temperament mattered, but the kind of people who left with Asquith were not just those who disliked Lloyd George, they were people whose heart was never in total war to start with. And, unlike Lloyd George, they despised many of those with whom they were obliged to coalesce.

This was damaging enough but the war did the Party even more profound harm. It significantly weakened nonconformity, Liberalism's indispensable social base. Nonconformity, like the Party, was split over the war and the split was almost exactly the same as that in the Party. Lloyd George took important sections of nonconformity with him—especially Robertson Nicholl and the *British Weekly*, and much of Wesleyan Methodism—while the smaller nonconformist faiths tended to stand by Asquith. And these political–religious divisions were difficult to repair. Physically, the war undermined the nonconformist congregations and did much to disengage young men, particularly, from the chapels.[58] It also undermined political nonconformity and those causes upon which political nonconformity depended—not least the role of religion in the educational system[59]—and did much, therefore,

[55] Lloyd George told Harold Nicolson that Asquith was an ideal peacetime prime minister but about the 'worst War Minister there could be, "since . . . he hated war" ' (H. Nicolson, *Diaries and Letters, 1930–1939*, London, 1966), 268.

[56] For a brief but still very good analysis of the Liberal Party's ideological and organizational disruption, see T. Wilson, *The Downfall of the Liberal Party, 1914–1935* (London, 1966), 23–48.

[57] For the fall of Asquith's government see J. Turner, *British Politics and the Great War* (New Haven and London, 1992), 138–48.

[58] Doyle, 'Urban Liberalism and the "Lost Generation" ', 631.

[59] The 'question' did not disappear but transformed itself. It now became a problem for the Labour Party given the significance of Roman Catholics in the Labour electorate. For the way the Catholic interest virtually wrecked C. P. Trevelyan's 1930 education bill, see D. W. Dean, 'Difficulties of a Labour Educational Policy: the Failure of the Trevelyan Bill, 1929–1931', *British Journal of Educational Studies* 17 (1969). For the transference of the political allegiances of nonconformity, see below, 91–2.

to weaken the Liberal Party's very *raison d'être*. Nonconformity
did not, of course, disappear. In many parts of the country its
social networks continued more or less intact but these networks
increasingly were to withdraw from an active political Liberalism into
a rather passive Conservatism.[60] Furthermore, as Packer has pointed
out, the war largely removed the necessary conditions for a successful
land campaign: landlordism, low wages, and private housing. The
huge land sales of the war and immediate post-war years made it
very difficulty to mount an attack on an aristocratic landlord class;
the war and its aftermath transformed the problems of agriculture
from one of rural poverty due to low wages to one of a depressed
industry as a whole; unemployment rather than low wages became
the central 'problem' of urban life; and the 'solution' to the housing
question increasingly became the responsibility of both the central
and local state, not that of the private landlord.[61] This did not mean
that the Liberals ceased to have a land policy; rather they ceased to
have a land policy on which a stable urban or rural base could be
built, assuming such a policy existed anyway.[62] This failure in turn
weakened the Liberal Party in a more fundamental sense and to that
we shall return.

The circumstances of the war were much more favourable to
the Conservatives. War itself was favourable to the Conservatives:
especially a war against Germany, which by 1914 came naturally to
them. They were, as I have suggested, not especially good at fighting
wars, but they were the party of war and the fighting services—which
is why the great majority of MPs who joined the services were
Tories.[63] They had nothing to prove. To the extent that they were
divided during the war the divisions were over who could fight it most
fiercely. This is something we expect. But if the Conservative Party

[60] I have discussed this elsewhere: McKibbin, *Classes and Cultures*, 90–2. And below,
91–2.

[61] Packer, *Lloyd George, Liberalism and the Land*, 182–93.

[62] For Liberal attempts to devise a land policy in the 1920s, see M. Dawson,
'The Liberal Land Policy, 1924–9: Electoral Strategy and Internal Division', *Twentieth
Century British History* 2, 3 (1991), 272–90.

[63] In 1914 a much larger number of Conservative than Liberal MPs had served in the
army: 53 against 15 (Ramsden, *Age of Balfour and Baldwin*, 98).

were the party of war it was also the party of property. Not in the sense that Conservative MPs were conspicuously more representative of property than the Liberals—though they represented different kinds of property[64]—but that they had a stronger ideological sense of the inviolability of property than the Liberals, as was to be expected of the anti-socialist party *par excellence*. Wars, furthermore, both threaten and destroy property and for much of the Conservative Party's natural constituency—as we shall see—the financial consequences of the war were anything but favourable.[65] In a prudent Conservative Party there would have been more 'Lansdowne letters'—an expression of the view that the European propertied classes stood to gain nothing from this war.[66] But patriotism and imperialism, a seeming readiness to fight the war until the end, trumped prudence: a marked contrast to the Party's behaviour in the 1930s. Had it not done so the war would have been much more divisive—a conflict between the defenders of honour and the 'national interest' on the one side and the defenders of property on the other.

The politics of the war also strongly favoured the Conservatives. In 1914 they were in opposition with no immediate prospect of becoming a government or certainty of winning the next election. The war, however, permitted them in two stages to become the predominant party of government without ever fighting an election. The first coalition government (May 1915), which was designed to rescue Asquith from his political difficulties, while disproportionately Liberal, nonetheless was the first step.[67] The formation of the second coalition (December, 1916) immensely strengthened them. The

[64] Conservative MPs were, for example, significantly more likely to have had landed backgrounds than the Liberals, who were significantly more likely to have had backgrounds in industry.

[65] See below, 41–3.

[66] Lord Lansdowne, former Conservative foreign secretary and leader of the Party in the House of Lords, had written to the *Daily Telegraph* on Nov. 29, 1917 urging a negotiated peace. For the circumstances of the letter see Turner, *British Politics and the Great War*, 252.

[67] The Liberals held most ministerial posts and the crucial ones—the premiership, the foreign office (Grey), the exchequer (McKenna), the home office (Simon) and munitions (Lloyd George). The Tory leader, Bonar Law, was colonial secretary—not traditionally one of the major offices of state.

withdrawal of the Asquithian Liberals left a ministerial vacuum only the Conservatives could fill. Apart from Lloyd George himself as prime minister no Liberal held a major post—except perhaps Christopher Addison, who as minister of munitions held a post of temporary significance. Lloyd George himself was the only Liberal in the small war cabinet. Although he held great personal authority this coalition was a Conservative government in all but name even when Churchill and Edwin Montagu (both still Liberals) later joined it. The Tories had thus staged a *coup d'état* by perfectly constitutional means. The general election of 1918, a triumph for them, simply confirmed what had already happened.

The war also profoundly altered the conditions of partisan politics, again to the benefit of the Conservatives. The collapse of the Liberal land campaign[68] removed what appeared to be the greatest threat to the Conservative Party's electoral standing. The Irish question had certainly not been solved but it no longer implicated the Conservatives in dangerous constitutional manoeuvres: the solution was now as damaging to the Liberal Party as anyone else. Furthermore, war and victory tended to reinforce a Conservative conception of England and the status order represented by the Conservatives: all those fundamental institutions of the English state—monarchy, the armed services, the established church, a particular form of parliamentary government—survived the war not merely intact but strengthened. In this survival, as we shall see, lay the central paradox and failure of post-war English (and British) politics. The institutional shell of Edwardian politics remained, as did its outward forms, while the dynamic of Edwardian politics, the only thing that gave it life, the progressive coalition, decayed and then collapsed.

The Conservatives were not only the ideological beneficiaries of the war; they were the main beneficiaries of the wartime failure to reconstruct the British political and electoral system on a democratic basis. We tend to think that the 1918 Representation of the People Act, since it nearly trebled the electorate and radically redefined

[68] See above, 11.

constituency boundaries, transformed the political system. In fact, the 1918 Act was the most conservative piece of legislation that could have been devised in the circumstances. Enfranchisement of all males was inescapable; but women's enfranchisement, probably also inescapable, was anything but democratic, based as it was on the old municipal franchise, itself fundamentally a property franchise. It also discriminated by age. Many justified their conversion to women's suffrage, not least Asquith, by a declared admiration for the wartime work of women, in munitions plants, in transport, on the land. Yet these women, predominantly young, were precisely those who were not enfranchised. They were not given the vote because they were below the age of thirty: the minimum age established by the Act for women's enfranchisement. Compare this with the treatment of young men. All those nineteen-year old males and the comparatively small number of women in the forces on active duty were conceded the vote. (The minimum age for all other men was twenty-one.) To have denied them enfranchisement would, it was said, have belittled their part in the country's defence. Of the women munition workers nothing similar was said. Proposals to reform the method of election all failed and the antique method of first-past-the-post in single-member constituencies was retained.[69] The plural vote was preserved (though less generously), as was separate representation of the City of London and the universities.[70] The House of Lords was untouched and the troops returned from the front line having successfully defended a parliament whose upper chamber consisted almost exclusively of hereditary peers. Those who were not were all state appointees: Anglican bishops and judges. Only in one way did the Act go beyond the minimum it had to do and that was to enfranchise those who had been in receipt of poor relief—something both

[69] The bill originally proposed large multi-member seats in the big cities whose members would be elected on the basis of a single-transferable vote. In all other single-member seats the alternative vote was to operate—something the Labour Party particularly favoured. Neither survived Conservative opposition either in the House of Commons or the House of Lords. For a detailed discussion, see Pugh, *Electoral Reform in War and Peace, passim.*

[70] Though the members for the universities were elected on the basis of the single transferable vote.

the Majority and Minority Reports of the Royal Commission on the Poor Laws had recommended in 1909. We thus find, both by what it did and did not do, that the English political elite had imposed on Great Britain a constitutional–political arrangement markedly biased towards the Conservative Party, franchise legislation weighted towards property and property rights, an upper house weighted even more towards property which retained formidable obstructive powers used wholly in the Conservative interest, and an un-representative voting system—first-past-the-post—which favoured entrenched blocs and electoral polarization, both of which worked to the Conservative Party's advantage. The elimination of propor-tional representation and the alternative vote as the price for getting the Representation of the People Act passed at all was, as Pugh points out, 'the most significant decision of the war, for it pro-duced a Conservative hegemony in British government that lasted until 1945'.[71]

The other obvious beneficiary of the war was the Labour Party. But it was a beneficiary as much by what the war did not do as what it did. The Party did not split, unlike the Liberal Party, though given its ideological affinity with Liberalism and the ambivalent attitude to the war by a number of its leaders (most notably Ramsay MacDonald) it could well have done. Nor did it follow the Continental model: socialist parties fundamentally divided by the war whose divisions never healed. It avoided both these disasters because its trade union base held together and because, within the labour movement, the unions were more important than the parliamentary party and less likely to fracture. The longer the war continued the more significant this was to be. Furthermore, unlike many of the Continental parties, Labour had never been wracked by the 'revisonist controversy' which opened divisions within Continental socialism only papered over before 1914.[72] To the degree that

[71] Pugh, *Electoral Reform in War and Peace*, ix.

[72] The revisionist controversy concerned the extent to which socialist parties departed from what was understood to be a 'pure' Marxism. The founding text of revisionism, Eduard Bernstein's *Evolutionary Socialism* (first published in English in 1901, but in

Labour had such a controversy—how far should it be an ally of the Liberals—the First World War largely solved rather than inflamed it. The bilateral loyalties of many Labour leaders, to trade unionism on the one hand and a form of radical internationalism on the other, meant they had a foot in both camps. A comparison of Asquith and Arthur Henderson, the Labour Party's secretary and then its leading figure, is instructive. After his resignation in 1916 Asquith gave no direction to the Party he still notionally led. When Henderson resigned from the Lloyd George government in 1917 he immediately set about reorganizing the Labour Party as the second party of the state.[73] But Labour did not leave the coalition government, nor did Henderson think it should. He was able to act as he did because he was both a patriot and an internationalist. Despite widespread hostility to the Party's so-called 'pacifists' (like Ramsay MacDonald and Philip Snowden) Labour in this way nearly, but not quite, got the best of both worlds.

The war also served both Labour's ideological and tactical interests. It settled (more or less) the vexed question of Labour's relationship with the Liberals. And the decision to break the old informal-semi-formal relationship with the Liberal Party was finally taken in circumstances that made it riskier and, so to speak, thus even more decisive. When Henderson originally drafted Labour's new constitution and persuaded the Party to contest the great majority of constituencies he did so on the assumption that the next parliament would be elected by the alternative vote, which would minimize the likelihood that three-cornered contests would give the

German in 1898 in *Die Neue Zeit*, and then in book form in 1899) was written in England and was significantly influenced by English experience. For a good account of the controversy, see J. Joll, *The Second International, 1889–1914* (New York, 1966), 77–105.

[73] The issue that forced Henderson's resignation, or dismissal as Henderson saw it, was whether the British labour movement should be represented at an international socialist conference in Stockholm at which German socialists would also be represented. Lloyd George had once favoured such representation as a way of supporting Russia's provisional government. He later changed his mind. Henderson, however, continued to believe that Britain should be represented and this was the ground on which Lloyd George manoeuvred him out of the war cabinet. (C. Wrigley, *Arthur Henderson* (Cardiff, 1990), 114–19; F. Leventhal, *Arthur Henderson* (Manchester, 1989), 64–70. See also Turner, *British Politics and the Great War*, 206–9.)

Conservatives large numbers of 'progressive' seats. 'In the majority of cases [Henderson told C. P. Scott] he would depend on the alternative vote and a friendly understanding between Liberalism and Labour to give each other their second choice.'[74] To go ahead anyway, despite the disappearance of the alternative vote, was a demonstration of how irrevocable was the break with Liberalism. That break, even without the alternative vote, was made possible because the war enormously advanced the political and social importance of the industrial working class and the status of the trade unions, who became simultaneously representatives of labour and arms of the state. Wartime social policies and 'reconstruction' were more associated with Labour than any other party. By 1918, on paper anyway, Labour's social programme entirely superseded the narrower New Liberalism, since improvement of working-class life chances was Labour's principal *raison d'être*. As Duncan Tanner has argued:

Unlike the elements of the Labour Party, the Liberals did not share a fundamental commitment to improving working-class living standards which could hold the party together whatever the divisions over the war. There was a form of social democracy more usually associated with Liberal thinkers and reformers, which in wartime conditions, was less resilient than the social democracy practised by Labour.[75]

In other fundamental respects the war also favoured both the Conservative and Labour Parties. They became in large measure class parties, whereas by 1918 the Liberal Party was not. Bernard Waites has argued that the war was responsible for what he calls the 'homogenization' of classes: the middle class became more middle class, the working class, particularly, more working class.[76] During the war the classes drifted apart while the war's industrial politics—especially in the munitions industries—actualized the

[74] T. Wilson (ed.), *The Political Diaries of C. P. Scott, 1911–1928* (London, 1970), 317.

[75] Tanner, *Political Change and the Labour Party*, 431.

[76] B. Waites, *A Class Society at War: England 1914–1918* (Leamington Spa, 1987), 279.

potential for class conflict which already existed. Although Waites possibly exaggerates the degree of working-class homogenization and underrates that of the middle class, there is much truth to this argument, as we shall see. The effect of such class homogenization was to give the Conservative and Labour Parties an irreducible core of social support. In the case of the Conservatives, of course, that support went way beyond the middle class, but that does not alter the fact that in its essentials it was a middle-class party. A similar core of class support was increasingly denied to the Liberals, for which the war was largely, though not entirely, responsible.

The Liberal Party was further weakened by its accelerating detachment from the state. It was almost immediately apparent after the war how distant so many Liberals—particularly Asquithians—now were from the state and alarmed at the new scope of its activity (and expenditure). The Party's relation to the state had, in fact, always been ambivalent: on the one hand, it was a party of reform, what the French called 'the party of movement', which looked to the state; but on the other, much of Liberalism's historic electorate was nonconformist and defined itself against the Church of England, the official and established religion of the English state. Before 1914 this ambivalence could be a source of strength; but rarely after 1918. Nor did the Liberal Party any longer seriously represent powerful interests within the state. More especially, it no longer represented either labour or capital. Although individual trade unionists continued to vote Liberal, if in diminishing numbers, no large union after 1918 had any formal or even informal connections to the Liberal Party. 'Business' Liberals, like Lord Rhondda, who had followed Lloyd George into government, increasingly stood for business rather than Liberalism, and some, like Alfred Mond of Brunner, Mond, soon to be ICI, were en route to the Conservative Party. Once it became divorced from state action it ceased to be a likely party of government, which is probably what Taylor meant when he said that *laissez-faire* was the cause of its downfall. The Conservative Party, of course, was equally suspicious of the state; but suspicion of the state as an economic agent was natural to it and an indispensable part of its technique of electoral mobilization. Given the decay of political nonconformity, however, without the state the Liberal Party, its social base declining and unstable, struggled to survive as a third party. And when it did present itself as a party apparently committed to state action—as in 1929—it found the ground, at least rhetorically, already occupied by Labour.[77]

Much of what has been said in this chapter is necessarily a kind of guess-work. One conclusion, nonetheless, seems more than mere guess-work. Although pre-1914 politics are sufficiently open to make confident predictions difficult, we can reasonably argue that the survival of the progressive alliance, and thus the viability of Edwardian politics, was dependent upon two highly contingent assumptions. First, that politics would continue to be determined by issues on which the Labour and Liberal Parties could agree. Second, that Labour would always remain subordinate to the Liberals within the party system. How long these assumptions would remain true, however, was uncertain. The war ended such uncertainty. It eliminated both assumptions and so weakened the historic Liberal Party almost irreparably.

[77] See below, 66–7.

2

Unstable Equilibrium, 1918–1929

However much we might disagree about the ultimate political effects of the First World War most would agree they were disruptive. Furthermore, although such disruption was thought possible by some in 1914—as one of a number of possibilities—few would then have predicted its speed and extent. The war fragmented the Liberal Party, re-established the political predominance of the Conservatives, whose future in 1914 was so uncertain, and broke the progressive alliance by permitting the Labour Party to claim that political independence which was its original *raison d'être*, but which the course of Edwardian politics persistently frustrated. The electorate had been reshaped (though in a flawed way) such that about 80 per cent of it had never voted before, and the war profoundly, if only temporarily, reordered the economic status of that electorate. But the disruption was not creative. Although Lloyd George and many of his Conservative colleagues intended the coalition government he had formed in December 1916 to be the core of a wholly rebuilt party system such did not happen. On the contrary, what emerged was a restored Edwardian politics, together with many of its mental habits and rhetoric, but without the one thing—the progressive alliance—which gave it life and coherence. Even though the purpose of politics in the 1920s was an attempt to prop it up, this was a system increasingly out of alignment with the society it was supposed to represent and was swept away in the financial and political crisis of 1931.

There were, however, three more 'logical' outcomes of the war: political forms more appropriate to the kind of society England had become and more consonant with its post-war political structures.

They were complete fusion of the Conservative and Liberal Parties (which many thought desirable and necessary); or the abandonment of free trade and the reshaping of the country's political economy behind protection; or the creation of a cross-class alliance of 'producers' against 'rentiers', the useful against the useless; or a combination of the three. None of them occurred, though all might have. Of the three the most likely was fusion. The Conservative Party and Lloyd George's half of the Liberal Party had fought and won the 1918 election overwhelmingly on a more or less common programme.[1] The coalition carried with it the prestige of both military and electoral victory. Its leaders, both Liberal and Conservative, believed in its permanence and fusion was undoubtedly the best solution to Lloyd George's problem—where did his political future now lie? To many the emergence of a Labour Party for the first time explicitly committed to a 'socialist objective' rendered the old conflicts redundant. There was a well-known international precedent. In 1909 the Australian free trade and protectionist parties had fused in face of the rapid growth of the Labor Party, undoubtedly a rational reaction. Within the Conservative Party the strongest proponent of fusion was Austen Chamberlain, Joseph's son and, after Bonar Law's retirement in March 1921, its leader. Chamberlain believed that the Conservative Party alone could not defeat Labour: anyone who thought so, he said in 1922, was living in a 'fool's paradise'.[2] The threat from Labour was such that the old causes—religious education, the fiscal

---

[1] The general election (14 December) was the first to be held on one day. The Coalition won 473 seats (389 in England) while another 20 Conservatives were elected independently of the government, and 53 per cent of the votes. Labour won 57 seats (42 in England) and 22.7 per cent of the votes. The independent Liberals (the Asquithian wing) won 36 seats (25 in England) and 14.7 per cent of the votes. (Asquith lost his Scottish seat to an independent Conservative.) The Labour vote was smaller than expected and not much more than the 20 per cent Philip Snowden guessed was the real Labour vote in 1914. The turnout was low (55.7 per cent), largely because of a low service vote. The actual electorate, therefore, was untypically middle-class and feminine, which probably magnified the coalition vote and minimized Labour's. Labour did significantly better in Wales where the turnout was higher (66 per cent). But that was almost certainly due to the overall significance of the miners' vote in Wales.

[2] Quoted in M. Cowling, *The Impact of Labour, 1920–24* (Cambridge, 1971), 181.

system (i.e. free trade or protection)—were now anachronisms.[3] This belief, that the Conservatives alone could not resist Labour, that their support was fragile, was not confined to Chamberlain. It was widely held among Tories in the 1920s—and thereafter[4]—even by those who did not necessarily favour fusion—and was based upon a view of self-interest (a sensible working man would obviously vote Labour) that many working men and women did not in fact have. Chamberlain's argument for fusion was driven by the centrality of anti-socialism to the Conservative Party after 1918[5]—itself a result of a changed attitude to the working class and its institutions.

Before 1914 the organized working class was not much loved in the Conservative Party; but there were nonetheless many Tory trade unionists—even in the unions' highest ranks[6]—and against the stereotype of the selfish member of an aggressive trade union, there was an almost equally strong stereotype of the patriotic, individualistic working man in whose hands the defence of empire was safe. Furthermore, there were many Edwardian Tories who regarded the labour movement as an almost apolitical 'interest' not to be alienated and who were anxious to keep it that way. As a result of the war, however, Tory attitudes became much less benign. In 1918 the unions had twice the membership of 1914. They had, it seemed, successfully used their power in a wartime economy to force wages up and working hours down. They had struck, it was thought, regardless of the consequences to the men at the front, while the unions were apparently responsible for the pauperization of much of the middle class to the benefit of the organized working class. Simultaneously, other working-class institutions, like the Labour Party and the co-ops,

---

[3] Ibid. 145.

[4] M. Kinnear, *The Fall of Lloyd George: The Political Crisis of 1922* (London, 1973), 50–4; D. Jarvis, 'The Shaping of Conservative Electoral Hegemony, 1918–139', in J. Lawrence and M. Taylor (eds.), *Party, State and Society* (Aldershot, 1998), 131–2, 144; and Jarvis, 'British Conservatism and Class Politics in the 1920s', *English Historical Review* CXI (1996), 59–84.

[5] E. H. H. Green, *Ideologies of Conservatism* (Oxford, 2002), 126.

[6] Like James Mawdsley, secretary of the Operative Cotton Spinners' Association, who stood with Churchill as a Tory candidate for Oldham in a double by-election in July 1899.

had emerged much strengthened—especially the co-ops, in the eyes of many Conservatives even more dangerous than the Labour Party.[7]

Experience of war, indeed differential experience of war, reinforced resentment and hostility. It was the case that a higher proportion of middle than working-class men fought and died since working men were more likely to be in reserved occupations—that is, occupations thought essential to the war effort—and their enthusiasm for fighting and dying was more tempered.[8] Although after the war England remained more civilian than most European societies, and its life usually less militarized, the front had made many middle-class men think as soldiers. The language of anti-Labour politics in the 1920s was suffused with the vocabulary of struggle and 'national service'. As soon as the war was over both private individuals as well as the government began to form militarized strike-breaking organizations which had more in common with post-war Italy than with the civil traditions of British industrial relations. Even by the end of 1918, Gregory notes, 'all of the poisonous ingredients of extreme right-wing politics existed in Britain—particularly southern England'.[9] Their golden moment came with the general strike of 1926[10] but they were equally prepared to act as strike-breakers as early as 1921 had a sympathetic strike in support of the miners actually occurred. (It didn't.)[11] The government then called on 'loyal citizens' to join a new 'Defence Force' and 75,000 did so within ten days.[12]

The logic of post-war anti-socialism, as C. L. Mowat noted fifty years ago,[13] the centrality of the working class and its demands

---

[7] J. W. B. Bates, 'The Conservative Party in the Constituencies, 1918–1939', unpublished Oxford D.Phil. thesis 1994, 230–1.

[8] A. Gregory, *The Last Great War: British Society and the First World War* (Cambridge, 2008), 81, 116.

[9] Ibid. 267.   [10] For the general strike see below 54.

[11] This was the famous 'Black Friday', 15 April 1921—the failure of the so-called Triple Alliance (Miners, Railwaymen, and Transport Workers) to act together in support of the Miners. (For Black Friday, see Clegg, *A History of British Trade Unions since 1889*, 298–302.)

[12] There is a good account of the atmosphere of April 1921 and the formation of these semi-militarized units in C. L. Mowat, *Britain Between the Wars* (London, 1956), 120–3.

[13] Ibid. 133.

to the popular idea of politics and the sense that the old party cries were meaningless pointed, therefore, to fusion as an inevitable consequence of war. Yet there was no fusion. Broad co-operation short of fusion was usually acceptable to many Tories and Liberals, which to them seemed to make fusion unnecessary. The evidence suggests that even those most hostile to Lloyd George's coalition government were not particularly hostile to 'co-operation'—which mostly meant electoral pacts against Labour, both at national and local level. Stanley Baldwin—the only member of the coalition cabinet to disown it publicly[14]—hoped that his first government would be as broadly based as the coalition. He had suggested to Bonar Law that Reginald McKenna, Asquith's last chancellor, should be offered the exchequer in 1922 and he himself was to offer the post to Robert Horne, Lloyd George's last chancellor, in 1923.[15] This suggests that in practice he saw little ideological difference between the two parties or between coalitionists and anti-coalitionists. Indeed, it is apparent that his surprisingly passionate intervention at the Carlton Club meeting was due primarily to a personal antipathy to Lloyd George and his method of government. Many Tories were willing to support a renewed coalition as long as it was led by a Tory: was, in effect, a Conservative government.

Lloyd George himself was a serious problem. Very few ordinary members of the Conservative Party were ready to fuse with him. They tended to have long memories, to defer to a local leadership often technically very Unionist, and thus to be dismayed by the Irish Treaty of 1922.[16] To them Ireland and the 1909 budget were living issues. Austen Chamberlain was probably right to say that the local associations were 'full of old pre-war Tories, who have learnt nothing and forgotten nothing'.[17] For them even the wartime coalition was illegitimate. Much of the Tory peerage and

[14] At the meeting of the Conservative Party at the Carlton Club on 19 October 1922 which brought down the coalition. (Kinnear, *Fall of Lloyd George*, 120–34; P. Williamson, *Stanley Baldwin* (Cambridge, 1999), 24–5.)

[15] Both refused. McKenna's refusal meant that the post went to Baldwin himself.

[16] Which was negotiated by Lloyd George and brought into being the Irish Free State.

[17] Green, *Ideologies of Conservatism*, 128.

gentry affected by post-war land sales were very anti-Lloyd George and it was often their 'connections' which were responsible for the rapid spread of the rebellion against Lloyd George in 1922. As Jonathan Bates has observed, Conservative parliamentary candidates 'were drawn from a small and well-connected pool' and he notes, for example, the way in which Lord Sandon's connections in three counties operated in an almost eighteenth-century way against Lloyd George.[18] Those who disliked Lloyd George's favourites and the not-so-mild smell of corruption that emanated from his government were cultivating well-tilled land. In these circumstances it is surprising that so many Conservative members of the coalition thought that its life under Lloyd George could be prolonged. The ease with which Sir George Younger, the chairman of the National Union and boss of the Conservative Party's organization, had destroyed proposals for an election at the beginning of 1922 should have disabused them.[19]

But Lloyd George was not the only problem. Fusion would probably have demanded union with the Asquithian Liberals as well. Politically that was not impossible. As long as the Conservatives did not threaten full-scale protection and once the Irish treaty was signed (1922) there was little to choose between Conservative and Independent Liberal policies—particularly and crucially on attitudes to government expenditure. Nevertheless, although among ordinary Conservatives hostility to Lloyd George was most intense, feelings towards Asquith and his allies were little warmer. Lloyd George had at least won the war; aside from his pre-war enormities Asquith also had to carry the burden of apparent wartime failure. The mean-minded but successful attempt to deprive him of the chancellorship of Oxford University in 1925 was an instance of how unforgiving the Tory memory was.[20]

But it takes more than one party to fuse. Apart from the coalition Liberals themselves, especially Lloyd George, Churchill and

[18] Bates, 'Conservative Party', 42.
[19] For this episode, see Ramsden, *Age of Balfour and Baldwin*, 158–9.
[20] For his defeat see R. Jenkins, *Asquith* (London, 1964), 510–12.

Christopher Addison, who after the war were largely partyless,[21] there were few in the Liberal Party as a whole who were happy to fuse with the Conservatives: less happy to fuse with the Conservatives than vote for them. Although Asquith was largely a lifeless leader when he returned to parliament in 1920[22] he still nourished a well-developed antipathy not just to Lloyd George but to the Tories who had deserted his government and himself in 1916. This antipathy was shared by the other leading opposition Liberals and only slowly discarded. Although, as I have suggested, the social and religious forces which sustained popular Liberalism had been much damaged by the war they still hung on, and the social worlds of local Anglicanism and Nonconformity remained largely distinct. What remained of the Liberal associations were, like the Conservative associations, dominated by Edwardians with long memories. For many active Liberals the coalition government was a union of apostates and traditional enemies. The Liberal Party never fully recovered from such apostasy, even in 1923 when its two wings were united in defence of free trade. Personal relations between the Liberals were always fraught—'thoughts too deep for tears' as Lord Curzon said of one meeting addressed by both Lloyd George and Asquith[23]—and the unity of the Party became increasingly fragile until it finally disintegrated in the 1929 parliament.[24]

The fundamental difficulty was that the Conservative and Liberal Parties, even though the latter was divided and decaying, were ideologically and historically well-entrenched; unlike the shallow-rooted protectionist and free trade parties in Australia. For many Tories, as a result, even the coalition demanded unacceptable sacrifices: Conservative agents and candidates, not to speak of the membership

[21] K. O. Morgan, *Consensus and Disunity: the Lloyd George Government 1918–1922* (Oxford, 1979), 182.

[22] He won a by-election for the seat of Paisley. Not one member of Lloyd George's coalition congratulated him.

[23] Quoted in M. Bentley, *The Liberal Mind, 1914–1929* (Cambridge, 1977), 89. In October 1925 C. P. Scott recorded Sir Donald Maclean as saying 'that there was no real reconciliation. Asquith's language in private about Lloyd George was lurid' (*Political Diaries of C. P. Scott*, 482–3).

[24] See below, 92–4.

of the Conservative associations, deeply resented having to cede constituencies to their coalition partners, often with dire consequences
to Tory organization. Moreover, it is likely that Conservative constituency parties never shared the Tory leadership's extreme fear
of Labour. The leadership (both those who favoured the coalition
and those who did not) always exaggerated the threat from Labour:
for coalitionists like Austen Chamberlain that threat was the main
argument for fusion. But many Tories were never convinced there
was such a threat, or if there were thought the Conservative Party
itself best placed to defeat it. Fusion made sense only if it were
clear that Labour was winning a majority of the working-class vote.
But with the working-class vote obviously still scattered—the Tories
had after all won a majority of it at the 1918 election—the case
for fusion was proportionately weakened. It was, in fact, the success of an anti-coalition Conservative in defeating Labour at a
by-election in Newport (a predominantly working-class seat) on the
eve of the Carlton Club meeting that persuaded many Tory MPs
that the coalition—let alone fusion—was not needed to hold off
Labour.[25] W. G. Runciman may exaggerate the extent to which
alternatives were foreclosed, but it is difficult to disagree with him
that what he calls the 'selective pressures' of English politics pointed
to the restoration of partisan politics on something like a pre-war
pattern.[26]

Fusion as an anti-socialist union demanded some kind of social
unity or commonality of economic experience on the part of the
anti-socialists, but the social base of the coalition fragmented before
such a union could be achieved. As Kenneth Morgan has argued,
the point of the coalition was to keep the class war at bay,[27] to
devise a political-economic system that would accommodate both
the middle and working classes, employers and employees, rentiers

---

[25] It was generally expected that Labour would win and Austen Chamberlain did
everything he could to impede the anti-coalition Conservative, Reginald Clary. (For the
by-election, see Kinnear, *Fall of Lloyd George*, 64.)

[26] W. G. Runciman, *A Treatise on Social Theory: Vol III Applied Social Theory*
(Cambridge, 1997), 177.

[27] Morgan, *Consensus and Disunity*, 76.

and professionals. In the immediate post-war years, however, such a strategy, though not impossible, was unlikely to succeed, as Lloyd George's government discovered. Rather, the coalition was under relentless pressure from its largest component, the Conservative Party, to satisfy its own constituency first. Once it began to do so, as it did from 1920 onwards, the coalition destroyed itself and left the future to moderate anti-coalitionists like Baldwin, who were determined to preserve the integrity of the Conservative Party but not to alienate unnecessarily what remained of the Liberal electorate.

How did this come about? The answer lies largely in the redistribution of wealth and property which occurred between 1914 and 1920. These years saw the most significant re-ordering of wealth in recent English history. There was via inflation, taxation and the pressures of the wartime labour market a general redistribution of wealth downwards: all, more or less, gained at the expense of those immediately above them.[28] The ultimate beneficiary in the short term was the man (and sometimes the woman) at the bottom: the unskilled manual working class. In the middle-class mind this meant, inaccurately but revealingly, the trade unionized working class, though in practice those who did best in the longer run tended not to be unionized. If this alone were what happened then the case for a two-party system based upon competition between those who lost and those who won—a fusion party and the Labour Party—would have been strong. But wealth redistribution was more complicated than this: although much went downwards as much went sideways. The details of loss and gain do not yield easy generalizations. Those, for example, who owned foreign bonds or equities were very likely to lose; and the owners of Russian bonds lost the lot. Those who owned houses subject to rent control after 1915 lost heavily while their tenants gained.[29] Those who owned stock in utility companies

[28] I have discussed this elsewhere. See McKibbin, *Classes and Cultures*, 50–9. There is a detailed discussion of changes in income and property in Waites, *Class Society at War*, 76–119.

[29] When the government introduced rent restriction legislation, fundamentally to buy the goodwill of those working in the armaments industries but also to mollify soldiers and their families.

(as many did) saw the real value of their return reduced by about half. Those who owned British government war debt lost and then gained. Shareholders in railway companies (again of whom there were many), due to the way the government compensated the companies after the war, lost while railway employees gained. Those on salaries, fixed pensions or fixed interest income, like long-term leases or debentures and had no alternative sources of income, all lost. The tendency of businesses to finance expansion from retained profits (and thus to reduce dividends) and the collapse of profits after 1919–20 probably added to the misery.[30] A. L. Bowley thought those who suffered most were 'the elderly members of the middle class whose investments were completed before 1913 (and usually at a fixed rate of interest) and pensioners'.[31] These losses were felt by much of the middle class and were the inevitable consequences not just of changes in the political balance of power—munitions workers are more necessary in a war than accountants—but by the way the war was partly financed, that is by inflation. Inflation, however, does not harm everyone equally; some it does not harm at all. Those whose income is derived from short-time bargains are affected least: brokers, dealers, shopkeepers were all able to protect themselves. The bigger the shopkeeper the better he did. Lord Leverhulme (Keynes's *bête noire*)[32] did not suffer. Nor did those in some way involved in war production—though the government moderated their good fortune via excess profits duties. These were the 'hard-faced men', the beneficiaries of government war contracts, who Stanley Baldwin thought were so over-represented in the House of Commons elected in 1918. It was they who encouraged people to see the post-war

[30] So Keynes thought (Waites, *Class Society at War*, 97). Although the average rate of dividend did not fall all that much.

[31] A. L. Bowley, *Some Economic Consequences of the Great War* (London, 1930), 76–7.

[32] See Keynes's comments on Leverhulme in the private sessions of the Macmillan Committee: 'I think [the post-war boom] was made possible by the megalomania of Lord Leverhulme and others'. Committee on Finance and Industry [usually called the Macmillan Committee], Private Session, (31 Oct. 1930), 8. This sitting is not recorded in the Royal Economic Society's edition of Keynes's *Collected Writings*.

world as divided between 'winners' and 'losers'. 'We began life again', Mrs Peel wrote,

in a world inhabited by what came to be known as the new rich and the new poor: the former those who had made money during the war and were sometimes rightly and sometimes unjustly called profiteers; the latter the landed gentry, professional classes and others whose incomes had been reduced or at best remained stationary in amount though practically halved in purchasing power.[33]

The political consequences of this fragmentation of wealth were very damaging to the coalition. They would have damaged any government in such circumstances but were especially harmful to one whose claim was to hold the ring, to rule in the interests of everyone. Like all the participants, after the First World War, England experienced class tensions hitherto unknown. There was the familiar war between the working and the not-working classes, but also a more complicated war between one part of the not-working class and another, between those who had done their bit during the war and had apparently lost thereby and those, the 'profiteer' or the 'rentier', who had not done their bit and had apparently gained thereby. These two words were among the most polemically charged in the political rhetoric of the immediate post-war period.[34] The word 'profiteer' was first used, not insignificantly, just before the outbreak of the First World War, and a few years after the word 'plutocrat' (a late-nineteenth-century word which acquired anti-semitic overtones during the Boer War) became widely used. By 1917 'profiteering' had become a central concept in the discourse of the war'.[35]

How potent the idea of the profiteer was can be seen from cartoons in almost any number of *Punch* in the early 1920s. The profiteer is depicted as sleek and elaborately dressed; his wife is bejewelled and befurred; both are conveyed to fashionable pleasure resorts in large

---

[33] Mrs C. S. Peel, *How We Lived Then, 1914–1918* (London, 1929), 6. Among the winners Mrs Peel included those working men who remained in work—but not those who became unemployed.

[34] I have also discussed this in *Classes and Cultures*, 54–7.

[35] Gregory, *Last Great War*, 139.

cars.[36] That they look stereotypically Jewish almost goes without saying. The word 'rentier' is of older vintage. By the end of the nineteenth century it was used to describe, more or less neutrally, anyone who lived mainly off investment income. After the war usage was less neutral. The rentier was now primarily a holder of government debt to whom a huge proportion of the annual budget was being paid. C. F. G. Masterman wrote of middle-class attitudes to the holders of government debt:

In two half-yearly lumps the Government pays out interest on over six thousand million pounds, owned by the men who stayed at home while the war was won. Some of their own kith and kin were thought to have assisted in that winning—now lying in half-forgotten graves; but now the six thousand millions are on their backs.[37]

That this debt was real, particularly after the rapid fall in prices which began in 1920, is not in doubt. By 1925 38.7 per cent of the annual budget was spent on debt-service compared with 12.4 per cent in 1912.[38] The word rentier came to connote the same sense of moral disapproval as profiteer or plutocrat. Rentiers, like profiteers, were socially useless people who did little for their country during the war except to lend it money for which they were to be repaid till the end of time.

Lloyd George's government was well aware of the power of words. In 1919 the Ministry of Labour argued that the 'popular adoption of the word "profiteering" was a widely used slogan which, if rather imprecise as an economic concept, as a moral commentary tended to bring profit into wider disrepute'.[39] The Treasury believed that

[36] The furs and jewels of the women munition workers or the wives of certain workingmen was also part of urban legend. The Revd Andrew Clark's daughter wrote to him from Scotland (14 Jan. 1917) that 'the wealthiest people of the period are the dockers at Invergordon many of whom are earning £8 a week and never less than £4. They hire motor cars on Sundays and go for long excursions over the country with their wives resplendent in furs and jewels.' (J. Munson (ed.), *Echoes of the Great War: The Diary of the Reverend Andrew Clark 1914–1919* (Oxford, 1985), 178–9.)

[37] C. F. G. Masterman, *England After War* (London, n.d. ?1922), 65.

[38] Waites, *Class Society at War*, 112.

[39] Quoted in R. Whiting, 'Taxation and the Working Class, 1915–1924', *Historical Journal* 33 (1990), 912.

without a capital levy[40] 'the rentier will be the subject of perpetual jealousy and perpetual attack'.[41] The great advantage of a levy on 'war wealth' to Austen Chamberlain was that 'it would meet the widespread feeling that the Profiteers have not contributed their share and (this is to me the strongest reason) thus avert from capital in general the prejudice aroused by the sight of such big fortunes made during the War'. Churchill suggested that unless some kind of wealth tax were introduced the coalition would 'become a plutocratic and not a national government'.[42] Coalition tax policy, therefore, was an attempt to devise a fair and so legitimate system of taxation which would at the same time not undermine the moral basis of a capitalist economy. Such was the origins of the Excess Profits Duty which at its height was levied at a rate of 60 per cent on profits deemed to be above 'normal'—a duty which survived until 1921.

A 'fair' system of taxation was politically imperative because it was demanded by the Tory electorate as well as the trade unions. When Churchill spoke of the dangers of plutocratic government he meant a government disliked as much by the middle as the working class. On the whole, the 'rich' were acceptable to the middle class. Plutocrats, or Mrs Peel's 'new rich', however, were not. These years were among the few occasions in modern English history when many members of the middle class were hostile to some forms of property and some kinds of capitalism. The working class might have been equally hostile but the anti-profiteering committees which sprang up in the south of England after 1918 were not staffed by working men or women. The coalition government fell, and with it the possibility of fusion, because it was subject to pressures which could only destroy it. Its crucial electorate—the Conservative-voting middle class—demanded of it policies which would weaken both trade unionism and speculative and/or rentier capitalism to the benefit of

---

[40] For which, see below, 50–2.

[41] Quoted in M. Daunton, 'How to Pay for the War: State, Society and Taxation in Britain, 1917–1924', *English Historical Review* 111 (1996), 892.

[42] Ibid. 904–6.

the salaried middle class, and it was the Conservative Party which acted as its political agent and Bonar Law and Baldwin, particularly, as its political representatives. In practice that class wanted, and eventually got, deflationary policies which restored the pre-war ratio of wages to salaries.[43]

What strikes the historian now is not only how vehement was this hostility to the plutocracy and the working class but also the familiarity of the language in which it was expressed. An important element in late-Victorian and Edwardian political rhetoric and literature was a sense that bourgeois society was living on the edge, that in the lower depths was a proletariat waiting to overwhelm it.[44] But so it was in the early 1920s. Much of the popular middle-class literature of the period differs little from the Edwardian literature of imperial crisis and decline. A striking instance of this was C. F. G. Masterman's accounts of the mood of the middle class in 1909 and again the early 1920s. In 1909, then Liberal MP for West Ham, he wrote:

The rich despise the working people: the Middle Classes fear them. Fear is the . . . motive power behind each successive uprising. In feverish hordes the suburbs swarm to the polling booth to vote against a truculent Proletariat. The Middle Class elector is becoming irritated and indignant against working-class legislation. He is growing tired of the plaint of the unemployed and the insistent crying of the poor. The spectacle of a Labour Party triumphant in the House of Commons . . . fills him with profound disgust . . . He has difficulty with the plumber in jerry-built houses needing continuous patching and mending. His wife is harassed by the indifference or insolence of the domestic servant. From a blend of these two he has constructed in imagination the image of Democracy—a loud-voiced, independent, arrogant figure, with a thirst for drink and imperfect standards of decency, and a determination to be supported at someone else's expense . . . He gazes darkly from his pleasant hill villa upon the huge and smoky area of tumbled tenements which

---

[43] McKibbin, *Classes and Cultures*, 58–9.
[44] For examples of this, see G. Stedman Jones, *Outcast London* (Oxford, 1971), 281–314.

stretches at his feet . . . Every hour he anticipates the boiling over of the cauldron.[45]

In 1921 he described the attitudes of the same class as follows:[46]

Richford [a middle-class suburb] hates and despises the working classes . . . partly because it has contempt for them, and partly because it has fear of them . . . Just on its borders, and always prepared seemingly to engulf it, are those great masses of humanity which accept none of its standards and maintain life on a totally different plane . . . Labour only enters its kingdom as a coal supply rendered ever more limited and expensive by the insatiable demands of the coal-miners to work short hours for immense wages; or the increase of its necessary season-ticket to 'town' owing to the demand of the railway workers for higher wages; or as the plumber, who is unable to mend its jerry-built houses; or the bricklayer who refuses to build any alternatives. It can walk but a few yards and it is in, say, Hoxditch [clearly in the East End—presumably an amalgam of Hoxton and Shoreditch], where all the inhabitants are dingy and all the houses are drab and over-crowded with swarms of discoloured children; and the public houses flare at every corner; and it realizes that this is the 'Labour' against which it is warned by all the supporters of things as they are.[47]

The second of these pieces should undoubtedly be treated with some care. Masterman always had an overdramatic style, and there could well have been an element of autobiography in it.[48] Nonetheless, *England After War* was meant to be a 'sequel' to the *Condition of England*: the chapter on the middle classes in the former 'picked

[45] Masterman, *Condition of England*, 71–2.

[46] It is not clear exactly when the book was written but internal evidence suggests it was 1920 or 1921.

[47] Masterman, *England After War*, 54–5.

[48] Masterman, having lost his government post at the end of the war, and no longer an MP, had no fixed income other than his journalism. His wife later wrote: 'I think these three years, 1921, 1922, 1923 were the hardest we had . . . Costs of living were still high and above all the uncertainty and unevenness of earning harassed him'. (L. Masterman, *C. F. G. Masterman* (London, 1939), 318–27.) For an interesting discussion of *England After War*, see S. Hynes, *A War Imagined: The First World War and English Culture* (London, 1990), 314–21. Masterman's post-war world, he writes 'was a dark vacancy, emptied of values, emptied even of imagination. He could see no positive force there, no political movement, and no vital faith' (p. 319). But what Masterman wrote in *The Condition of England* suggests that a 'dark vacancy' was not in his mind a consequence only of the First World War.

up the theme' of the same chapter in the latter.[49] There is thus no reason to doubt that what Masterman described in 1920 is what he saw, and what he saw in 1920 is very much what he saw in 1909, even down to the plumbers and the jerry-built houses. Masterman's assumption that many thought of immediate post-war England—and in a sense 'experienced' it—in Edwardian terms seems to me right and was of fundamental importance to post-war politics.

The most spectacular manifestation of the mood Masterman describes was the Anti-Waste movement, the press-led attack on 'wasteful' public expenditure: in Masterman's words, the middle classes' 'last desperate hope of survival'.[50] Balderston has argued that the 'virulent' Anti-Waste and other 'economy' movements were a result of the inflationary effects of the war on the balance of taxation. 'Without conscious design', he writes, 'the war thus broke the compact which had protected the broad mass of income tax payers since 1852.' The burden of direct taxation was increased by 'fiscal drag' and so therefore was the burden of public spending financed by direct taxation.[51] There is obvious truth in this. Many taxpayers must have seen a connection between the hugely increased levels of public expenditure and higher levels of taxation. To see Anti-Waste only in these terms, however, is either to exaggerate its specificity or to underestimate the breadth of its target. It was a movement not just against 'squandermania' but a whole way of life and a post-war settlement which (it was thought) disproportionately favoured shirkers of whatever class. In this view the coalition was a government which served the interests of shirkers, and by the end of 1920 many plainly thought this. In November 1920 an anti-spending independent (Lord Rothermere's son, Esmond Harmsworth) won the Wrekin by-election; in January 1921 another anti-spending independent supported by Lord Rothermere won Dover from the Conservatives, and in June 1921 official Anti-Waste candidates won

    [49] L. Masterman, *Masterman*, 318–27.   [50] Masterman, *England After War*, 56.
    [51] T. Balderston, 'War Finance and Inflation in Britain and Germany, 1914–1918', *Economic History Review*, 2nd series, 42, 2 (1989), 235.

Westminster St George's and Hertford from coalition Conservatives.[52] The government was eventually, if reluctantly, driven to recognize the strength of the 'economy' movement. It did not wish to alienate the working classes, nor was there much it could do about its association in the public mind with dubious financiers or shady war contractors, but it had little alternative than to embrace 'economy' and the famous 'Geddes Axe' was the result.[53] Once, however, it began to buckle under pressure from Anti-Waste and the Conservative (and Liberal)[54] grassroots, as it did from the beginning of 1920, the coalition became increasingly anachronistic: an expedient to see Britain through the war and immediate post-war whose existence could not be prolonged once cross-class alliances and heterodox policies ceased to be possible. Fusion died even before Lloyd George's government, and did so because the coalition's social and ideological base disintegrated once the war was won. Circumstances forbade a government of all the classes. As they did a government which united all property, since all property could not be united in the early 1920s.

The second alternative, akin to the first, was the construction of a two-party system founded upon a conflict between 'producers' and 'rentiers': roughly speaking between useful and useless members of society. This was a kind of Keynesian conflict. To the extent that there is a theory of political behaviour in *The General Theory* this is it. A society based upon the interests of the rentier was functionally defective: one of the consequences of its defects, Keynes argued, was a consistent tendency for economies to operate below productive capacity and thus with high levels of unemployment. The dethronement of the rentier—his 'gradual euthanasia' in Keynes's words—should therefore be the aim of public policy.[55] Although

[52] The defeated Conservatives also identified themselves as 'anti-waste'.

[53] For the appointment of the 'Geddes Committee', see Morgan, *Consensus and Disunity*, 245. For its report, 288–95. The government, of course, did not accept all the committee's recommendations, and could hardly have done so given the size of the cuts recommended.

[54] Asquith and Reginald McKenna were both strong critics of the government's level of spending as were most Asquithian Liberals.

[55] J. M. Keynes, *The General Theory of Employment, Interest and Money* (London, Royal Economic Society edn, 1973), 376. See more generally chapter 24: 'Concluding

Keynes did not argue explicitly that the interests of the rentier and those of productive society were politically antithetical, this was certainly the implication of his argument.[56] If it were the case that the interests of society and the rentier were opposed, that would indeed be the basis of an antagonistic two-party system. Throughout the 1920s the construction of a party of the useful was one of the ambitions of the Labour Party.

After its reorganization in 1918 and the adoption of its new constitution Labour followed two strategies. One was to be unambiguously a party of the working class—to protect its interests and institutions before anything else. The other was to be a party of the useful classes; people of goodwill who by their productive efforts served the wider interests of society. It was pursuit of the second strategy that encouraged Arthur Henderson to suggest in his first draft of Labour's new constitution that it might be renamed the People's Party,[57] and it was, as we shall see, the Party's inability to pursue either of these strategies consistently, or any other, that led to the disaster of 1931. Either strategy, however, appeared to exclude the rentier, who was neither working class nor useful.

The main financial instrument of the Labour Party's attempt to become a producers' party was, as Martin Daunton notes, the capital levy.[58] The capital levy was tax not on income but on wealth in kind. It was a levy on equities and fixed-interest stock and was specifically designed to pay off a substantial proportion of the now colossal national debt. In effect, it was a tax on the principal holders of that debt. The levy was not Labour Party policy alone. The Treasury had once favoured it, as had some members of the coalition government. But it was identified with Labour and was for a time Labour policy. And the capital levy helps to explain why Labour did not emerge in

Notes on the Social Philosophy towards which the General Theory might lead' (372–84).

[56] Though he came close to making it explicit. See *The Collected Writings of John Maynard Keynes*, Vol. XX (London, 1981), Macmillan Committee, Private Session (21 Feb. 1930), 68.

[57] McKibbin, *The Evolution of the Labour Party*, 93–4.

[58] Daunton, 'How to Pay for the War', 891.

the 1920s as a producers' party, the party of the useful. Technically, it was a difficult tax. It would have been hard for the markets to have absorbed such large amounts of stock as would have appeared, and though Labour was ready to tax the 'bondholder' it was increasingly reluctant to upset the ordered working of the market. Furthermore, a large proportion of the debt was held by institutions like insurance companies and building societies which were central to the national life.[59] How would they be taxed and with what consequence? It was for these reasons that the Treasury abandoned the levy. Such political gains as the levy might have won were outweighed, it argued, by the likely fiscal losses. The Labour Party also discovered that the levy seemed to have little attraction to working-class voters. This may have been because of the tax's expropriationary implication; something perhaps unpopular even with those who had nothing to expropriate. Or because the working class was itself a larger holder of the debt than people thought.[60] Whatever the reason Labour gave up the tax and so unquestionably weakened its stance as a producers' party. It was left only with a rhetorical appeal to the useful. Richard Whiting has argued that 'support for . . . capital taxation was strongest when an essentially nineteenth-century radical argument could be launched about the burdens of the *rentier* and the bondholder upon the rest of the population. It was a case of rescuing a rather small state from the consequences of debt. This worked especially well after the First World War; it had much less impact after the Second.'[61] As a rhetorical strategy it undoubtedly had some success during and after

[59] Waites, *Class Society at War*, 112.

[60] If true, it was probably a result of the purchase of war savings certificates by wage-earners (Waites, *Class Society at War*, 104). The Revd Andrew Clark recorded in his diary for 6 June 1918 that 'M. E. Hughes called this evening. He said: When the local War Savings Association was first suggested to him by Canon O. W. Tancock he threw cold water on it, not believing that people in Great and Little Leighs would have any savings to invest. He has been greatly surprised by the number of members who have joined, and at the amount they have paid in. All his indoor servants, and almost all his outdoor men are regular contributors.' (Munson (ed.), *Echoes of the Great War*, 239.) Clark's comment stands in contrast to Gregory's conclusion that the savers of rural England were not especially patriotic (Gregory, *Last Great War*, 137).

[61] R. Whiting, 'The Boundaries of Taxation', in S. J. D. Green and R. C. Whiting (eds.), *The Boundaries of the State in Modern Britain* (Cambridge, 1996), 149.

the First World War. In practice, however, as an agent of policy, it was much less successful.

In any case, as the Treasury asked on a number of occasions, who were the rentiers and the profiteers, and was that all they were? These were fluid categories. The individual holders of government debt were a mixed bunch and few lived entirely off its receipts. Many members of the salaried or professional middle class were themselves owners of fixed-interest government stock, patriotically bought, as were businessmen and industrialists who by most definitions were in fact producers. Keynes himself recognized that, at least for purposes of taxation, it was difficult to distinguish between the rentier and the 'enterpriser'.[62] Their interests as one might conflict with their interests as the other. However effective as political vocabulary were the terms 'rentier' and 'profiteer', as partly ideological constructions they were not safe foundations for a new party system. Thus some kind of cross-class alliance dependent upon a simple functional definition of society was always going to be difficult. In the circumstances of the 1920s, furthermore, the Labour Party of all parties could not have become the base of such an alliance. A more likely outcome was a cross-class alliance *against* Labour. The failure of fusion and Labour's inability to become a producers' party were, therefore, closely related: a result of the survival of two historic parties (though one much weakened), the degree of antipathy to 'socialism,' and the multiplicity of economic role typical of any modern economy.

The third alternative was to abandon free trade. This was not a narrow question of customs' duties: the free-trade fiscal system was the pole around which British politics had moved for eighty years. It underlay a form of liberal government and social and economic relationships central to British life and very difficult to defy—as the Conservatives found to their cost in 1906. Its abandonment would have involved, therefore, more than just the imposition of customs'

---

[62] Macmillan Committee, Private Session (24 Oct. 1930), 21. This sitting is not included in the Royal Economic Society's edition of Keynes's *Collected Writings*.

duties; it implied a significant reconstruction of the whole political system, of its economic authority (which mattered most, finance or industry?) and its mental and psychological underpinnings—as it was to do in the 1930s. It would also have been the most powerful symbolic break with Edwardian politics conceivable. There were already good arguments for doing it. Most of the conditions which permitted the (more or less) effective working of free trade before the war had gone. Even before 1914 Britain's had been the only fully 'open' economy. But then it was financially and industrially strong enough to sustain that role. After 1918, itself much weaker and the world now even more protectionist, it could no longer do so. Even setting a 'good example' to the rest of the world—something which many urged—was now beyond her. In the 1920s the only country strong enough to set a good example was the United States, which had no intention of doing so. The benefits, therefore, which Britain derived from free trade were now much less obvious, and as unemployment rose to unprecedented levels after 1920, protection—particularly of industries like iron and steel—seemed one of the few job-creating policies immediately to hand. As a result, the intellectual and economic interest-group defences of free trade were now much weaker.[63] Thus people like Keynes or Reginald McKenna, free traders to a man before 1914, were edging towards some form of protection. Indeed the first steps had already been taken. In 1915 McKenna himself, as chancellor of the exchequer, was responsible for imposing duties on imported 'luxury' goods (the so-called McKenna Duties), and the importation of certain goods like dyes or scientific or optical instruments had been embargoed during the war.[64] The Corn Production Act was designed to give British agriculture some protection during the war, though it had been repealed, controversially, after it. The Safeguarding of Industries Act (1921) provided a form of protection for a limited number of industries (though more limited than

---

[63] For this, see F. Trentmann, *Free Trade Nation* (Oxford, 2008), 241–330.
[64] Though the embargo had been allowed to run out in 1919.

many wanted) and the state was using types of quasi-protection, like bounties, more than it did before the war. Finally, Britain's adherence to that indispensable prop of international free trade, the gold standard, had been ended in 1919, and though it was understood that Great Britain would return to gold in due course, she experienced sufficient time off it to make return (certainly at par) always contentious.[65]

The collapse of employment in the great 'staple' industries after 1920 provided protection with its historic opportunity. In effect what happened was what Joseph Chamberlain always said would happen; though before 1914 it never did. Furthermore, the Conservatives, having overthrown the coalition in October 1922 for essentially negative reasons, were rather bereft of anything positive. Bonar Law, who became prime minister on Lloyd George's resignation, had fought and won an election on the policy of 'tranquillity', which, while undoubtedly eschewing the excitements of Lloyd George's premiership, promised little else.[66] 'The only way forward', as Ramsden has written, 'seemed to be to go back to the politics of tariff reform, the party's only positive contribution to political economy, its only real point of positive belief, and a policy that might have been made popular by years of depression.'[67] Stanley Baldwin, who had succeeded Bonar Law as prime minister in May 1923, chose to seize the moment. Baldwin, the son of a West Midlands ironmaster, was an old protectionist and in October 1923 declared himself in favour of tariffs. After some dithering, he sought the approval of the electorate in December to introduce them. Although Baldwin no doubt saw this as a way of restoring coalitionist Tories to the Party—many like

[65] In that year the free export of gold had been stopped and the exchange value of sterling left to the markets.

[66] In the election (15 Nov. 1922) the Conservatives won 344 seats (307 in England), Labour 142 (95 in England), the Asquithian Liberals 64 (44 in England), the Lloyd George Liberals 53 (31 in England). There were 10 independents: most Conservatives of one sort or another. One Communist was elected in Scotland—J. T. Walton Newbold, really the Labour candidate. But a number of Lloyd George Liberals were elected without Conservative opposition on a Conservative vote, and there were a number of anti-Labour agreements between Liberals and Conservatives more generally.

[67] Ramsden, *Age of Balfour and Baldwin*, 177.

Austen Chamberlain strongly protectionist—this was incidental. He undoubtedly thought protection the most efficacious way of reducing unemployment[68] and that he would win an election on such a programme.

Baldwin, however, failed to win a parliamentary majority. The result of his action was to reunite the Liberal Party as the historic defender of free trade with both Asquith and Lloyd George signing its manifesto, and to provide the Labour Party with another opportunity to advance in industrial England.[69] Given the plausibility of the arguments for protection, why did it fail? First, because it became clear that the Conservative Party and its press supporters were more divided on the issue (or more indifferent) than Baldwin assumed. Lords Rothermere and Beaverbrook were opposed to simple protection, which Baldwin was offering or appeared to offer. They wanted imperial preference, which Joseph Chamberlain offered in 1903. The *Daily Mail* thus supported Lloyd George and the *Daily Express*'s support was tepid at best. The Party's small number of free traders, like Lord Salisbury and his brother Lord Robert Cecil, the 'free fooders' of Edwardian days, remained opposed, but did not actually leave the Party.[70] Lancashire Toryism retained its free trade allegiances, based as they were on the cotton industry's fiscal traditions; and they partly explain the heavy Conservative losses to the Liberals in Lancashire. Much of suburban England also turned out to be surprisingly hostile. Although many of the coalition protectionists did return to the Party its unity was not restored; it was merely fractured in a different way.

Second, protection failed because the Labour Party and most of its electorate remained free trade. Free-trade socialism was still,

---

[68] For this, see ibid. 177–81; R. Self, 'Conservative Reunion and the General Election of 1923', *Twentieth Century British History* 3, 3 (1992); N. Smart, 'Baldwin's Blunder? The General Election of 1923', and rejoinder by Self in *Twentieth Century British History* 7, 1 (1996).

[69] The result of the election was Conservative 258 seats (221 in England), Labour 191 (138 in England), Liberal 158 (123 in England). The Conservatives won 38 per cent of the vote, Labour 30.7 per cent and the Liberals 29.7 per cent.

[70] Though it was the occasion for Lord Robert Cecil's retirement from the House of Commons. (Viscount Cecil of Chelwood, *All the Way* (London, 1949), 179–80.)

for better or worse, the dominant form of English socialism. For this reason Balderston's argument that the damage done to the Edwardian taxation system by wartime inflation destroyed 'the free trade consensus' seems clearly wrong.[71] As an ideology free trade remained politically central to both middle and working-class politics. Trentmann probably exaggerates the scepticism with which simple free trade was regarded in the electorate at large and some of the evidence he adduces to support his view is not entirely convincing.[72] But its survival also introduced another element of incoherence into the party structure and forms of political representation. Once Baldwin accepted that protection was electorally dead (at least in the short term) Britain was left with a fiscal system in which the largest party, the Conservative Party, had little or no belief, to which the second largest party (Labour) was committed although free trade was incompatible with almost all its other policies except free collective bargaining and even that was primarily a union policy, and whose only unqualified supporter, the Liberal Party, was the weakest of the three parties, the one almost certainly on the wrong side of history.

The failure of protection committed England in the 1920s to a largely futile politics which was increasingly distant from the structure and economy of English society. It postponed for a decade that re-adjustment of politics to society which eventually occurred after 1931 under a protectionist regime, but which the Tories could not do in the 1920s. The maintenance of free trade precluded the Conservatives from making a quasi-Chamberlainite appeal to the working

[71] Balderston, 'War Finance and Inflation', 235.

[72] For example, he cites the exemplary case of the constituencies of Sheffield Hillsborough and Paisley. In Sheffield Hillsborough A. V. Alexander, the Labour and Co-op candidate, defeated a free-trade Liberal, simply because he was the Labour candidate not because his form of free trade was more popular than the Liberal's. No Liberal could have won Hillsborough after 1922. As to Paisley (the constituency which had returned Asquith to parliament in 1920) it is not clear what Trentmann is arguing. Asquith had always been elected and re-elected in Paisley only as a result of divisions within the local Labour Party, and he was defeated (in 1924) once these divisions had been healed (Trentmann, *Free Trade Nation*, 223–5). The suggestion that in the early 1920s free trade was 'feeble and mostly silent' (p. 306) is also, in my view, an exaggeration.

class—'tariff reform means jobs for all'—until the 1930s; just as it precluded the Australian justification for protection—protected wages in a protected market.[73]

Its failure also committed England to a largely sterile system of industrial relations whose most pointless expression was the general strike of 1926: a sympathetic strike undertaken by the TUC without hope in expectation of failure.[74] Although the union movement was dominated by the right, attempts to devise an alternative form of industrial relations were never fulfilled. For this the unions were by no means wholly to blame. The failure of the so-called Mond–Turner talks was a result of employer obstruction at least as much as union inertia,[75] but their failure left industrial relations frozen. The abandonment of free trade could have released the labour movement from its ideological overcommitment to free collective bargaining and from that ambivalence towards the state which hobbled the Labour Party and within a few years came close to wrecking it.

The electoral failure of protection eliminated other possibilities and made certain something hitherto only likely—the return of

[73] The assistant secretary of the cabinet, Thomas Jones, thought there was 'no champion in the Government ranks comparable to Joseph Chamberlain. I saw no one with the ability and drive to make the case [for protection]'. (Thomas Jones, *Whitehall Diary 1916–1925*, 249.)

[74] The literature on the general strike is abundant. The best single account remains G. A. Phillips, *The General Strike* (London, 1976).

[75] The Mond–Turner talks were the result of an approach by Sir Alfred Mond, chairman of ICI, to the TUC whose aim was to recast British industrial relations on the basis of union recognition, conciliation and arbitration, industrial rationalization, and the encouragement of economic policies more favourable to industry as a whole. The TUC, rather battered after the general strike, was ready to participate. The talks, which began in January 1928, were alternately chaired by Mond and Ben Turner, chairman of the general council of the TUC. Had it been left to the elites of both the employers' organizations and the unions something might have been achieved. But the smaller employers and management, especially those who had to deal with the unions on the shopfloor, were strongly opposed to union recognition and compulsory conciliation. Nor was it likely that the proposals would have had much support among the union rank and file. In any case, the onset of depression (and Mond's death) so altered the industrial climate that the talks petered out. (For Mond–Turner, see Clegg, *History of British Trade Unions*, 464–71; H. F. Gospel, 'Employers and Managers: Organisation and Strategy, 1914–1939', in C. Wrigley (ed.), *A History of British Industrial Relations Vol II: 1914–1939* (Brighton, 1987), 173–7.)

the pound to the gold standard at the pre-war parity.[76] Protection was heterodox; to have formally abandoned free trade would have made possible a different monetary policy. The preservation of free trade permitted the re-enthronement of gold which in turn implied (indeed few denied it) that the perceived needs of the London money market would have priority over other economic desiderata: high levels of employment for example. How far the return to gold at par weakened the British economy in the 1920s is a matter of dispute. Keynes thought it overvalued the pound by about 10 per cent, a figure now thought to be too high. And few would agree with him that the coalminers paid the price for overvaluation or that the general strike was its immediate consequence. The coal industry was in desperate straits before 1925 and, in any case, there was no significant overall fall in British real wages between 1925 and 1929. (Though, equally, there was no recouping the relative losses of the years 1920–4.) What it did was to encourage a caste of mind which came close to paralysing policy after 1929 when the relatively benign international circumstances of 1925 disappeared, and a rigid, often irrational association between free trade, the gold standard and the impossibility of devaluation—not least among the leadership of the Labour Party. Such irrationality lay behind Philip Snowden's notorious comments to the cabinet on 22 August 1931, at the height of the crisis:

The Chancellor of the Exchequer informed the Cabinet of the nature of the consequences that would follow a departure from the gold standard. So far as he was concerned, he had no doubt whatever if he was compelled to choose between retaining the Labour movement in its present form and reducing the standard of living of the workman by 50 per cent, which would be the effect of departing from the gold standard, he knew where his duty would lie.[77]

---

[76] That is at $4.86—the rate of the pound against the dollar in 1914.

[77] This is discussed in D. E. Moggridge, *British Monetary Policy 1924–1931* (Cambridge, 1972), 228–33. None of Snowden's former ministerial colleagues publicly reminded him of these comments when as chancellor in the National government he was responsible for taking the pound off gold. Snowden's comment here might be set

Despite its consequences, free trade had unquestionably won the 1923 election, and the Liberals had little option but to put Labour, as the larger of the two free-trade parties, into office.[78] The first Labour government, which lasted for nine months in 1924, was, despite its brief life, significant for two reasons. The first was largely to destroy whatever hopes people had for the reconstruction of the progressive alliance. In terms of policy there was unquestionably much in common between Radical Liberals, like C. P. Scott of the *Manchester Guardian*, and Labour. But in putting Labour into office Asquith set no conditions and secured no agreements. Nor would he have got any had he tried. On the contrary, Ramsay MacDonald, the new prime minister, spent much of his first ministry complaining of the parliamentary behaviour of the Liberals and of their general impossibility.[79] This dismayed those who saw in MacDonald's government an opportunity to mobilize a new progressive majority. What explains this? One explanation is that it was the result of electoral competition: both parties were competing for the same progressive territory. Labour thus had no interest in encouraging a rival. But it is questionable how far they were competing for the same territory. They were perhaps competing for the same free-trade electorate—but that is quite different. Much of the Liberal electorate of 1923 was not 'progressive'; and much of the Liberal front bench no longer was. Labour's behaviour is better explained by the history of Liberal–Labour relations. The fact is Labour's enforced subservience

next to his wife's reply to Keynes on proposals to modify the fiscal system. On 1 March 1931 Keynes sent Snowden a copy of his 'Proposals for a Revenue Tariff'. A few days later Mrs Snowden replied. 'I grieve', she wrote, 'to have to return your article unread by my husband, but he is really too ill to give his mind to anything. I have read your article, and will tell him the contents when he is able to listen. I dare say he will feel as sad as I do that you should think it necessary to take this line, for we are as strongly convinced that it is as wrong (taking a long view) as you are that it is right'. (Ethel Snowden to Keynes, 7 March, 1931 in *Collected Writings of John Maynard Keynes*, Vol. XX. 488–9.) For the 1931 crisis, see below, 69–70 n.

[78] The most recent study of the first Labour government is J. Shepherd and K. Laybourn, *Britain's First Labour Government* (Basingstoke, 2006). The older book by R. W. Lyman, *The First Labour Government 1924* (London, 1957) is still useful.

[79] For good examples of MacDonald's attitudes, see *The Political Diaries of C. P. Scott*, 448–78, esp. 448–9; also D. Marquand, *Ramsay MacDonald* (London, 1977), 320–1.

to the Liberals before 1914 was always resented at a personal level by Labour MPs, even those like MacDonald and Henderson who felt there was little alternative. MacDonald was particularly touchy about these perceived slights. Even before the 1924 government had been formed he told C. P. Scott that 'there must be an end to the flaunting of Labour's dependence [on the Liberals]. It might be tolerated once, it might be tolerated twice, but after that, if repeated, he would speak out strongly.' He showed, Scott thought, 'a curious sensitiveness on this and spoke with feeling, as though this were a matter of deep importance'. Scott concluded that it was probably the matter 'on which his party feels most and on which he would be most exposed to attack'.[80] What was true of the parliamentary party was almost certainly true of much of the Party's national membership—many of whom had never shared the parliamentary party's readiness to co-operate with the Liberals, even before 1914 when there really were few alternatives.

In any case, how much was there to co-operate on? Except in the sphere of foreign policy, where the government had a reasonably clear idea what it wanted and for whom the successful carrying of the Dawes Plan was important,[81] it is unclear exactly what MacDonald and his colleagues intended or how long a life they thought the government had. Certainly no long-term programme was envisaged and MacDonald himself was vague about the government's future. Although Snowden was very critical of MacDonald's leadership and thought there was no reason why the government should have ended when it did,[82] most members of the Party, like MacDonald, seem to have thought of the government as a kind of public relations exercise

---

[80] *Political Diaries of C. P. Scott*, 453 (6 Jan. 1924).

[81] For the Dawes Plan, see Shepherd and Laybourn, *Britain's First Labour Government*, op. cit.

[82] For Snowden's views, see Marquand, *MacDonald*, 391–2; *Political Diaries of C. P. Scott*, 472 (13 Jan. 1925). There is little doubt that MacDonald's handling of the Zinoviev letter affair was incompetent; but he was hardly helped by the Foreign Office. Although he agreed that a sub-committee of the outgoing Labour cabinet should enquire into the circumstances of the affair at his insistence the role of the civil service was excluded from its terms of reference, though in private he was very critical of the Foreign Office.

designed to show that Labour could govern without disaster, and seem happy to have brought its short life to an end.[83]

The second reason for the government's significance was in confirming the role of anti-socialism in both entrenching Conservatism and undermining the Liberal Party and a more traditional radical progressivism. The first Labour government thus brought to an end—at least temporarily—a period of party confusion by fashioning the party system around an anti-socialist Conservative Party. Baldwin soon found that while protection was unpopular anti-bolshevism was not. From the moment Labour took office and Baldwin foreswore protection the electorate began to polarize partly around Labour but much more around the Conservatives. Furthermore, the circumstances in which the 1924 election was fought could hardly have been more favourable to the Tories.[84] Forced to bring into being a Labour government, Asquith was then forced to fight another election on an issue—Labour's relationships with the Communist Party and with the Soviet Union—which was uniquely favourable to the Conservatives. Circumstances and Tory demagoguery had so contrived it that for much of the electorate in 1924 the choice was between 'socialism' and 'anti-socialism'—and there was only one winner if that were the choice. Daunton has argued that the Conservative Party met the challenge of Labour's attempt to construct

[83] Particularly as they thought the government was likely to be defeated in the near future anyway on the trade treaty with the Soviet Union. See n. 84 below.

[84] The government chose to be defeated in a vote on the Campbell case. The Attorney-General, Sir Patrick Hastings, had intended to prosecute for sedition the editor of the Communist *Workers' Weekly*, J. R. Campbell (a wounded ex-serviceman, a matter of some importance), for articles that apparently called on British servicemen not to fire on their fellow workmen either in war or peace. The decision to prosecute—probably a mistake anyway—was unpopular with many Labour MPs and Hastings admitted that before he withdrew the prosecution (as he did) both MacDonald and Henderson (home secretary) had suggested that the prosecution was unwise. The Conservatives decided to move a vote of censure; the Liberals an amendment: that a committee of the House of Commons be appointed to enquire into the government's actions. MacDonald chose to treat both the motion and amendment as matters of confidence. The Conservatives unexpectedly withdrew their motion and the government was defeated on the Liberal amendment. At the same time as Communist sedition was being worked up as an issue the government was negotiating a trade treaty with the Soviet Union which was strongly attacked by the Conservatives, Lloyd George, and some other Liberals.

a 'producers' party (which Labour had in fact abandoned by 1924) by becoming an alliance of small and large property, as it obviously did.[85] But that is not how the Conservative Party presented itself to people who had no property. 'Socialism' was not only about property or threats to property, it was about threats to the constitution. The Conservative Party of the 1920s is best understood as the party of the constitution and, unlike the pre-war years, that was a plausible self-description.[86] Furthermore, Baldwin's constitutionalism had a moderating effect on the Conservative Party and especially its press. For Baldwin, Schwarz argues, there was a crucial distinction between 'public opinion' and 'propaganda'. Left to themselves the press lords practised an unacceptable propaganda: under Baldwin's influence they represented 'public opinion'.[87] Churchill is a good example of Baldwinian constitutionalism. In 1923 he was defeated as a free-trade Liberal in Leicester. In March 1924 (two months after the formation of the first Labour government) he stood in a by-election for the Westminster Abbey constituency as an 'Independent Anti-Socialist' with much Tory and press support.[88] In the general election of October 1924 he stood in Epping and was elected as a 'Constitutionalist'. He immediately joined Baldwin's second government as chancellor of the exchequer.

The Labour government was defeated in the House of Commons on 8 October and the general election was held 29 October. In a significantly higher turnout than 1923 (77% as against 71.1% in 1923) the Conservatives won a victory which exceeded even their victory at the 'khaki election' of 1900.[89] The size of the victory was largely due to the significant decline in the Liberal vote; a decline

---

[85] Daunton, 'How to Pay for the War', 894.

[86] I have discussed this elsewhere. McKibbin, *Classes and Cultures*, 58–9.

[87] B. Schwarz, 'The Language of Constitutionalism: Baldwinite Conservatism', in *Formations of Nation and People* (London, 1984), 1–9.

[88] He stood against an official Conservative who only narrowly beat him. The result of Churchill's intervention was that the Labour candidate, Emanuel Shinwell, bizarrely, came close to winning.

[89] The Conservatives won 412 seats (347 in England, to which should be added seven 'Constitutionalists'), Labour 151 (109 in England), the Liberals 40 (19 in England).

magnified by the sharp fall in the number of Liberal candidacies.[90] Former Liberal voters favoured the Conservatives over Labour by about two to one. The Labour vote rose from 30.7 per cent (29.9% in England) to 33.3 per cent (32.9% in England) but since there was a significant increase in the number of Labour candidacies—from 427 to 514 (350 to 414 in England) the vote per Labour candidate did not in practice increase markedly. More generally, the first Labour government, the 1924 election and Baldwin's second government (1924–9) seemed to establish that, when compelled to choose, most Liberal voters preferred the Conservatives to Labour: a cardinal fact of interwar politics. That in turn suggested that a renewed progressive alliance was almost impossible. The potential for alliance building had moved from the left to the right: from an anti-Conservative to an anti-Labour front. An essentially conservative (and Conservative) definition of 'constitutionalism'—even if one already widely held in the labour movement[91]—was entrenched and became largely unchallengeable. 'Constitutional' behaviour became identified with parliamentary behaviour. Strikes, even more sympathetic strikes, apparently designed to compel a constitutionally elected government to enforce wage-increases or changes to conditions of work were defined as illegitimate and therefore unconstitutional. That was the significance of the general strike. It was defeated because the TUC and the Labour Party (to the extent that the Labour Party's views mattered) could think of no convincing way to argue that it was not unconstitutional; not designed to force a constitutionally elected government to change its policies via unparliamentary action.

[90] The Conservative share vote rose from 38 per cent (39.8% in England) in 1923 to 46.8 per cent (47.6% in England). The Liberal share fell to 17.8 per cent (17.6% in England) from 29.7 per cent in 1923 (29.9% in England). The fall in the number of Liberal candidacies was largely a result of Lloyd George's unwillingness to use his political fund to support a greater number.

[91] Schwarz argues that Baldwinite Conservatism depended, above all, on the education of Labour into an acceptance of constitutionalism (Schwarz, 'Language of Constitutionalism', 9). But the suggestion that Labour had to be educated into constitutionalism is misleading. However much people doubted it, the labour movement as a whole was always committed to a widely accepted definition of constitutionalism, which is why it got itself into such a tangle during the general strike.

The 1924 election also established, in broad terms, the victory of the middle class over the working class. It represented a successful struggle to re-establish the social *status quo ante bellum*. That struggle had been central to British politics from 1920 on. It had brought down the coalition government, was responsible for Baldwin's emergence as Conservative leader, and determined the tax policies of both Conservative and Labour governments. The decision of both the Treasury and the Labour Party to forgo a capital levy and then the excess profits duties allowed the restoration of an essentially Edwardian tax system. Although people certainly paid more tax than in 1914—especially the rich—the structure of taxation was fundamentally that built by Lloyd George between 1909 and 1914 and remained very favourable to the middle class as a whole. Labour's acceptance of this and of the return of the pound to the gold standard at par showed how ready it was to acquiesce in policies which often did not favour its electorate.

In the short term, all this had a semi-stabilizing effect. Like the Edwardian system the political system of the 1920s was based upon a delicate equipoise. It more or less worked, and it had in 'anti-socialism' and 'socialism' some kind of organizing unity. People knew what politics was about. But the elements of instability were more pronounced: no one could safely bet on the system's future. It represented an attempt to restore Edwardian party-politics and political language although the major structural supports for such a system now hardly existed. It had enough life not to die immediately, but no more. Free collective bargaining, for example, was strong enough to resist any general attempt to force down British labour costs after the return to gold in 1925 but was too weak to do anything helpful for the miners or anyone else working in the old heavily depressed staple industries. The 1920s system imposed free trade on the country at a time when the argument for protection was probably stronger than it had ever been. And the unions allowed themselves to be dragged by Baldwin into the cul-de-sac of the general strike.

Furthermore, it only worked when there were two parties of almost equal size. But the Labour Party, despite its apparent rapid growth after 1918, was, for whatever reason, simply never strong enough to slip into the role the Liberals had vacated. Even at its best the Labour Party in the 1920s never got much more than one-third of the votes. In other words, it was less successful in mobilizing its potential electorate than the Liberals had been before 1914. But the Liberals, like the system, still had a half-life. Had they been able to contest more seats they would almost certainly have got about 20 per cent of the votes even in the unfavourable circumstances of 1924. There was a decaying nonconformist electorate which still remained attached to the Party and it found a new role: as a kind of middle-class protest party.

By 1929 it had become apparent that the electorate created by Baldwin in 1924 had to some extent fragmented and the Liberals, rather willy nilly, were one of the beneficiaries.[92] Given the success of his anti-socialist and constitutional strategies during the 1924 elections and the general strike, that Baldwin's electorate fragmented in 1929 is at first sight surprising. The re-establishment, however, of a quasi-Edwardian system, free trade and all, hobbled the Tories as much as anyone else. Thus the Conservative majority was shakier than it appeared. In pursuit of constitutionalism Baldwin had to take risks, which he undoubtedly did, provoking the general strike being one. And though the government won the strike hands down it proved difficult to consolidate the 'victory' by legislation, other than via the petty 1927 Trades Disputes Act, which violated 'fairness' since the its principal victim was actually the Labour Party. The government's 'constructive' legislation, for example the widows', orphans' and old age pensions legislation (1925) and the major reforms to local government introduced by Neville Chamberlain in 1928, were insufficient to hold the Party's 1924 electorate together. Nor had Baldwin devised a way of permanently incorporating the Liberal vote within the anti-socialist bloc.[93] Baldwin's second government

[92] Lloyd George did, however, try to devise a genuine rural policy. See M. Dawson, 'Liberal Land Policy, 1924–1929', *Twentieth Century British History* 2, 3 (1991).

[93] It has been suggested to me that the Prayer Book controversy, by emphasizing the Conservative Party's continuing Anglican character, might have alienated otherwise

was, therefore, not able to exploit the potential of constitutional anti-socialism as the Tories did after 1931.[94] In the 1929 election, which the Conservatives fought under the slogan 'Safety First', the Conservative vote in England declined by 9 per cent, and some of that loss went to the Liberals, whose vote rose by 6 per cent. Much of that 6 per cent was simply a result of an increased number of candidates: though this in turn demonstrated how many people would still vote Liberal if they had a Liberal to vote for. Liberal gains were most marked in rural and, to some extent, suburban England and suggested that Baldwin's moderate Tory anti-socialism still had to find a permanent home in parts of the country, especially where there were discontented farmers and active nonconformists.[95] The Liberals, by siphoning off enough votes from the Conservative Party, propelled Labour into office in 1929 as they had done in January 1924. The electoral system, however, which consistently under-represented them, denied the Liberals the opportunity to convert short-term protests and a residual nonconformist vote into longer-term political power: it repeatedly forced the electorate to choose between two larger class-based parties.

Labour's 'victory' in the 1929 election, when for the first time it became the largest party in the House of Commons, pointed to nearly all the flaws in the post-war political settlement. Victory was only partly a result of its own efforts. The Liberal Party, once again well funded by Lloyd George, and, as we have seen, contesting many more seats than in 1924, cost the Tories perhaps two million votes which otherwise would have been theirs. Nor was there much symmetry

sympathetic nonconformist voters, and there could be truth to that. (For the controversy, see McKibbin, *Classes and Cultures*, 277–8.)

[94] See the following chapter.

[95] The results of the 1929 election, held on 30 May 1929, were: Labour 287 seats (226 in England), Conservative 260 (221 in England), Liberals 59 (35 in England). The Conservatives won 38.1per cent of the votes (38.8% in England), Labour 37.1 per cent (36.9% in England), the Liberals 23.6 per cent (23.6% in England.) The Liberals contested 174 more seats and Labour 55 more. The 1929 election was the first to be held under universal suffrage—all women were enfranchised in 1928—and this probably favoured Labour by diluting the middle-class and elderly character of the female electorate.

between the Liberal programme and its voters. Lloyd George, as is well known, fought the 1929 election on a semi-Keynesian 'reconstructionist' programme, *We Can Conquer Unemployment*. But the unemployed on the whole did not vote Liberal. Nor were most of the Liberal Party's new voters 'reconstructionists'. They were former Liberals who had voted Conservative in 1924 and who had little interest in radical economic policies, except in so far as they helped the farmer. Lloyd George mined about as much of the traditional nonconformist and 'provincial' Liberal electorate as still existed. Nor, as was to become clear, were most Liberal MPs much interested in radical policies. The 1929 election therefore brought into office a party which owed its victory largely to the intervention of another party which fought the election on a programme neither the majority of its voters nor its MPs believed in. These were not happy circumstances in which to take office.

In a sense, those who have argued either that the First World War changed nothing or that it changed everything are both right. The dynamic of Edwardian politics was provided by the progressive alliance: an alliance driven by a still viable free-trade fiscal system and dominated by the Liberal Party. In this relationship Labour was a necessary but subordinate partner. Furthermore, Masterman in the first of the passages quoted above (p. 46), exaggerated the extent to which the Edwardian middle class was unprotected from the greed and hostility of the working class. The Liberal government, in fact, had been surprisingly successful in holding the demons of Edwardian politics at bay. The war, however, by unshackling Labour, released these demons and so destroyed the progressive alliance. There was thus no 'progressive majority' after 1918 and those who thought it might be remade were constantly disappointed. If obliged to choose between them, as increasingly they were, most Liberals preferred the Conservatives to Labour. The Labour victories of 1924 and 1929 were therefore merely artefacts of an electoral system which inadequately reflected the preferences of the majority of voters. At no time in the 1920s would that majority have voted Labour. The war thus did change everything: it destroyed the progressive alliance.

But a quasi-Edwardian politics was, nonetheless, restored. To that extent the war changed nothing. The paradox is resolved however if we remember that the restored system was actually a shell: its most vital element, the party of progress, destroyed. The restored free-trade economy was also a kind of souvenir: it evoked happy memories which could not be relived. Both the restored politics and the restored economy vanished in 1931.

3

The Crisis of Labour
and the Conservative Hegemony,
1929–1939

I have suggested that despite the Edwardian system's underlying instability and the corrosive effect of the First World War it had still not been completely destroyed by the end of the 1920s. The reformed Labour Party mobilized enough of the working-class vote to disrupt the system, but not enough to give the Party any real authority. The Conservative Party, was recognizably the same; its leadership in fact almost identical. The Liberal Party hung on, recovery always (but not quite) around the corner, trapping much political talent that could have been put to better use. An attempt had been made to restore the pre-1914 economy. The Edwardian political economy therefore still stood, but shakily. In the 1930s, however, there was nothing provisional about England's political system and, unlike the 1920s, it represented economic and social reality.

In this chapter I will try to explain how this happened by examining the origins and consequences of the 1931 crisis—the financial crisis of August 1931 which felled the second Labour government (1929–31) and brought to power a National government dominated by the Conservatives.[1] The year 1931 is pivotal for a number of

---

[1] The 1931 crisis: the crisis which brought down the second Labour government in August 1931 was the result of three separate 'crises' coming together. The first was a budgetary one. The British budget was in deficit—largely it was thought by the increasing cost of unemployment benefit—and predominant contemporary opinion held this deficit, whose size was exaggerated, to be unacceptable. The second was the European banking crisis into which Britain had been sucked (though its own

reasons. Fusion, the will-o'-the-wisp of the 1920s, was effectively achieved and on terms set by the Conservatives. Free trade was at last abandoned and protection introduced. Free-trade Liberalism was eliminated as a serious rival to the Conservative Party. Similarly free-trade socialism was effectively destroyed and a chapter in the history of the Labour Party closed. And the crisis was responsible for that remarkable Conservative hegemony which lasted unchallengeable until the Second World War. In trying to account for these changes, which few predicted, we should ask two questions about the crisis and its outcome: are we explaining Labour weakness or Tory strength (the more difficult question)? And was what happened, the second question, merely the result of luck, good or bad?

Most admit that fate had a part to play, and few would deny that the Labour Party was very unlucky to be in office in 1931 and the Tories very lucky not to be. But some doubt that it was luck alone. In 1967 Robert Skidelsky argued that the second Labour government was not just a victim of luck but of its own failure to adopt policies it was free to choose. It did not choose them, he argued then, because it held to a utopian socialism which blinded it to the power of the state as an economic actor and committed the government in practice

banks were perfectly sound) by the lending policies of the Bank of England. The third was a balance of payments–currency crisis: a consequence partly of the first two crises. In mid-1931 there began a 'run' on the pound as foreign holders of sterling lost confidence in British finances. (In 1925 the pound had been returned to the gold standard at a fixed rate (the pre-1914 rate) against the dollar, which meant that claims against sterling had to be redeemed in gold.) In defending the pound, the Bank of England lost much of the country's gold stock. It was thought necessary to borrow abroad in order to protect the pound's value against the dollar, and the price to be paid for this was severe cuts in public expenditure. The second Labour government agreed to many cuts, but almost half the cabinet, led by the foreign secretary, Arthur Henderson, refused to accept cuts in unemployment benefit. The government resigned and the prime minister, Ramsay MacDonald, thereupon formed a so-called National government, which included himself and Philip Snowden (as chancellor of the exchequer) and the leaders of the Conservative and Liberal Parties. This government made the necessary budgetary cuts; but they failed in their purpose—partly because foreigners were worried about popular reaction to such cuts—and on 21 September it was forced to abandon the gold standard and allowed the pound to 'float' against other currencies. None of the predicted disasters occurred and on 27 October 1931, the National government won an overwhelming victory in a general election as the saviour of the nation.

to the status quo.[2] He later conceded that utopian socialism might not have been the problem,[3] but continues to argue that a 'lack of education and talent, [and] bad administrative arrangements' tended to make Labour ministers 'timid when they should have been bold. But irrelevant doctrine exposed their intellectual vacuity to the civil servants who, in effect, took over the running of the country.'[4] I was always sceptical of this argument. I did not believe that effective policies were freely available to anyone who had the wit to see them, and even if they were, I doubted that the educated classes were any more likely to adopt them than Labour ministers.[5] I still think that is so.[6]

Skidelsky's argument does, however, raise two political sub-questions. Why did the Labour government allow itself to be driven from office in 1931 in almost the worst possible circumstances and to fight an election it could never win—though few imagined the extent of the defeat—when almost *any* reasonably calculated strategy would have been less disastrous? Why was Labour, apparently *the* party of the state, not prepared to use the state or at least the experience of government, if not to effect a transformation of the economy, which was hardly possible, at least to preserve its own electorate intact, which was? What surprises the historian is the comparative scarcity of debate within the Party, the degree to which MacDonald's leadership and Philip Snowden's chancellorship remained unquestioned almost to the end.[7] Dissidence was not absent,

[2] R. Skidelsky, *Politicians and the Slump: The Labour Government 1929–1931* (London, 1967).

[3] *Society for the Study of Labour History Bulletin*, 21 (1970), 6–7.

[4] R. Skidelsky, *Politicians and the Slump: The Labour Government 1929–1931* (London, 1994 edn), xxiii.

[5] R. McKibbin, 'The Economic Policy of the Second Labour Government', in McKibbin, *Ideologies of Class*, 197–227.

[6] Skidelsky suggests that our difference 'boils down to whether there existed some room for manoeuvre by a government sufficiently determined to do something about unemployment. I say yes; McKibbin says no.' (*Politicians and the Slump* (1994 edn), xxvii.) I would not, however, deny that there was some room for manoeuvre. Our difference is whether there was enough room to make much difference; and that I doubt.

[7] D. Howell, *MacDonald's Party: Labour Identities and Crisis 1922–1931* (London, 2002), 54.

as the vote on Mosley's proposals in 1930 suggest,[8] but compared with other parties in other countries, socialist or non-socialist, it was tame stuff.

In the last chapter I suggested that there were competing strategies open to the Labour Party: one was to be the party of the whole working class; another to be the party of useful citizens. The strategy of the useful citizen drew upon an older ILP tradition which emphasized fellowship and community, a tradition which strongly influenced MacDonald and Snowden. But it also drew upon the Fabian conception of the 'brainworker', a formulation that found its way into what became clause IV of the Party's 1918 constitution and was designed to appeal to the professional middle class.[9] There was, however, a third strategy for Labour: to be a party which served the specific interests of the unions and their members. But those who devised the Party's programme in the 1920s were unsure which strategy to follow and tended to try all three. As a result, Labour's policies in the 1920s were designed primarily for the working class, and could hardly be otherwise, but were also designed not to offend anyone else. In a surprisingly optimistic interpretation of this strategy (if that is what it was) Duncan Tanner writes that in the 1920s 'Labour had to prove itself a practical party, capable of providing security and opportunity . . . wartime changes and new structural circumstances [the extended franchise?] helped; but Labour had to adopt the right image and approach for these circumstances to yield results.' Labour 'engaged in a process of learning and adaption.

[8] Oswald Mosley had been appointed chancellor of the Duchy of Lancaster with a brief to help J. H. Thomas in the development of an employment policy. Mosley devised a programme based on domestic reconstruction, large-scale (by contemporary standards) public works programmes and a scheme of retirement pensions to encourage people to leave the workforce. Although Mosley was hostile to notions that recovery could be export-led, he later developed proposals for Empire Unity which were not unlike Joseph Chamberlain's pre-war policies. Snowden and the Treasury were inevitably hostile to Mosley's plan and he resigned from the government in May 1930. Nonetheless his proposals were only narrowly defeated at the Party conference in October 1930. There is a sympathetic discussion of Mosley's policies in R. Skidelsky, *Oswald Mosley* (London, 1975), 199–233. See also Howell, *MacDonald's Party*, 79–80, 299–300.

[9] I have discussed this elsewhere. See McKibbin, *Evolution of the Labour Party*, 96–8. The formulation was 'producers by hand or brain'.

In 1929 it appeared to have learnt a great deal and consequently mobilized support across a variety of communities.'[10] But neither of these propositions—that Labour needed to move beyond its working-class base and that by 1929 had successfully done so—is true. There is little evidence that Labour had moved significantly beyond its working-class base in the 1920s; nor in the most working-class country in the world did it need to—except to the extent that it failed to secure the whole working-class vote. And in the interwar years Labour (at best) won no more than half the working-class vote: the second cardinal fact of interwar politics.[11] Here there was a kind of regression. The more it failed to win the bulk of the working-class vote, the more it sought to find votes elsewhere—in rural England for example.[12] The more it sought votes elsewhere the less able was it to extend its industrial working-class electorate by aligning it with the policies of the Labour Party. The principal reason for this strategic muddle lies in the structure of the reformed Labour Party, which was, as soon became clear, badly flawed. When Arthur Henderson presented the new constitution to the Labour Party in 1918 he confessed that were Labour able to start anew he would have preferred it to do so on the strength of a mass individual membership alone—in other words, to be a broad-based democratic party.[13] But, as he recognized, so central to the Party were the unions already, this was hardly possible. Indeed, it is difficult to imagine the Party without the unions. They provided most of the membership and the money, and trade unionists of whatever social class were more likely to vote Labour than anyone else. Thus in most parliamentary

[10] D. Tanner, 'Class Voting and Radical Politics. The Liberal and Labour Parties, 1910–1931', in J. Lawrence and M. Taylor (eds.), *Party, State and Society: Electoral Behaviour in Britain since 1820* (London, 1997), 124.

[11] For the first cardinal fact see above, 63.

[12] For this, see C. V. Griffiths, *Labour and the Countryside: The Politics of Rural Britain 1918–1939* (Oxford, 2007), 109–285 particularly. It is worth noting that although many in the Labour Party believed that power could not be won without the support of rural England, the Party was actually reluctant (or unable) to provide the resources that might have made this possible.

[13] For Henderson's speech and its reception, see Labour Party *Conference Report*, January 1918, 98–104.

constituencies Labour's success was proportionate to the number of trade unionists. The core of Labour's local networks were the union branches, even more than the co-ops or the working-men's clubs. Furthermore, rather fraudulently, the unions could claim to represent the whole working class simply because, however badly they treated those not their members, no one else was going to treat them any better.

Yet in the 1920s the unions never seriously tried to dominate the Labour Party or even use it in a constructive way. The union–Party joint bodies, established with such high hopes in 1918, were all dissolved in the mid-1920s.[14] The first Labour government (1924), in its determination to seem even-handed, was disappointing to the unions; not least disappointing was Henderson as home secretary.[15] Thereafter the unions kept their distance. During the general strike they virtually ignored the Party, to the annoyance of its leaders, and it was to be the principal victim of their actions.[16] One consequence of this distance, the widespread feeling in the unions that industrial action was superior to political, was that for many trade-union sponsored MPs the House of Commons was a kind of retirement home, and union representatives on the Party's ruling bodies tended to be second rank, especially since members of the general council of the TUC were barred from sitting on the national executive of the Labour Party. The other consequence was that Henderson's

[14] For these bodies, see McKibbin, *Evolution of the Labour Party*, 206–14. For their dissolution, N. Riddell, *Labour in Crisis: The Second Labour Government: 1929–1931* (Manchester, 1999), 10–11, 59.

[15] Henderson was particularly criticized for his failure to re-instate the Liverpool policemen who had been dismissed for their part in the police strike of 1919 and for a rather heavy-handed intervention in industrial disputes. For Henderson's record see M. Worley, *Labour Inside the Gate* (London and New York, 2005), 79; Shepherd and Laybourn, *Britain's First Labour Government*, 92–3; C. Wrigley, *Arthur Henderson*, 144–9.

[16] The 1927 Trades Disputes Act, the Baldwin government's response to the general strike, which outlawed sympathetic strikes, also introduced 'opting in'. Under the 1913 legislation, which overturned the Osborne Judgement, those trade unionists who did not wish to contribute to a union's political fund had to 'opt out'. Inertia thus favoured the Labour Party. Under the 1927 Act those who wished to contribute to the political fund had to 'opt in'. Inertia now worked against the Labour Party whose finances suffered significantly.

hope that within the unified labour movement the political needs of the Party, which in his view best represented the working class, would necessarily override the sectarianism of the unions was never fulfilled.

Given the insistence of the unions in 1917–18 that their authority in the reformed party was to be decisive—it was their votes which were to elect the NEC and their delegates who were to dominate the annual conference—their behaviour is at first sight puzzling. A party designed by the unions to be their instrument was in fact rarely used by them as such. But the reason for this is not hard to find. The unions, as we have seen, were always ambivalent about any political action which might imply state involvement in industrial relations (and most political action did) and above all by their determination to preserve free collective bargaining and the extra-legal privileges they were given by the 1906 Trades Disputes Act—which even the 1927 legislation did not seriously infringe. Not all unions, certainly, were as committed to this view as the skilled unions. Ernest Bevin, the general secretary of the Transport and General Workers Union, the largest and fastest-growing union, was sceptical of some received wisdoms about the undesirability of state intervention and had strongly supported Keynes on the Macmillan Committee.[17] Nonetheless, even he, as an instance, was opposed to family allowances since they were payments which by-passed the normal procedures of wage-bargaining. He was always suspicious of parliamentary politics: a suspicion no doubt confirmed by his astonishing failure at Gateshead in the 1931 elections—a seat Labour had held at a by-election in the same year;[18] and he temporized over protection. By being compelled to cede many of their welfare functions to the state—unemployment benefits for example—the unions further confined their actions to the defence of free collective bargaining and relieved themselves of the obligation

[17] For Bevin and the Macmillan Committee see A. Bullock, *The Life and Times of Ernest Bevin*, I (London, 1960), 425–34.

[18] Bevin was beaten by 12,239. Labour had won by 16,749 in 1929 and 9,336 in 1924. It was probably Labour's worst result even in a year of catastrophic results.

to think seriously about policy in the widest sense. The resulting narrowness of vision is well known: the opposition, for instance to anything that might undermine the primacy of the wage as the source of family income or anything that might redistribute income within the working-class household—that is, from men to women.[19] Even the fiscal system was spared. A. G. Walkden's attempt in 1930 to persuade the general council of the TUC to abandon free trade was defeated by 17 votes to 5.[20] The following year, the general council again reaffirmed its commitment to the international trading system and, by implication, to free trade at a moment when Britain's continued adherence to it was virtually indefensible. This is even odder since the trade unions' evidence to the Macmillan and May Committees—written by the TUC's research department—blamed deflationary policies after 1920 and the return to gold in 1925 for the severity of the depression, and on almost strictly Keynesian grounds. But they never tried to impose reflation or devaluation on the Labour Party, even in 1931 when people were aware that devaluation and/or protection were at least plausible possibilities. Even after 1931, when the unions really were in a position to impose policies on the Party, they 'fudged the issue' of the fiscal system and never consistently supported reflationary policies.[21] This seemingly inexplicable behaviour is a result of the fact that for most union leaders free trade and unfettered collective bargaining went together: you could not have one without the other.

The unions, therefore, in defence of a certain version of industrial relations, which had worked well for them and their members before 1914, isolated themselves not just from the state but from the Labour Party. Since, however, the Labour Party was deliberately designed around trade union power this left a political vacuum which was

---

[19] Howell, *MacDonald's Party*, 368–76.   [20] Riddell, *Labour in Crisis*, 85–6.
[21] Cronin, *Politics of State Expansion*, 127–8. As Cronin points out, they never showed much interest in the expansionary policies devised by Continental socialists and known to the unions through the International Federation of Free Trade Unions. And they certainly knew of Keynes's policies. The Parliamentary Labour Party even voted against the National government's first protectionist measures, though that is the last time the Party seriously defended free trade before 1939.

unfilled, except at the end of the second Labour government, by anyone or any particular strategy. The Party's individual members might have filled this gap, but the membership was still too small and politically too weak. Since, furthermore, a high proportion of members were male trade unionists in work, they had the same ambivalence towards the state as their leaders. Labour lost twice by this relationship. It suffered electorally by its association with the trade unions, but the unions gave that relationship no coherence or political direction.

In one sphere alone was the membership and eventually the leadership of the unions prepared to act politically—in defence of the unemployed. In so far as the unemployed had a politics it was to maintain the money value of benefit and an unrestricted right to receive it. In this they had much sympathy within the labour movement. It was almost universally believed that since the state seemed unable to find the unemployed work it was obliged to give them a reasonable standard of life. The attitude of the unions to the unemployed was then, and since has been, much criticized. James Cronin has called it 'shameful'[22] and many of the unemployed themselves despaired of the unions.[23] But the two occasions before the 1931 crisis itself when the unions did put strong pressure on the parliamentary Labour Party were both in defence of the right of the unemployed to full benefit.[24] It is true that the unions' motives were not purely altruistic,[25] yet the sympathy for the unemployed

[22] Ibid.

[23] See McKibbin, 'The "Social Psychology" of Unemployment in Interwar Britain', in *Ideologies of Class*, 245.

[24] The two occasions were the recommendations of the Interim Report of the Royal Commission on Unemployment Insurance (June 1931) when the unions successfully campaigned against the recommended cuts in benefit (W. R. Garside, *British Unemployment, 1919–1939* (Cambridge, 1990), 54–5) and their hostility to a rigorous interpretation of the 'genuinely seeking work' clauses of unemployment insurance (D. King, *Actively Seeking Work: The Politics of Unemployment and Welfare Policy in the United States and Great Britain* (Chicago and London, 1995), 80).

[25] In defending the money value of unemployment benefit they were also trying to defend the money value of wages, that is, the money income of those *in* work; in their eyes an attack on one presaged an attack on the other. The dole had become, in effect, a de facto minimum wage. But in defending the full benefit of the unemployed male

in the union movement as a whole was genuine, and it is no accident that the 1931 crisis centred so much on the money value of the dole.

More generally, it has been argued that the labour movement's culture of loyalty to its leaders worked against the unorthodox and reinforced the authority of a cautious and essentially conservative leadership. That such a culture existed is undeniable. Robert Michels, who had little regard for the political capacity of the 'masses', thought it characteristic of social democracy, as much in England as anywhere else.[26] Riddell has described the loyalty to the Labour leadership as 'hero-worship'.[27] The three main defectors in 1931, Ramsay MacDonald, Philip Snowden, and J. H. Thomas, had significant support in their own constituencies, and in the 1931 elections took many Labour voters with them, though only in Thomas's case was this lasting.[28] The loyalty to MacDonald, even from those who had close dealings with him, was well known: a tribute to his rhetorical platform skills and a carefully cultivated history of radical martyrdom.[29] But MacDonald only took a handful of MPs with him in 1931 and most Labour voters stayed Labour voters. The 1931 crisis within the labour movement was, in fact, as much a conflict of loyalties as a conflict of policies. The way the crisis developed compelled the Labour Party to choose between loyalties: loyalty to MacDonald, that is to abandon the Party, or loyalty to the movement on terms set by the unions. Henderson and those who supported him

worker the unions acquiesced in the so-called Anomalies Act, which denied benefit to many unemployed women.

[26] R. Michels, *Political Parties* (New York and London, 1962), 93–7 and *passim*. Of England Michels wrote: '[The] English socialists entrust the salvation of democracy solely to the good will and to the insight of the leaders'(113).

[27] Riddell, *Labour in Crisis*, 226–7.

[28] MacDonald, to his own surprise, held his Durham seat (Seaham) by 5, 951 in 1931 but was defeated in 1935 by over 20,000 by Manny Shinwell. Snowden did not contest Colne Valley in 1931 and the seat was won by a Liberal. Labour, however, regained it in 1935. In Derby, traditionally a Labour stronghold, Thomas still had a majority of over 12,000 in 1935—much of that vote probably from railwaymen who remembered with sympathy his record as trade union leader. His seat was lost to Labour in 1936 when he was forced to resign after leaking budget secrets. (For an example of this sympathy see H. R. S. Phillpott, *The Right Hon. J. H. Thomas* (London, undated, 1932?), 121–32.)

[29] For examples, see Howell, *MacDonald's Party*, 51.

opted for the second, though Henderson had frequently despaired of the unions and never accepted their version of what the Labour Party was to be.[30] It was that version, however, to which most MPs and Party members were loyal in 1931.

The relationship between the unions and the Labour Party was thus in practice damaging. Almost equally damaging was the institutional relationship of the parliamentary party [PLP] to the leadership. The procedures of the PLP were anything but democratic, and neither the 1918 constitution nor the PLP's standing orders did much to correct this. Although the leader of the Party was elected by MPs and in opposition so was the parliamentary executive (a kind of shadow cabinet), this was not so in government. MacDonald (more or less) had to recognize the claims of his senior colleagues, though some grudgingly,[31] but he was otherwise free to choose his ministers as he wished—and in 1924 chose two who were not even members of the Labour Party.[32] The PLP, broadly speaking, was kept informed of government policy and on occasion (again unemployment policy) forced changes on the cabinet, but it had no formal right to modify or reject policy. Standing orders did not permit the PLP to act as a 'caucus' nor did they allow the brutally effective institution of the 'spill' which kept Australian ministers on their toes.[33] MacDonald rarely

[30] The best single study of the Labour Party during the crisis is Riddell, *Labour in Crisis*. But see also A. Thorpe, *The British General Election of 1931* (Oxford, 1991), 63–87.

[31] In 1924, for instance, he only reluctantly offered Henderson a cabinet post—a man who was his equal in the wider labour movement.

[32] The two were Lord Chelmsford (first lord of the admiralty) and Lord Parmoor (C. A. Cripps, a former Tory MP), Lord President of the Council. Parmoor did join the Labour Party and remained a loyal member. Lord Haldane, the lord chancellor, a former senior Liberal minister, was technically a member of the Party. In fairness to MacDonald we should note that both convention and the constitution required a certain number of ministers to sit in the House of Lords at a time when Labour's representation there was negligible and hostility to 'Labour' creations still strong. (For this, see P. Williamson, 'The Labour Party and the House of Lords, 1918–1931', *Parliamentary History* 10, 2 (1991), 320–4.)

[33] The 'spill' was a device by which at a meeting of the parliamentary party a member could move that all offices be declared vacant. If the motion was carried, all officers, including the Party leader, had to be re-elected. It still operates in both major Australian parties. Whether a spill would ever actually have been used in Britain is another question.

attended meetings of the PLP or the NEC and was plainly irritated at having to consult them during the 1931 crisis itself. Nor was there much else for MPs to do since the institutional weakness of the House of Commons reinforced that of the PLP. This encouraged a passivity among MPs and, like the unions, an unwillingness to think seriously about policy. It also encouraged resort to the House of Commons bars, home of the powerless backbencher throughout the ages.

At bottom, Skidelsky's criticism of the Labour Party is intellectual: it had the wrong ideas (or no ideas). This was also Keynes's view: people were in an intellectual 'muddle'. If they had possessed the right ideas, they would not have been muddled and much unnecessary suffering could have been avoided. And if Labour ministers had had the right intellectual equipment or training they would have acquired the right ideas. This, however, is tricky ground. Education and talent, as I suggested earlier, are no guarantee of the unorthodox. Indeed, in the 1920s and 1930s, the economic ideas of Britain's educated classes were almost entirely orthodox. Furthermore, the Labour government was always reluctant to take active deflationary measures, and resisted them till the last minute. In this sense it was not a particularly orthodox government.[34] The real criticism we might make of MacDonald and Snowden, especially Snowden, was that in 1931, far from rejecting the educated classes, they were too respectful of education and those who had it. They were easily impressed by the smoothness and plausibility of the City and civil service, and Snowden had a credulous belief in the disinterestedness of the Bank of England's advice.[35]

MacDonald, however, was less credulous, and less dogmatically attached to Snowden's simple fiscal rules. Whereas the May Committee was appointed by the Treasury under Snowden's direction and its profoundly orthodox majority report entirely predictable,[36]

---

[34] I have argued this elsewhere. See *Ideologies of Class*, 217–18.

[35] See James Cronin's comment on Snowden: 'As a young man he worked for the Inland Revenue and never lost the tax collector's mentality' (Cronin, *Politics of State Expansion*, 99).

[36] The May Committee on National Expenditure was appointed in February 1931 as a temporizing measure to buy continued Liberal support for the government. Its

the membership of the Economic Advisory Council, appointed by MacDonald in early 1930, was much more diverse: both Keynes and Bevin sat on it, as they did on the Macmillan Committee whose membership was almost stellar.[37] MacDonald also knew what a dead weight Snowden was but could think of no safe way to remove him.[38] Indeed in December 1930 Keynes included MacDonald in the party of economic advance, together with Lloyd George, Bevin, and Mosley. 'For, assuredly, if we think their temperaments back twenty years or imagine them occupying positions of "more freedom and less responsibility" Mr Lloyd George and Mr Ramsay MacDonald would be where Mosley is.'[39] On 2 August 1931 MacDonald wrote unprompted to Keynes asking for anything that he might write on the May Committee's Report 'as I should like very much to have your views for my guidance'.[40] We know that MacDonald did not use Keynes's advice, despite seeking it, and the question is why.

It has been suggested to me that MacDonald 'needed' Snowden to protect him from radical policies which, when it came to the point, frightened him or he thought half-baked since Snowden 'was much better at the kind of confrontational politics needed to keep such ideas at bay than MacDonald was, and MacDonald knew it'.[41]

chairman, Sir George May, was a former secretary of the Prudential Assurance Company and its membership markedly business and financial. It was the publication of its deeply pessimistic (and inaccurate) report on Britain's budgetary position in July 1931 that helped accelerate the financial crisis.

[37] Its membership included Keynes, Bevin, T. E. Gregory, Lord Bradbury (a former senior Treasury official), Reginald McKenna, R. H. Brand (a distinguished banker). But it also included the former Communist MP J. T. Walton Newbold, an eccentric appointment if ever there were one.

[38] He probably also needed Snowden's support in his increasingly acrimonious relations with Arthur Henderson over foreign policy. His growing hostility to and suspicion of Henderson played some part in the 1931 crisis. For this, see D. Carlton, *MacDonald versus Henderson: The Foreign Policy of the Second Labour Government* (London, 1970).

[39] Keynes was commenting on the so-called Mosley Memorandum (*Collected Writings of John Maynard Keynes*, XX, 476). He put Snowden in the same party as Sir Herbert Samuel—in other words in the party of the die-hard free traders.

[40] In ibid., 589. Keynes replied that he did not intend to publish anything about the Report 'because my views are not fit for publication' (590).

[41] A comment by one of the anonymous readers of the original manuscript of this book.

I think there is some truth to that view as there is to Tanner's that the 'tariff crisis'—the failed attempt to modify the government's adherence to free trade tied MacDonald to Snowden 'irrevocably'.[42] Nonetheless, the answer is political, not primarily intellectual, not in MacDonald's fear of radical policies, and lies in the tradition of socialism in which he was nourished: it blinded him to the realities of political power. Of the senior members of the cabinet during the 1931 crisis only Henderson seems to have had a clear idea both of the potential power of the unions within the Labour movement and the way the crisis was being consciously manipulated by Labour's opponents for their own benefit.[43] MacDonald, however, was all too ready to believe in the good faith of the opposition leaders. The determination of the Conservatives to force an election regardless of its political and financial consequences appears to have surprised him.[44] His kind of socialism concealed the fact that in 1931 there were social and ideological conflicts which could not be wished away by talk of equality of sacrifice. MacDonald was probably as much a socialist in 1931 as he always had been—he certainly thought so—but though he had a sense of what a socialist society might look like, he had little idea of how you got there, and little awareness that others might wish that you didn't. As a socialist, he was the logical opposite of Marx, who had little idea of what a socialist society might look like but a strong sense of how you got there, and particularly what were the obstacles on the way. Nonetheless, as a tradition it did not deny the existence of intellectual alternatives, however much MacDonald behaved during the crisis itself; and MacDonald was clearly aware of them.[45]

---

[42] D. Tanner, 'Political Leadership, Intellectual Debate and Economic Policy during the Second Labour Government, 1929–1931', in E. H. H. Green and D. Tanner (eds.), *The Strange Survival of Liberal England* (Cambridge, 2007), 140.

[43] Thorpe, *British General Election of 1931*, 81–3.

[44] P. Williamson, *National Crisis and National Government: British Politics, the Economy and Empire 1926–1932* (London, 1992), 410–11.

[45] G. D. H. Cole, who knew MacDonald well and was on the Economic Advisory Council, thought MacDonald 'loved playing with ideas and policies, and fancying how he could put them across' but lacked the intellectual self-confidence or political clear-sightedness to adopt them (Cole, *History of the Labour Party*, 257).

Yet MacDonald was not alone in 'failing' in 1931. So also did the other four members of the 'big five'—Henderson, Snowden, Thomas, and Clynes. These were the men who had dominated the Labour Party since its foundation in 1900 and who were primarily responsible for 1931. Contemporaries struggled to explain why this happened; why men, formidable politicians in many ways, should have so mishandled events. An obvious explanation, of course, is that events were beyond the experience of most men, and that their failure was hardly a surprise. Another explanation is that their kind of socialism (as in the case of MacDonald) was unsuited to the circumstances. This also has some truth. But their socialism was not, however, the same. MacDonald and Snowden, on the one hand, and Henderson, Thomas and Clynes, on the other, came from different traditions. MacDonald and Snowden were products of the ethical socialism of the ILP; Henderson and Thomas[46] of trade-union collectivism; and Clynes of both.[47] If these traditions 'failed' they failed in different ways. A more convincing, if more depressing conclusion is that their failure represented the failure of 'outsider' politics. Outsiders were not just working class. MacDonald and Snowden, both outsiders, were not altogether working-class figures (but perhaps even more outsiders precisely because of this, their social marginality); but many were. All came from outside the system and found it difficult to cope with the political and social elites as equals or with confidence. (And in the second Labour government the one who coped best, Henderson, was immured in the Foreign Office.) No senior member of MacDonald's government was from the middle class; it was the most working-class cabinet Britain has had, and it showed.[48] Those working-class outsiders who did have confidence

[46] Thorpe has suggested that Thomas, unlike Henderson, should be regarded as a 'Tory socialist' or 'Tory democrat', which seems to me right. He also suggests that Thomas was anxious to join the National government because he could not afford to lose a cabinet minister's salary. (A. Thorpe, ' "I am in the Cabinet": J. H. Thomas's Decision to Join the National Government in 1931', *Historical Research* 64 (1991), 389–402.)

[47] There is an incisive analysis of these traditions in Howell, *MacDonald's Party*, 8–13, 21–53.

[48] The cabinet certainly had 'middle-class' members, but none, not even Sidney Webb, carried much weight. The only middle-class member of the cabinet known with certainty

in their own judgement, like Ernest Bevin, consciously distanced themselves from the government, with damaging consequences. The year 1931 also represented the failure of the autodidactic tradition in British politics. MacDonald and Snowden were conspicuous examples of this tradition, though they were not alone. It had been very effective in familiarizing a generation with the cultural canon and the norms and practices of political life, but had, in a sense, over-socialized them.[49] It made them too respectful of the bearers of the dominant political culture and too ready to defer to them. It also exposed the limitations of a kind of socialism, the socialism of fellowship and ethical improvement, that had been so important in shaping MacDonald's and Snowden's political personalities. One almost inevitable consequence of 1931 was, as we shall see, to weaken in the Labour Party a politics which drew both upon the autodidact tradition and the socialism of fellowship.

That the leading members of the Labour government were in some way intellectually ill-fitted to cope with 1931 is so self-evident as to be truistic. But no party had the right 'ideas' in 1931 and the Labour leaders were hardly more ill-fitted than the others, though less opportunist. As Williamson notes: 'Virtually all other financial, business and economic advice to [Labour] ministers, whether so-licited or unsolicited, whether private or published, supported the Bank of England.'[50] The Labour Party's failure lay not in having the wrong ideas but in allowing itself to be driven from office in *politically* the worst possible way. Its leaders made the politician's worst mistake: they did not act politically, and even those who did, like Henderson, left it too late. The reason was, as I have suggested, partly structural: the Party's institutions did not fill the roles assigned

to have voted against cuts in unemployment benefit in 1931 was Christopher Addison. (See K. and J. Morgan, *Portrait of a Progressive: The Political Career of Christopher, Viscount Addison* (Oxford, 1980), 202–4.) H. Lees-Smith, the president of the Board of Education, and like Addison a former Liberal, might have been the other.

[49] There is a sympathetic and detailed, but ultimately unconvincing treatment of the autodidact in J. Rose, *The Intellectual Life of the British Working Classes* (New Haven and London, 2001).

[50] Williamson, *National Crisis*, 293.

them in the 1918 constitution or act in the manner expected by those who wrote it. The trade unions did not run the Party; were indeed only intermittently interested in it. Nor, despite what they said, did they represent the whole working class. The NEC, formally the Party's policy-making institution, did not make policy. The annual conference, increasingly stage-managed, was not as it was supposed to be—the parliament of the labour movement. The PLP was largely passive and had few formal rights. The leader of the Party thus had probably more autonomy—for better or worse and in 1931 for worse—than the leaders of the other parties. During the 1929 parliament, for example, Baldwin had more trouble with the Conservative Party than MacDonald did with Labour. On the other hand, the unions did not *not* intervene, and most people accepted (however reluctantly) that they had a particular standing in the Party shared by no one else. Nor did many question that doubtful claim to represent the whole working class. There were, furthermore, limits to the inertia of the PLP and the NEC—something not always understood by MacDonald, though deeply resented by him when he did. The result was an institutional impasse which, though it permitted two years of evasion, left the Party at sea when decisions had to be made, which they did in August 1931. The second Labour government was, therefore, subject to a series of weak but contradictory institutional pressures whose only outcome could be drift rather than the adoption of the 'right' ideas, and in 1931 to very strong pressures from outside whose only outcome could be orthodoxy.

But the failure was also ideological. MacDonald was not alone in his political over-socialization. Too many in the Labour Party believed in the neutrality of the state and the country's dominant financial and political institutions, and in the primacy of the 'non-political' sphere in social life.[51] Nor did they think much about how

---

[51] There is a touching example of this in the memoirs of Bob Smillie, president of the Miners' Federation of Great Britain and a man on the Labour Party's left: 'Having acquired some reputation as a batsman, I helped to start the Larkhall Cricket Club, and it was with a glow of pride I read my name in the *Larkhall Press* as top-scorer for my side . . . I can see a crowd of us lads waiting outside the printing office for the paper to

the power of these institutions might be used against them. You did not need the right ideas, or in fact, many ideas at all, to be suspicious of advice that came from the Treasury or the Bank of England, or to assume that the interests of the working class (or the country) might not be served by such advice, but it was very late in the day that men like Bevin and Citrine came to that position. It was political instinct rather than ideas which was missing. Skidelsky has, I think, the relationship between ideas and politics in the wrong order. He in effect argues that the right ideas would have lead to the right politics. I would argue the reverse: that the right politics, that is an actively partisan politics, *might* have led to the right ideas. But in so far as the 'right' policies had to be—in Skidelsky's sense—effective policies there is no certainty even the 'right ideas' would have produced them.[52]

Whatever we conclude, the results of the general election on 27 October 1931 confirmed just how badly the Labour government contrived its political departure. Labour was certain to lose whatever happened; but the results were very much worse than anyone expected. The Conservatives and their allies won 67 per cent of the votes and 554 seats; a victory without precedent in the history of the modern British party system.[53] Labour won only 52 seats (including three ILP MPs and three other independent Labour MPs) and only 30 per cent of the vote. The Labour leadership was decapitated: not only had MacDonald, Snowden, and Thomas left the Party, its other two leading members, Henderson and Clynes, both lost their seats. Only one member of the Labour cabinet, George Lansbury, survived. With the exception of South Wales, some mining seats in England and some seats in the East End the Conservatives and

appear, mainly for the joy of seeing our names in print. I have seen it often since, but have never been able to recapture that fine rapture when it appeared not as the name of a rabid "Socialist" and "national peril", but as a flannelled cricketer.' (*My Life for Labour*, (London, 1924), 25.)

[52] S. N. Broadberry, *The British Economy between the Wars: A Macroeconomic Survey* (Oxford, 1986), 154–6.

[53] The allies in 1931, of course, included the free trade Liberals under Herbert Samuel who left the government in 1932.

their allies won overwhelmingly everywhere. Labour did very badly in places, like Birmingham, where it had recently made significant gains[54] but also in areas of traditional strength, like the North East where its vote almost collapsed.[55] Yet these results, though bad, were not atypical. In seats contested only by Conservative and Labour in 1929 and 1931 the Conservative vote rose by 38.1 per cent and the Labour vote fell by 28.6 per cent.[56] The election accelerated the drift of Liberal voters to the Conservatives, to the detriment of Labour. And most of the Liberals who switched to the Conservatives in 1931 stayed there. This new pattern of electoral behaviour was confirmed at the 1935 election. Though the overall Labour vote almost returned to its 1929 level, the Conservative majority was still a huge 247 and was based upon the extraordinary weakness of the Labour vote in urban England. In 1935, for example, the principal cities of England returned 44 Labour members and 103 non-Labour.[57] In the ten double member constituencies, all with the exception of Brighton heavily working class, Labour won no seats.[58]

The 1931 and 1935 elections thus completed what 1924 had begun: the creation of a large anti-Labour majority with the Conservative Party at its centre. How far was this achieved by luck? Undoubtedly the 1929 election was a good one to lose. In particular defeat allowed the Tories to escape any responsibility for the financial crisis of 1931. In addition, they were fortunate that the last great attempt at deflation failed in its purpose so quickly.[59] The National

[54] In 1929 Labour won 6 of Birmingham's 12 seats—all of them for the first time. In 1931 Labour lost all 12 seats: none narrowly.

[55] It lost, for example, nine of its eleven Durham county seats—nearly all of them mining.

[56] D. H. Close, 'The Realignment of the British Electorate in 1931', *Historical Journal*, 67 (1982), 393. For the results see also Thorpe, *British General Election of 1931*, 255–71.

[57] They were: London, Birmingham (no Labour members), Liverpool, Manchester and Salford, Sheffield, Leeds, Bristol, Newcastle (no Labour members), Bradford, Hull, Nottingham, Leicester (no Labour members), Plymouth (no Labour members), Stoke, and Wolverhampton (no Labour members).

[58] Brighton, Blackburn, Oldham, Bolton, Preston, Stockport, Derby, Norwich, Southampton, Sunderland.

[59] Snowden's emergency budget of 10 September 1931 and the so-called Economy Act were designed to balance the budget both by expenditure reduction and increased

government showed no embarrassment that it had failed or that the irretrievable ruin against which Snowden warned was nowhere to be seen. On the contrary ministers took modest pleasure in the new vistas that devaluation opened and less than modest credit for the achievement. This failure determined the National government's economic policies and the society they indirectly created for the rest of the decade. Nonetheless, we must remember that what the government tried to do at its formation was to save the political-economic regime established in the first half of the 1920s, not to have what happened: a managed currency, strict controls on capital exports, a weakened Bank of England, a marked decline in the standing of the City and its institutions, particularly the acceptance and discount houses, increasingly strict curbs on speculative currency movements, and a bank rate of 2 per cent throughout most of the decade. All of these were happy consequences of a failed policy. The only intended innovation—in fact an inevitable one—was protection and even that was at first smuggled in as an emergency measure. Whether the Tories, who were determined on protection anyway, realized how far tariffs themselves demanded the kind of controls put in place after 1931 is less certain. Probably not, but they willingly acquiesced in them anyway. In a sense what was restored was the 1920s without the mistakes. The politics of the 1930s 'fitted' social and economic reality as the politics of the 1920s did not. *The Times* called the Conservative victory in 1935 'a triumph of steadiness' which does not differ much from 'safety first', the Conservative slogan of 1929—except that in 1935 it succeeded.

How far the economic and financial system which developed after 1931 positively earned the Tories electoral support is hard to say. The strong recovery of the Conservative vote in Birmingham and the West Midlands can partly be attributed to protection, and protection probably had some appeal to the working class elsewhere. The partial

taxation, so to secure the loans necessary to maintain the pound on the gold standard at par. This policy failed with surprising speed. Gold withdrawals from the Bank continued such that Britain was forced to go off gold on 21 September 1931 and the pound allowed to find its own level on the exchanges. It was effectively devalued by about one-third.

protection and extensive subsidies given to agriculture—a policy in fact begun by the second Labour government—was gratefully received by the farmers. The overall financial regime established in 1931–2 undoubtedly favoured the quasi-consumption boom of the 1930s and the huge growth in new private housing. The (more or less) strictly balanced budgets of the 1930s possibly created an economic environment conducive to investment. The successful debt conversion of 1932 took pressure off government finances as did partial suspension of the sinking fund. A cyclical upswing and a marked improvement in the terms of trade (which encouraged consumption) were, however, equally important—though again the government understandably took credit for that.[60] What Conservative policies certainly did was to offend the fewest people, and those who were offended, the unemployed, served a useful political purpose.[61]

Nevertheless, many of those who supported the National government benefited little from its policies; not at least until rearmament became serious at the end of the decade. English prosperity was strongly biased by geography and class. Those in the wrong geography and the wrong class (like those in the North East) largely missed out. But they did accept the National government's historically plausible account of what happened. That was a story of economic recovery: a slow but continuous climb from the depths of 1931. It was a story of competence opposed to incompetence; of the fitness of one class to rule as against the unfitness of another. In his 1934 budget Chamberlain restored most of the cuts to benefits and salaries made in 1931. In doing so, he said, Britain was moving from *Bleak House* to *Great Expectations*. In other words, those who had not yet gained from the policies of the National government could

---

[60] The extent to which government policy contributed to economic recovery in 1930s has always been debatable. See, for example, Broadberry, *British Economy between the Wars*, 111–67; N. K. Buxton in Buxton and D. H. Aldcroft (eds.), *British Industry between the Wars* (London, 1979), 9–22; S. Howson, *Domestic Monetary Management in Britain 1919–38* (Cambridge, 1975), 90–145; S. Glynn and J. Oxborrow, *Interwar Britain: A Social and Economic History* (London, 1976).

[61] See below, 101–2.

expect to do so. This was an interpretation with which most were prepared to agree.

The story of economic recovery, however, was not by itself enough. Much of what happened in the 1930s, after all, was a result of the run of events—few foreseen by the Conservatives. But they exploited these events and devised a form of social politics driven partly by an overt anti-socialism and partly by a broadening of the Party's elites. As a policy it was as much ideological and rhetorical as an appeal to the self-interest of those who supported it. As a way of combining people who might in fact have had differing interests it was peculiarly successful. At the highest level, as W. D. Rubinstein notes with only some exaggeration, '*all* of Britain's elites were politically unified within the Conservative party'[62]—the end of a process by which the Tory Party became the party of all property. This is the more remarkable in that much of the industrial elite believed they had been sacrificed to the financial elite in 1925 (when Britain returned to the gold standard) as the preliminary evidence of the Federation of British Industry to the Macmillan Committee demonstrated all too clearly.[63] Furthermore, in the 1920s many industrialists, especially in textiles, were still free trade, if unenthusiastically. However, if we accept, as I have suggested elsewhere, that businessmen 'took the same view of politics as anyone else outside the working class' this unification of property is less surprising. More than most they 'had reason to believe that the "working class" was a unionized working class with whom they were perpetually in conflict and for whose greed they would have to pay'.[64] For this reason, though not the only one, Mond-Turnerism failed, and for this reason the final version of the Federation of British Industry's evidence to

[62] W. D. Rubinstein, 'Britain's Elites in the Interwar Period', in A. Kidd and D. Nicholls (eds.), *The Making of the British Middle Class? Studies of Regional and Cultural Diversity since the Eighteenth Century* (London, 1998), 188.

[63] After noting the ways in which British monetary policy had worked against industry the Federation said that 'from the point of view of British industry and commerce the essential prerequisite of a proper functioning of the gold standard is to a certain extent a questioning of weighing the interests of one group against those of the others'. (Macmillan Committee, *Minutes of Evidence*, I, 188.)

[64] McKibbin, *Ideologies of Class*, 283.

the Macmillan Committee was more unwilling to admit that the interests of finance and of industry might not be harmonious. To those huddling together against the bitter wind the Conservative Party seemed the best shelter.

The country's elites were not alone in acting this way. Much of the middle class came together in a form of anti-working-class politics: small businessmen, professionals, most members of the new white-collar occupations, the farming community. These groups, like the elites, still had 'objective' conflicts of interest and culture. There was a 'traditional' and 'non-traditional' middle class; a 'northern' and 'southern' middle class; an upper and lower middle class. Nor had the National government treated them even-handedly: the tax regime introduced in 1931 disproportionately favoured the upper middle class and equally disfavoured the 'ordinary' middle class. Although there was a developing uniformity of 'middle-class' culture which promoted political integration, something which gave both provincial and metropolitan middle classes a common world view,[65] this by itself had probably not gone far enough to turn the Conservative party into a mass middle-class party. What did so was the readiness of the nonconformist middle class to be enrolled in an anti-working-class, anti-socialist union. Before 1914 nonconformity was not absent from the Tory Party. Joseph Chamberlain was in effect a Tory, though a peculiar one, and the willingness of Wesleyans to make their peace with the Tories (and vice versa) was well known. But the course of Edwardian politics actually strengthened the Anglicanism of the Conservative Party. Socially, as we have seen, Anglicanism and nonconformity rarely mixed and this remained so throughout the interwar years. But even active nonconformists could distinguish between social and political relationships: you did not have to drink with people who shared your views on socialism. In any case, Baldwin's own easy-going Anglicanism, a kind of ecumenical

[65] S. Gunn, 'Class Identity and the Urban: The Middle Class in England, c. 1790–1850', in Kidd and Nicholls (eds.), *The Making of the British Middle Class?*, 29–47; R. Trainor, 'Neither Metropolitan nor Provincial: The Interwar Middle Class', in ibid., 203–13.

Protestantism, made him an honorary nonconformist and eased the transition:

The [Conservative] party, now formally committed to conventional economics and conventional morality and broadly non-denominational in its Christianity, became a party for which a large non-aligned element and parts of the old Nonconformist, Liberal constituency could vote. It was this support, critically absent in 1923 and 1929, that was the difference between winning and losing elections.[66]

The incorporation of nonconformity, therefore, meant the incorporation of Liberalism. For many of the older generation of Liberals that simply meant a withdrawal from active politics since 'as one of them said, they could not accept "that in fighting Conservatives [they] had been wasting [their] time" '.[67] For others, one element of that incorporation was the belief that 'conventional economics' could include protection. From the moment parliament met in 1929 the Liberal Party, still under the notional leadership of Lloyd George,[68] began to disintegrate. The policy of supporting the Labour government was increasingly divisive in a party the bulk of whose voters and the majority of whose MPs were fundamentally anti-socialist. The representative Liberal leader was thus not Lloyd George but Sir John Simon—attorney general and home secretary in Asquith's government. Simon had maintained his radical credentials by his opposition to conscription (and resignation as home secretary in January 1916) and after the war by his campaign against the Lloyd George government's policy in Ireland. But from 1922 onwards (when he returned to the House of Commons) it was his developing hostility to the Labour Party which marked his career. During the general strike he had made a celebrated parliamentary intervention which argued the strike's illegality. The speech's significance, however, was not legal—since it was in fact poorly argued—but political: Simon

---

[66] Bates, 'Conservative Party in the Constituencies', 263.

[67] Doyle, 'Urban Liberalism and the "Lost Generation" ', 632.

[68] Lloyd George had succeeded to the leadership after Asquith, who had lost his seat in the 1924 election, retired in 1926.

was asserting his anti-socialist credentials. From 1929 he became increasingly distant from Lloyd George's policy of supporting the Labour government and increasingly sceptical of the political or economic value of free trade. In June 1931, under his leadership, about half the Liberal Party's MPs effectively left the Party and took the name Liberal Nationals—usually called by contemporaries Simonite Liberals. Although—probably to his surprise—he was not included in the first National government, he received his reward when he became foreign secretary in November 1931.[69] Even when the free trade Liberals, led by Sir Herbert Samuel, left the National government in 1932 the Simonite Liberals stayed. Simon, like his followers, was attracted by Baldwin's anti-socialist but moderate Conservatism. In 1935 he wrote in his diary that Baldwin 'was an entirely acceptable chief—he represents our general attitude completely and there is nothing of the high and dry Tory about him'.[70] Most Liberals felt the same. The majority of Liberals who voted Conservative in 1931 did not return to the Liberal Party.[71] But a party acceptable to Simon was not the Tory Party of 1914. The acceptable party was, as we have seen, Baldwin's: primmer, calmer, more even-tempered, less obviously a brewers' front. And less imperial. In the early 1920s the empire mattered much to the Tory membership, and on three occasions they revolted against Party policy.[72] But each revolt was weaker than the last. Someone like Simon, who played an important part in India's constitutional development, could not have been associated with a full-blooded imperialist party.[73] In some of the country the old Liberal elites—those who no longer called themselves Liberals—still had local electoral success as 'independents' but were known to be

---

[69] For Simon's career see D. Dutton, *Simon: A Political Biography of Sir John Simon* (London, 1992). Also Dutton's entry on Simon in the *Oxford Dictionary of National Biography*.

[70] Williamson, *Baldwin*, 354. It should be noted that this reference to Baldwin as his 'chief' was made when MacDonald was still prime minister.

[71] Close, 'The Realignment of the British Electorate in 1931', 404.

[72] Bates, 'The Conservative Party in the Constituencies', 127.

[73] In 1927 he accepted the Baldwin government's offer to chair a statutory commission on India's constitutional development. Attlee was also a member.

semi-detached members of the Conservative Party.[74] In much of rural England a type of one-party politics developed. Here everyone was a Conservative: an allegiance which lasted a generation. When W. M. Williams visited the rural village of Gosforth in the early 1950s he found that there had been no election to the parish council for years. Members of the council were 'non-political' because everyone was a Tory. People voted Conservative because 'we all do' or because 'me father did'. No one thought it necessary to give a political reason for doing so.[75] This is the more remarkable in that the Tory Party had not always been thought the farmer's friend and points to the decline of the Liberal Party as a provincial protest party, one of its roles in the 1920s.[76]

Throughout the 1930s the Conservatives further entrenched themselves within English life by informally colonizing its rapidly developing associational life. The Women's Institutes, the chambers of commerce, the National Farmers' Union, the British Legion, sporting associations, ratepayers' associations, though most officially non-political, all acted as secondary agents of Toryism, and often had overlapping memberships.[77] In some moods the Conservatives were suspicious of these agents. They were thought to compete with the

---

[74] F. Bealey, J. Blondel, and W. P. McCann, *Constituency Politics: A Study of Newcastle-under-Lyme* (London, 1965), 28.

[75] W. M. Williams, *The Sociology of an English Village: Gosforth* (London, 1956), 175–6.

[76] Where the Liberals had traditionally been a strong or the dominant party they may have continued to play this role. Trediga argues that in rural Cornwall in the late 1930s the Liberals were doing better than they had since the late 1920s, and suggests that farmers' discontent was responsible for this. (G. Trediga, 'Turning the Tide? A Case Study of the Liberal Party in Provincial Britain in the late 1930s', *History* 92, 307 (July 2007), 347–66.) It has also been suggested that Vernon Bartlett's success in winning Bridgewater (Somerset) as a quasi-Popular Front candidate at a by-election in November 1938 was also due to unhappy farmers rather than local opposition to appeasement. To the extent that this is so, Liberal success is likely to have been intermittent and superficial; or due to other variables like a residual nonconformist Liberalism—especially so in the West Country.

[77] McKibbin, *Classes and Cultures*, 96; Bealey et al., *Constituency Politics*, 52. They note that those who established the chamber of trade in Newcastle-under-Lyme in 1925 were almost exactly the same as the men who founded the Rotary Club in 1929. The 'coincidence of membership of the two bodies and of the council was quite striking'.

Conservative associations for membership and money and so obstruct attempts to unify the middle classes within the Conservative Party.[78] In fact, however, although an associational abundance could compete with the Party, Conservatives usually understood their importance to Conservatism and Tory activists were encouraged to join them.[79] They were 'non-political' places where new and old members of the Conservative Party could meet in apparent harmony. Baldwin always recognized their importance. Hence the extraordinary number of addresses he gave to 'non-political' organizations, usually on 'non-political' subjects: on literature, Englishness, music, rural life, fraternity, religion.[80] Where these societies flourished so did Conservatism. Where they did not, as in the new housing estates, Conservatism struggled.

The social unity of the Party was not, however, promiscuous: it had been adjusted to new political circumstances, but not transformed. It was not socially egalitarian and would have been a different party were that so. The constituency associations continued to be dominated by local elites and the class character of their committees was significantly different from that of their membership. Social occasions where the whole Conservative family met could definitely be awkward and were usually avoided.[81] But the carefully managed sociability and the well-defined hierarchies were acceptable to their membership, who would have it no other way. That was why they were members.

But given England's social structure even a politically united middle class would have been insufficient a base for the Conservative predominance. More remarkable than the Party's hold on the middle classes in the 1930s was its hold on much of the working class. In 1931 the Conservatives won about 55 per cent of the working-class vote; in 1935 about 50 per cent. More than Labour, the Conservative

---

[78] D. Jarvis, 'The Shaping of the Conservative Electoral Hegemony, 1918–1939', in Lawrence and Taylor (eds.), *Party, State and Society*, 145.

[79] Bates, 'Conservative Party in the Constituencies', 223–4.

[80] Williamson, *Baldwin*, 154.

[81] Bates, 'The Conservative Party in the Constituencies', 81; Stacey, *Tradition and Change*, 85–8.

Party in the 1930s was the party of the working class. For this there were a number of reasons. Frank Parkin's argument, that we would expect people to support a party which stood for the country's dominant value system, is one. Here trade unionism mattered. There were certain institutions, especially trade unions, which promoted alternative forms of social solidarity and were effective ideological counters to Toryism. Those working men outside these institutions, however, were mobilized by a specifically Tory social solidarity which, unlike working-class Liberalism, Labour found difficult to undermine. The Tory Party had long been entrenched as a working-class party. Henry Pelling calculated that between 1885 and 1910 almost half the enfranchised working class voted Tory.[82] The Conservative Party successfully exploited the defensiveness of working-class culture, the belief that the well-to-do had a fitness to govern denied the working class, and an essentially Tory conception of the English nation: imperial, Anglican and socially graded. Generational factors probably also mattered. Older working-class voters, politically socialized during the Edwardian period, were more likely to continue supporting a party they had always supported, or if pre-war non-voters, one they knew and understood.[83]

The Conservatives in the 1930s, it has been argued, did not pursue the working-class vote as such; but as the party of property pursued the votes of those working men with property, however small.[84] The Tories doubtless did this, but how successfully is questionable. Apart from the important exception of the unemployed[85] — if we assume that their political loyalties, in so far as they

[82] Pelling, *Social Geography of British Elections*, 420.

[83] M. Benney, A. P. Gray, and R. H. Pear, *How People Vote: A Study of Electoral Behaviour in Greenwich* (London, 1956), 104.

[84] Daunton, 'How to Pay for the War', 894; D. Jarvis, 'British Conservatism and Class Politics in the 1920s', *English Historical Review* 111 (1996), 83–4. Jarvis writes: 'Appeals to working-class savers, shoppers, tax-payers and property owners thus provided a vital counterpoint in Conservative discourse to the more blunt juxtaposition of "public" and working classes. They also highlighted a decisive shift of direction. Whatever mistakes it might make in the future, the Conservative party would never again waste its energies in chasing that alluring but illusory prize, the working-class vote.'

[85] See below, 101–2.

had them, were primarily to Labour—it would be surprising if the economic profiles of working-class Tory and Labour voters differed much. On Merseyside, for example, though working-class Tories probably did have more property (it would have been difficult not to), the reason why one voted Tory and the other Labour was primarily religious and ethnic. The differences between working-class Tory and working-class Labour in the 1930s were probably as much a result of historic, if waning, social and sectarian loyalties and local peculiarities as economic self-interest: something strongly argued by Trevor Griffiths.[86]

Hitherto, either explicitly or implicitly, we have been mainly talking about men. But the Conservative Party's success in the 1930s was even greater among women and they were disproportionately responsible for its success. In *every* social class the majority of women voted Tory. If women and men voted Conservative in the 1930s in the same relative proportion as they did in 1945[87] then a large majority of working-class women voted Conservative—a much higher proportion than men—and it is on this that the Tory electoral hegemony of the 1930s was ultimately based. Why did the Conservatives have such an advantage? One answer, it is suggested, lies in the superiority of the Conservative Party's formal propaganda.[88] There is perhaps some truth to this. The Tory appeal was snappier and did not make the mistake of overestimating the political education of the community. Labour's propaganda was thought, even by Labour, to be sometimes too 'highbrow'. In practice, however, the Tory approach to women differed little from Labour's. The propaganda of both was essentially domestic; both appealed to the 'chancellor of the exchequer' of the household; both insinuated that the housewife's struggle with the weekly budget enabled her to recognize the wisdom of one party and

---

[86] T. Griffiths, *The Lancashire Working Classes, c.1880–1930* (Oxford, 2001), 317–20 particularly.

[87] See below, pp. 173–4. As an absolute proportion, of course, many fewer men and women voted Conservative in 1945 than they did in 1935.

[88] D. Jarvis, 'Mrs Maggs and Betty: The Conservative Appeal to Women Voters in the 1920s', *Twentieth Century British History* 5, 2 (1994), 129–52.

the folly of the other. Labour probably did have a clearer vision of the modern, technologically assisted housewife ('Better Times for the Housewife'[89]) than the Conservatives and made an attempt to mobilize the single working-women, but with only mixed success.

Both in their membership were increasingly women's parties. From the early 1920s most new members of the Conservative Party were women, many recruited from the old Primrose League. By the 1930s, as far as we can tell, the majority of members of the Party were women.[90] But the Labour Party was not all that different. Women were not a majority, but were close.[91] In constituencies without strong union links women did most of the work and earned most of the money. In both parties women's role was essentially adjunct: whist drives, fetes, sales of work, the usual round of money-making. In both—especially the Conservative Party—women were conscious of the fact that however much they did men ran the show. Of local Conservatism, Bates has argued that 'there was considerable tension between men and women: while women made up the bulk of the membership and did most of the work, men contributed most of the funds and maintained effective control of the local parties'.[92] It is unlikely that the experience of women in the Labour Party was much different, though it is possible that the 'atmosphere' of the Conservative party was 'more congenial socially' for women than Labour.[93] In both parties the role of women was secondary, though the politically determined woman was best advised to join the Labour Party.[94]

---

[89] The title of a Labour pamphlet of 1923 officially attributed to Herbert Morrison.

[90] Bates, 'The Conservative Party in the Constituencies', 82.

[91] Worley, *Labour Inside the Gate*, 184. Worley suggests that about three-sevenths of Party members were women.

[92] Bates, 'The Conservative Party in the Constituencies', 64; N. R. McCrillis, *The British Conservative Party in the Age of Universal Suffrage: Popular Conservatism, 1918–1929* (Columbus, Ohio, 1998), 58. McCrillis has a full discussion of the Conservative Party's women's organizations.

[93] G. E. Maguire, *Conservative Women: A History of Women in the Conservative Party, 1874–1997* (London, 1998), 78.

[94] But not push her luck. In his introduction to Marion Phillips' pamphlet *Women in the Labour Party* (1918), Henderson attacked 'feminist agitation' which he said

Since in the 1930s 'women's issues' as such were not the common coin of politics the crucial determinant of the Tory success among women was both how the parties presented themselves to women and how women saw the parties. That a majority of middle-class women in the 1930s voted Conservative is not surprising; the class influences to which they were subject (whether they were married or not) were by themselves enough to explain that even if there were other contributing influences—Anglican churchgoing for example.[95] The tendency of working-class women to vote Tory in much higher numbers than men, however, needs more explanation. Here a perceived life experience frequently overrode class influences and shaped many women's view of politics. The sexual division of labour in often straitened working-class households placed a particular burden of individual responsibility on women: whether the household worked or not largely depended on them. Individualism was built into their lives. A party which emphasized individual responsibility and the individual above the social stood for the reality of life; unlike the Labour Party which, despite its attempts to woo the housewife, stood for the fecklessness and aggression of men. The Labour programme, especially in 1931, must for many women have seemed so far from reality as to be fantasy. In this way the common sense of the Tory Party appeared to be the common sense of life.[96]

There is also some truth to Selina Todd's argument that the trade unions, due to their comparative indifference to the female workforce,

had no place in the Labour Party. Andrew Flinn has noted, however, that the first generation of Labour women councillors in Manchester were much less ready to describe themselves as housewives than Conservative or Liberal women councillors. (Flinn, 'Labour's Family, Local Labour Parties, Trade Unions and Trades Councils in Cotton Lancashire, 1931–39', in M. Worley (ed.), *Labour's Grass Roots: Essays on the Activities of Local Labour Parties and Members, 1918–1945* (Aldershot, 2005), 84.)

[95] Just as active nonconformity might explain a middle-class woman's decision to continue voting Liberal.

[96] I would not wholly agree with Eccleshall here. He argues that 'far from pouring sheer lies into heads . . . the dominating [Conservative] ideology succeeds by misrepresenting the facts of ordinary life. In this way, its ideological content is hidden under the guise of common sense'. (R. Eccleshall, 'Ideology as Common Sense: The Case of British Conservatism', *Radical Philosophy*, Summer 1980 (25), 3.) The Conservatives in this case did not misreport the 'facts' of ordinary life. What they misreported was how these facts might be changed.

failed to mobilize a work-based political radicalism which undoubt-edly existed. The disputes, she notes, 'in which young women were involved clearly drew upon the workplace culture that . . . they themselves evolved. Women's workplace networks could be turned to political purposes.'[97] But on the whole they were not.

The way women then acquired political knowledge might also have reinforced the bias against Labour. In their study of Greenwich in 1951—as chronologically close to the 1930s as such research can take us—Benney and his colleagues were struck by how far women obtained their political knowledge indirectly or through their families, or not at all, while men derived their knowledge from work or the outside world. Women's knowledge was acquired privately, men's publicly.[98] Furthermore, the implication is that even women in full-time work, since they anticipated marriage and domesticity, in effect acquired their knowledge privately. The result was a kind of delayed knowledge. For women, as with older men, Labour, it is argued, was an unknown party and voting Labour still a comparative novelty. Largely excluded from the 'public' sphere—by their own will or others'—they voted for a familiar party whose view of life seemed similar to their own.

After 1931, therefore, the Conservatives assembled a highly diverse electoral coalition which socially had little in common. What held it together was an ill-defined, but often strongly held, anti-socialism. Comparing the pre-1914 and post-1918 worlds the Conservative MP Noel Skelton wrote that the Edwardian political battles were 'fought on a narrow front and by small armies of professionals, whose passage through the life of the nation affected it hardly more than a charabanc disturbs the countryside today. But socialism fights on the broadest of fronts, and this breadth of front must dominate the strategy and tactics of the new era; for envelopment and crushing

---

[97] S. Todd, *Young Women, Work and Family in England, 1980–1950* (Oxford, 2005), 185. Todd emphasizes the significance of this against those, like Trevor Griffiths, who emphasize 'gender and generational divisions in working-class life' (227). I am sympathetic to this argument but would not take it as far as she does.

[98] Benney et al., 'How People Vote', 108.

defeat . . . form the danger against which Conservatives must guard in the great battles ahead.'[99] If a moderate Conservative like Skelton could argue this it is not surprising that many others did as well. 'Socialism' could be several things: nationalization, authoritarianism, subversion, a movement to destroy the family and religion, or even, as it was to many in the 1930s, simple incompetence. Though naive it was not totally unreasonable to associate the Labour Party with these things. Labour was in favour of nationalization and fought the 1931 election on a programme that must have seemed to many 'bolshevism run mad' (Snowden's famous description of it);[100] Labour was the most secular of the parties and the one where unconventional views of marriage were more likely to be found; a number of its leaders were thought by many to have behaved unpatriotically during the war—and the conspicuously patriotic behaviour of two of those most suspect during the war, MacDonald and Snowden, in 1931 further damaged the Party they left behind. Nor should we underestimate the strength with which anti-socialism was held. Despite Baldwin's easy-going manner, for example, his anti-socialism was real enough. In 1926 he was as responsible for provoking the general strike as anyone and he made no attempt to forestall the 1927 Trade Disputes Act.[101] He had a long pedigree as an anti-socialist: in 1931 he told his wife 'that the great thing this time [the 1931 election] is to give Socialism a really smashing defeat'.[102] A casual glance at the Conservative press during the 1931 election can leave no doubt how many agreed with Baldwin.

Socialism could also mean support for the undeserving; for those outside the claims of moral worth; or if inside, just. Conspicuously absent from the list of possible beneficiaries of the National government's policies were the long-term unemployed. In October 1931,

---

[99] Quoted in McCrillis, *The British Conservative Party*, 224–5. Skelton was a Scottish MP, but there is no reason to think that his view were unrepresentative of Tory opinion generally.

[100] For this programme see Thorpe, *The British General Election of 1931*, 159–60. The programme, it should be noted, represented the last gasp of free-trade socialism. In this sense, it was the one and only time Labour fought an election on its 'maximal' 1920s programme: clause IV plus free trade.

[101] See above, 63.   [102] Quoted in Williamson, *Baldwin*, 44.

for the first time since the First World War, unemployment was not mentioned in the King's speech. Although the National government eventually devised a labour transfer scheme and tinkered with the 'special areas'—areas of high and persistent unemployment—nothing had much success until the rearmament programmes in the late 1930s. Nor was the government much bothered with this. It, like its Conservative and Labour predecessors, preferred the dole which kept the unemployed both alive and quiescent.[103] Nonetheless, there were some boundaries the second Labour government would not cross. Nor would the labour movement have permitted it to do so.[104] But the National government not only cut unemployment benefit, it introduced the means test which, by linking benefit to total household income, not only reduced the already exiguous living standards of many working-class families but broke them up or made young wage-earners financially responsible for the rest of the family. Whatever its economic futility this tightening of the screw was not politically pointless. The ideological centrality of unemployment benefit and the absolute determination of the Conservative and Liberal Parties in 1931 that it should be cut strongly suggest that to the National government long-term unemployment was of less significance than the restabilization of the economy on terms which excluded the unemployed and was seen to do so. The National government can, indeed, be thought a coalition against the unemployed: an attempted mobilization of the working against the workless—a weapon in the battle against 'socialism'.

By 1939 England possessed a party-political structure that showed no sign of fragmentation. In much of the country a two-party system, Conservative and Labour had developed, modified only by pockets of surviving Liberalism in the English peripheries or by the personal popularity of individual Liberal MPs, like Geoffrey Mander in Wolverhampton[105] or Percy Harris in Bethnal Green. In parts

---

[103] I have discussed this elsewhere. See McKibbin, *Ideologies of Class*, 228–58.

[104] See above, 77–8.

[105] His popularity was not harmed by the fact that Mander's Paints was a large employer in Wolverhampton.

of rural and provincial England there was really only one party, the Conservative Party, whatever it happened to be called. Both the Labour and Conservative political families were coalitions but the Conservative one was much larger. Both had pure types of voters: people we would expect to vote Labour or Conservative in almost any circumstances. The pure type of Labour voter was a young working-class male trade unionist in employment who despised religion. The pure type of Conservative voter was a middle-class widow living in a provincial town and a practising Anglican. The difference was that in the Labour family the number of people who differed from the core voter was comparatively small. Even so there were clear geographical biases to Labour's support. It was disproportionately strong in mining constituencies and (albeit less so) in other areas of high unemployment. It was reasonably strong and growing in London and in industrial and textile Yorkshire. It had virtually all the Irish vote, but apart from Merseyside there were yet too few on the English electoral rolls to be of much help, and the hostility they excited among the Protestant electorate was actually a hindrance. Although in 1935 Labour had in aggregate recovered its 1929 vote, in some of the country, like the West Midlands or Tyneside, its 1929 level was not reached again until 1945.[106] It was, as we have seen, weak in nearly all the major towns of England and had a majority of seats in only one, Sheffield. There was a host of industrial seats, whether 'old' industry like Barrow or 'new' industry like Coventry, which Labour failed to recover in 1935. Nor, apart perhaps from London and Sheffield, did Labour secure much advantage from such municipal success as it had. Indeed, in local as well as in parliamentary politics Labour was becalmed after 1935. As Davies and Morley note, while Labour recovered strongly after 1931, between 1935 and 1938 it suffered a marked reverse in local government elections. There was absolutely no sign in them of the huge gains Labour would make in 1945.[107] What Labour did secure was the likelihood that were the

---

[106] For the development of Labour's programme in the 1930s, see below, 142–4.

[107] S. Davies and B. Morley, *County and Borough Elections in England and Wales, 1919–1938: A Comparative Analysis* (Aldershot, 2006), 638–45.

National government to falter electorally the probable beneficiary would be it and no one else.

The Conservative family was much larger in breadth and depth. Although the parliamentary party was socially homogenous and the membership increasingly so, that was not true of the Party's voters. Aside from the mining seats, parts of Yorkshire, and bits of east and south London, there was nowhere in England they did not dominate. The cities, the suburbs, the industrial towns, the countryside, all were part of the Conservative family, and few showed signs before 1939 of leaving it. The by-elections in the 1935 parliament and the Gallup polls which the *News Chronicle* began to publish in 1938 suggested the Tories would win the next election with their majority almost unchanged.[108]

To return to the questions asked at the beginning of this chapter. First, are we explaining Tory strength or Labour weakness? This is difficult to answer since the two are, so to speak, dynamically related. What we can say is that the political failure of the second Labour government made possible the Conservative conquest of most of England, including much that was 'natural' Labour territory. That government offered no compelling reason why those who did not already vote Labour should do so, and the way it collapsed drove back into the Conservative family those traditionally Tory working men and women who had begun to vote Labour in the late 1920s—most conspicuously in Birmingham and the West Midlands. The reputation of the government, moreover, left Labour with little to work with for the rest of the decade—it, after all, gave socialism a bad name—until the fall of the Chamberlain government in 1940 was responsible for an unexpected party-political *bouleversement*. Its failure also cruelly exposed the autodidactic tradition, so strong in Labour's working-class leadership, as politically useless in the circumstances of 1931.[109]

---

[108] The average swing to Labour in these by-elections was 4 per cent—way below what Labour needed and a surprisingly small 'by-election effect'. For details, see C. Cook and J. Ramsden (eds.), *By-Elections in British Politics* (London, 1973), 9, 116–17.

[109] See above, 84.

Second, how much was due to luck, good or bad? Obviously a good deal. But the Tories also made their own luck. They manipulated the 1931 crisis such that Labour's electoral defeat was much heavier even than the by-elections earlier in the year foretold, and they consciously shaped themselves as a party acceptable to a majority of the population in ways which involved important changes in appearance and attitude. Baldwin's significance is that he encouraged and personified this refashioning. In summary, we might say that Labour was dealt a bad hand which it played badly; the Conservatives a good hand which they played well. The result was the electoral and ideological supremacy of the Conservative Party and the marginalization of Labour both ideologically and as a party of government.

4

The Party System Thrown Off Course

In the last chapter I argued that the Conservative Party had by 1939 established a political supremacy which seemed unchallengeable. All the evidence we have—by-elections and opinion polling—suggested that although the Labour Party had recovered most (though not all) of the ground lost in 1931 it was making no further advances. Yet in the general election of 1945 there was an overall swing of 12 per cent to Labour and in some areas a much larger one. In this chapter I wish not only to attempt an explanation of why that happened but also of what happened—what was involved in this change and what it meant to the electorate.

There are already several familiar explanations. Most have some truth, though others are, in Sibley's words, 'conceptually doubtful'.[1] One of the most familiar is that the ideological underpinnings of Labour's victory were already in place by the end of the 1930s: they represented, so to speak, the pre-history of wartime radicalism and the policies of the Attlee government. They are what Arthur Marwick many years ago called 'middle opinion'.[2] There had in the 1930s always been alternatives to the apparent orthodoxies of the National government and of 'unplanned' capitalism which had considerable cross-party support. Political and Economic Planning (PEP) and the Next Five Years' Group, whose theoretical statement *The Next*

---

[1] R. Sibley, 'The Swing to Labour during the Second World War: When and Why?' *Labour History Review* 55, 1 (Spring 1990), 23–4.

[2] A. Marwick, 'Middle Opinion in the Thirties: Planning, Progress and Political Agreement', *English Historical Review* 3, cccxi (1964) 285–98.

Five Years: An Essay in Political Agreement was published in 1935.[3] Both tried to find a compromise between brute socialism and laissez-faire capitalism. Indeed, the vocabulary of 'planning' was a commonplace in the 1930s. If Labour's victory in 1945 required such a vocabulary, it certainly existed before the war. There is also evidence that part of the population was 'radicalized' in the later 1930s by a loosely defined 'anti-fascism'. The extraordinary success of Victor Gollancz's Left Book Club and the Penguin Specials, both of which treated issues of the day 'progressively', the extent of support for the Spanish Republic (even if largely passive),[4] the very large membership of the League of Nations Union, and the huge sales of 'democratic' social reports like J. B. Priestley's *English Journey* (1934) or 'social reform' novels like A. J. Cronin's *The Citadel* (1937) do suggest that something was happening.[5] Even the government had to acknowledge this. The appointment of the Royal Commission on the Distribution of the Industrial Population (1937), the famous Barlow Commission, against the wishes of Neville Chamberlain,[6] whose recommendations were to be the basis of wartime location of industry legislation, was a good example.[7] Furthermore, the findings

[3] See also Harold Macmillan's *The Middle Way: A Study of the Problem of Economic and Social Progress in a Free and Democratic Society* (1938).

[4] According to a Gallup Poll of March 1938, 57 per cent of respondents favoured the Republic and only 7 per cent Franco. For a full treatment of this, see T. Buchanan, *Britain and the Spanish Civil War* (Cambridge, 1997), 22–36.

[5] For the Left Book Club, see S. Hodges, *Gollancz: The Story of a Publishing House* (London, 1978); J. Lewis, *The Left Book Club: An Historical Record* (London, 1970); for Penguin, N. Joicey, 'A Paperback Guide to Progress: Penguin Books, 1935-c.1951', *Twentieth Century British History* 4, 1 (1993); for Priestley, J. Baxendale, *Priestley's England: J.B. Priestley and English Culture* (Manchester, 2007); for Cronin, R. McKibbin, 'Politics and the Medical Hero: A. J. Cronin's *The Citadel*', *English Historical Review* CXXIII, 502 (2008).

[6] He thought its appointment would be a tacit admission that the labour policies of the National government had largely failed.

[7] The Report, which was not published until after the outbreak of the war, was (among other things) critical of the effect the government's labour transfer schemes had on the communities from which people left, and suggested that industry should be brought to labour rather than the reverse. John Stevenson calls it the 'planners' breakthrough'. (J. Stevenson in H. L. Smith (eds.), *War and Social Change: British Society in the Second World War* (Manchester 1986), 69.)

of the British Institute of Public Opinion (the British branch of the Gallup organization) suggested that the majority of the population supported 'Labour' social policies rather than those of the National government; just as the majority supported Republican Spain. Only a belief, it has been argued, that the government would keep Britain out of war, or if not, win the war, preserved an otherwise discredited Conservatism.[8]

On the whole, we should be sceptical of such arguments. Even if we agree that political change during the war favoured these 'centrist' organizations[9] only with difficulty can PEP or *The Middle Way* be seen as precursors of the Attlee government. PEP was closely associated with the MacDonald wing of the National government and probably did better duty as a research body than as political lobbyist. Macmillan, having left the Conservative Party in opposition to its employment policies, rejoined it in 1937, while the vocabulary of planning, as Daniel Ritschel has pointed out, concealed ideological fragmentation.[10] There was 'capitalist' planning, which had a good deal of support within the Conservative Party and often involved little more than the 'rationalization' of dying industries and industrial self-government; a kind of 'Liberal' planning associated with Lloyd George's 'New Deal' in the mid-1930s; 'technocratic' planning, found everywhere in Europe and the United States and on both the political right and left, as well as varieties of 'socialist' planning. They had little in common though Keynes was to give them some kind of unity, as he was to the warring factions of the Labour Party. As to popular preferences, that so much of the population should apparently support 'progressive' policies indeed might have had long-run importance. The problem is that they would not vote Labour to get them—and it is improbable that a belief that the Conservatives were more likely to keep them out of war was alone responsible for

---

[8] Sibley, 'Swing to Labour', 29.

[9] This has been argued by Malcolm Smith in B. Brivati and H. Jones (eds.), *What Difference did the War Make?* (Leicester, 1993), 44.

[10] D. Ritschel, *The Politics of Planning: The Debate on Economic Planning in Britain in the 1930s* (Oxford, 1997), 232.

this. In any case, these were not always Labour policies: although 67 per cent of the population said they were in favour of family allowances, Labour, as we have seen, was very divided over them. Furthermore, the electorate seemed no more likely to vote for a broad-based progressive candidate than for Labour.[11]

The wider significance of the Left Book Club, the Penguin Specials or Popular Frontism generally is difficult to assess. We do not altogether know who patronized them, though we can make reasonably well-informed guesses. Most were probably 'middle-class' or 'upper working-class'—some probably from the growing 'public' middle class, people employed by national or local government—and some from the 'writers' circles' and working-class literary self-help movements.[12] It was thought at the time that public professionals, especially teachers, were increasingly left wing (and increasingly likely to undermine the nation's fibre), and that it was they who belonged to the Left Book Club and bought Penguin Specials.[13] They may well have done, but it is also the case that in the 1930s and 1940s the majority of teachers were probably Conservatives.[14] The culture of

[11] In the first of the 'popular front' by-elections, Derby in 1936, Philip Noel-Baker, standing as the Labour candidate but with the support of *inter alia* Viscount Cecil, J. L. Hammond, J. A. Hobson, Keynes, and Eleanor Rathbone, narrowly won the seat; what was surprising, however, was how small his majority was in a constituency which had once been very safe Labour. In the celebrated Oxford by-election (1938) the Independent Progressive candidate did reduce the Conservative majority but probably not much more than one would expect in a by-election. In the Bridgewater by-election (1938) the independent progressive candidate, Vernon Bartlett, who won, undoubtedly did well—largely by mobilizing much of the normally non-voting population. But it was uncertain how much that was due to local discontent and how much opposition to the National government's policies—presumably a bit of both. The Duchess of Atholl resigned her seat (Kinross and West Perthshire) in 1939 to fight a by-election in opposition to appeasement, and especially the government's policies towards Spain, but lost to an official Conservative.

[12] There is an outstanding discussion of these movements in C. Hillyard, *To Exercise Our Talents: The Democratisation of Writing in Britain* (Cambridge, Mass., 2006).

[13] One Mass-Observer, 'Mrs Trowbridge' records a conversation with a well-off member of the middle class who attributed increasing indifference to empire to the influence of elementary school teachers, the 'duds' among their contemporaries, who had gone socialist since the salary cuts of 1931. They are not alone. 'Secondary and Grammar School teachers having gone all "Red" at the Universities deliberately infect their pupils with the same disease.' (D. Sheridan (ed.), *Wartime Women* (London, 1990, 154.)

[14] Evidence from the late 1940s suggests that about two-thirds of teachers voted Conservative. In this they differed little from others in equivalent professional occupations. (J.Bonham, *The Middle Class Vote* (London, 1954), 134–5.)

the Left Book Club and the Penguin Special, nonetheless, continued into the first years of the war—that famous anti-Conservative polemic *Guilty Men*[15] was one of its products and undoubtedly loaded the dice against the Conservatives. It, however, began to peter out towards the end of the war and died suddenly with the advent of the Attlee government. In 1945 an unusually high proportion of the middle class voted Labour (between 25% and 30%) and the progressive impulse of the late 1930s was probably in part responsible, but as a political culture it was not particularly sympathetic to Labour either before or after 1945.

The second, and in many ways the most attractive explanation, simply does away with the problem of 'conversion' (did people change their political allegiances during the war?) by arguing that Labour's victory was the delayed effect of generational and demographic change. It suggests that those who voted Conservative in 1935 mostly continued to do so, but in 1945 Labour was supported by a new cohort of voters who were politically socialized in the interwar years. The sociologist, Mark Abrams, noted that one-quarter of those who voted for the first time in 1945 had reached adulthood since 1935; in 1945 over half the voters had been born in the twentieth century while two-thirds of the voters in 1935 had been born in the nineteenth century.[16] In other words, a high proportion of those voting in 1945 reached political maturity after the Labour Party had become the second party of the state. Franklin and Ladner, who have argued this most strongly, write that after 1918 'Labour needed only the passage of time for those socialized in newly Labour supporting households to come of voting age'. And even if the new voters did not come from such households (as the majority did not) they were raised in Labour 'environments' or working-class neighbourhoods.[17] The

---

[15] See above, p. 107. Of the three authors of *Guilty Men*, one, Michael Foot, had been a Liberal and the others, Frank Owen and Peter Howard, were.

[16] M. Abrams, 'The Labour Vote in the General Election', in *Pilot Papers: Social Essays and Documents* 1, 1 (Jan. 1946), 24–5.

[17] M. Franklin and M. Lardner, 'The Undoing of Winston Churchill: Mobilisation and Conversion in the 1945 Realignment of British Voters', *British Journal of Political Science* 25 (1995), 436.

1945 election 'saw the coming of age of a new generation of voters, socialized into Labour partisanship during years in which the Labour Party was building its base of support. Perhaps combined with a general mobilization of the working class, this cohort simply swept all before it.'[18] Abrams has further suggested that the huge swings to Labour in the more prosperous parts of England—greater London and the West Midlands—were partly a long-term consequence of migration from the north of England.[19] Once again 'conversion' as an explanation is largely eliminated. A majority of first-time voters in 1945 certainly voted Labour—anything up to 67 per cent depending upon how one measures it—and this was true of men and probably of women.[20] It is also true, as is usually the case, that younger voters were more inclined to vote Labour than older ones. Furthermore, in 1945 there were ten years of new voters and ten years of dead voters which meant that the electorate in 1945 was significantly different from that of 1935. That in the age-group 30–49, according to Durant, there was apparently a huge difference in the way men and women appear to have voted (men 61% voted Labour, women 46%) might be explained, as I suggested in the previous chapter, by the different ways men and women were politically socialized.[21]

As a partial explanation the generational–demographic argument has value; as an explanation of everything it cannot really work. Were it to be true we would expect the change to be more gradual and more sign of it in parliamentary by-elections before the outbreak of war. Even if we allow for ageing registers the evidence is, on the contrary, that the Labour vote was 'stuck', and that forms of political socialization cited—schooling, neighbourhoods, work

[18] Ibid. 452.   [19] Abrams, 'The Labour Vote in the General Election', 25.

[20] Franklin and Ladner suggest the figure is 67.2 per cent ('The Undoing of Winston Churchill', 452). H. Durant suggests a lower figure, and one in the age group 30–49 markedly affected by gender (Durant, *Political Opinion* (London, 1949), 6–7).

[21] Durant, ibid. That gap, however, is worryingly large and might be statistically unsound. Given the circumstances we would expect a higher proportion of women in that age group to vote Labour and my guess is they did. It was thought at the time that women were more reluctant to disclose how they voted than men and that might be responsible for the gap. Or else for some reason the sample was skewed.

practices—were weak. The demographic argument—that Labour's gains in the south of England and the Midlands were a result of the long-term effects of migration—is surely exaggerated. Although migration from the north or Wales was undoubtedly to influence the political culture of Birmingham, Coventry, Oxford, Slough, Hayes, even Banbury (where the construction of an aluminium strip-rolling mill in 1930 transformed the character of a market town), it cannot explain the speed and size of the movement to Labour in 1945. In Birmingham, for instance, the proportion of skilled workers voting Labour seems to have doubled between 1935 and 1945.[22] And, while migration to the south might partly explain the decay of the Labour vote in the north-east in the 1930s, it obviously cannot account for the huge swing to Labour there in 1945.

A generational–demographic theory of political socialization allows for neither contingency nor political action. There is no reason, for instance, why schools or neighbourhoods should as such be Labour: it demands political actors to make them so. Nor does the history of the Labour Party in the 1930s, one after all of failure, suggest why younger generations in growing proportions should inevitably have supported it. It seems almost inconceivable that an event as profound in its social, economic, and physical consequences as the Second World War should simply wash over the electorate leaving only differential birth-rates or the local elementary school to decide political allegiances. Franklin and Ladner, in fact, concede this. They note that Labour had many more established than new voters in 1945. We cannot know, therefore, 'how those Labour supporters who were old enough to have voted in 1935 acquired their 1945 partisanship. It thus remains unclear whether Labour gained more by mobilization or as a result of switching by those who had originally supported another party.'[23] It is almost impossible, in practice, to explain the Labour victory in terms which do not allow for large-scale conversion during the war

---

[22] J. Bonham, *The Middle Class Vote* (London, 1954), 161.
[23] Franklin and Ladner, 'The Undoing of Winston Churchill', 446.

itself; something which, in their informal way, the mass-observers recorded.[24]

A once popular version of the 'wartime-change' explanation of the Labour victory was the radicalization of the armed forces; an assumption that there was something about military experience which radicalized men and women in ways life did not do for those still on civvy street. Support for this version is partly statistical and partly comparative or anecdotal. In those Commonwealth countries which had elections during the war and where the service vote was counted separately, the services emerge as undoubtedly more left wing than civilians. There was also the evidence of the mock elections held on troop convoys and in army camps to while away the time where the Conservative vote was usually embarrassingly low or non-existent.[25] All this, *prima facie*, suggests a marked radicalization, as do the proceedings of the famous Cairo 'parliament' (April 1944)—a body modelled on the old 'local parliaments' and made up of servicemen on leave or based in Cairo.[26] Many blamed such radicalization on the Army Bureau of Current Affairs (ABCA), whose lecturers were alleged to have bolshevized the services. Historians now tend to discount this as an explanation. Although there were 5.5 million members of the services in 1945 they cast only about 6 per cent of the total vote, and people were unsure of its overall significance.[27]

[24] See, for example, Muriel Green in S. Koa Wing (ed.), *Our Longest Days: A People's History of the Second World War* (London, 2008), 262: 'Several people told me they have voted Conservative all their life before and this time they were so disgusted with the conditions of pre-war, unemployment etc., that they decided long ago to vote Labour at the next election'; Beryl Johns in D. Sheridan (ed.), *Wartime Women* (London, 1990), 251: 'Many in outside queue [for an election meeting] said they had changed political views during the war and had veered to the left.'

[25] Jim Fyrth records that in his unit the results of the mock election held in 1945 were Labour 84, Communist 21, Liberal 11, Conservative 7. (J. Fyrth, 'Labour's Bright Morning—And Afternoon', in J. Fyrth (ed.), *Labour's High Noon: The Government and the Economy, 1945–1951* (London, 1993), 259.)

[26] The parliament was held in a popular off-base club called Music for All. On the night of its final meeting over 600 servicemen and women attended to hear the 'chancellor of the exchequer' (the late Leo Abse) present a bill to nationalize the Bank of England. (N. Grant, 'Citizen Soldiers: Army Education in World War II', in *Formations of Nations and People*, 180–5.)

[27] For details, R. B. McCallum and A. Readman, *The British General Election of 1945* (London, 1947), 43.

That it favoured Labour most agreed, and if a greater number of servicemen and women had actually voted—only 55 per cent did—the Labour majority would probably have been even bigger. Nonetheless, this could be explained by age-cohort. The armed forces contained a disproportionate number of young men—precisely that group most likely to vote Labour and the only fair comparison is with civilian voters of the same age and sex. Such a comparison is unlikely to show much difference between the two. Furthermore, the BIPO polls, which showed Labour well ahead of the Conservatives from the moment they were renewed in 1943, did not include in their samples members of the armed forces.[28] As for army education, there is a mass of evidence to suggest that the lectures were often given by sceptical officers to bored or sleeping squaddies[29] while the membership of the Cairo parliament, it is argued, was unrepresentative of the forces as a whole and became famous only because the War office insisted on closing it.[30]

These objections to the notion that the armed forces were peculiarly radicalized, as far as they go, have some validity but are not entirely convincing. It is possible, for instance, that the speed with which Chamberlainite Conservatism became discredited in 1940 had its origins partly in the services. In the crucial vote of confidence that felled Chamberlain in May 1940 a much higher proportion of Conservative MPs who were in the services voted against the government than non-serving members of the party. Paul Addison has further argued that the notion of the 'guilty men', the men who almost brought Britain to its knees, which was so damaging to the Tory party, began with the evacuees of Dunkirk and spread by word of mouth to the civilian population.[31] Harold Nicolson (now

---

[28] H. Pelling, 'The 1945 General Election Reconsidered', *Historical Journal* 23, 2 (1980), 410.

[29] J. A. Crang, 'Politics on Parade: Army Education and the 1945 General Election', *History* 81, 262 (April 1996), 223–7.

[30] Grant, 'Citizen Soldiers', 85. For the Cairo parliament see also Bill Davidson, 'The Cairo Forces Parliament', *Labour History Review* 55, 3 (1990), 20–6.

[31] P. Addison, *The Road to 1945: British Politics and the Second World War* (Pimlico edn, London, 1994), 111.

in the ministry of information) recorded in his diary in June 1940 that there was 'a growing feeling against . . . the "old gang" . . . the men who have come back from the front [i.e. Dunkirk] feel that Kingsley Wood and [Thomas] Inskip let them down and must go. Chamberlain would have to go too.'[32] Dunkirk, it thus could be said, completed what the debacle in Norway started. Norway began a revolt within the Conservative Party; Dunkirk began a revolt against the Conservative Party. Tom Harrisson, the co-founder of Mass-Observation, noted that the Mass-Observation evidence suggested that service personnel were more radical than civilians even though the BIPO polls were of civilians only,[33] while the military censors found in service correspondence 'a strong but unformed and not always coherent radicalism'.[34] Labour's very surprising victory in Winchester in 1945 was partly due to the large number of servicemen in barracks there. What seems to be the case is that the services were a special and heightened version of what happened in the civilian population—that the way politics was radicalized, often confused and inarticulate, makes it easy for us to overlook what happened, or even to deny that it happened. That is a theme to which we shall return.

Perhaps the most common interpretation of 1945 is to see the Labour victory as the result of a process, of the experience of war over the longer term; not something that happened suddenly. Contemporaries (and historians), for example, discerned a pattern in wartime by-elections which could support this interpretation.[35] In the first eighteen months or so of the war such by-elections as were contested (under the party electoral truce the three parties agreed not to stand against each other in by-elections) were usually fought by anti-war

[32] Nicolson, *Diary and Letters, 1939–1945*, 94. Kinglsey Wood was Secretary of State for Air, 1938–40 and Thomas Inskip was minister for the Co-ordination of Defence, 1936–9. Neither had been thought successes in these posts.

[33] T. Harrisson, 'Who'll Win?', *Political Quarterly* 15, 1 (Jan.–March 1944), 26.

[34] J. L. Hodson, *The Sea and the Land* (London, 1945), 302–3.

[35] For a contemporary view see P. G. Richards, 'The Political Temper', *Political Quarterly* 16, 1 (Jan. 1945), 64; also Sibley, 'The Swing to Labour during the Second World War', 26.

candidates of various stripes and usually against Conservatives. In the next couple of years most independent candidates who opposed Conservatives wanted the war waged more vigorously. Four independents were elected and it is in this period that the Tories began to worry about such losses. After the very safe seat of Skipton was lost the ban on cabinet ministers speaking in by-elections was actually lifted.[36] From January 1943 to the general election the majority of by-elections in Conservative seats were contested, now by candidates of definitely left-wing provenance, contests which unquestionably anticipated Labour's victory. It was the course of the by-elections which convinced some that the Conservatives could not win the next election. P. G. Richards, the *Political Quarterly*'s 'correspondent', though he was careful not to predict a Labour victory, argued that the by-elections showed that the 'swing to the Left is a great political reality'.[37] Tom Harrisson said in early 1944 that whoever led the Conservative party in the general election [he meant Churchill] the Tories could not win. 'That is about the first prediction I have ever dared make.'[38] The movement to Labour was by this interpretation gradual, a kind of cumulative radicalization. The legitimation of a 'Labour' view of society was the result of several years of war which had created a new status quo and whose very progress undermined by stages the Conservative hegemony. Home Intelligence attributed this 'home-made socialism' to a number of things: the levelling of classes, the result of bombing and rationing; the Russian successes; revulsion against 'vested interests, "privilege", the "old gang" etc; agreement that post-war life must be better'.[39] It can also be argued that the new status quo was a result of the state's actions. In the early stages of the war, Field argues, it was voluntary organizations which responded first:

But by 1945 the boundaries of public and private spheres, of state and society had been substantially redrawn. Family life was reshaped by a series of [state] interventions. Whether it was in fixing the calorific intake

---

[36] Richards, 'The Political Temper', 65.　　　[37] Ibid.
[38] Harrisson, 'Who'll Win?', 32　　　[39] Addison, *Road to 1945*, 163.

for occupational groups and family members under the rationing system; controlling rents; setting insurance rates for war injuries; providing nurseries, hostels, free vaccinations, and orange juice for children; or paying new types of allowances, the scope of state responsibility for the health and well-being of the population was greatly enlarged.[40]

Charles Madge, another founder of Mass-Observation, argued that it was the state's 'need' for the masses which had transformed politics: 'In peace-time, industry and the state did not need the masses: they were an embarrassment. There were too many of them. Now the need for them is very great. Hence the revision of the basic contract implicit in economic policy.'[41] In doing so, however, the state did things that correct opinion before the war insisted could not be done. In order to fight the war, therefore, the state progressively undermined the Conservative hegemony. We can see how this might have been so. The creation of a wartime political economy and, above all, the increasing intervention of the state in people's lives were not the achievements of a day.

Nonetheless, we are left with the awkward fact that, as I see it, the end of the Conservative political and ideological supremacy— regardless of who was the beneficiary—was extraordinarily sudden. On the eve of the House of Commons debate that brought him down (7–8 May) BIPO found support for Chamberlain largely unchanged. The Conservative press continued to support him strongly. Three days later only one-third of the population supported him. By July 77 per cent of respondents wanted him out of the government altogether. Given the genuine impregnability of the Conservatives well into 1940 (according to the BIPO polls) this collapse was remarkable. Maggie Joy Blunt, a Mass-Observation diarist, noted on 9 June that her 'championship of Chamberlain is short-lived . . . scarcely anyone but Fascists have a good word for him now, in fact one is suspected of Fascist tendencies if one says anything for him'.[42] To the historian

---

[40] G. Field, 'Perspectives on the Working-Class Family in Wartime Britain, 1939–1945', *International Labour and Working-Class History* 38 (Fall 1990), 5–6.

[41] C. Madge, *War-Time Pattern of Saving and Spending* (Cambridge, 1943), 6–7.

[42] S. Garfield (ed.), *We Are At War* (London, 2005), 253.

the second half of 1940 is a different world from September 1939. The kinds of things which were freely said in public about the evacuees in September 1939 (to which we shall return)[43] were more rarely said (at least in public) eight months later. Of this change there are striking instances. In July 1940 *The Times* in a leader wrote:

If we speak of democracy, we do not mean a democracy which maintains the right to vote but forgets the right to work and the right to live. If we speak of freedom, we do not mean a rugged individualism which excludes social organization and economic planning. If we speak of equality we do not mean a political equality nullified by social and economic privilege. If we speak of economic reconstruction, we less think of maximum production (though this too will be required) than of equitable distribution.[44]

This is simply not a leader *The Times* could or would have written a few months before. At the end of that month Lord Halifax, the foreign secretary, no reactionary but also no revolutionary and a leading member of Chamberlain's government, wrote to Duff Cooper, the minister for information:

We were all conscious . . . of the contrast between the readiness of the nation, and particularly the Treasury, to spend £9 million a day to protect a certain way of life and the unwillingness of the administrative authorities in peace to put up, shall we say, £10 million to assist in the reconditioning of Durham unless they could see the project earning a reasonable percentage . . . I am quite certain that the human conscience in this country is not going to stand for a system that permits large numbers of unemployed, and that the masses of the population in foreign countries are also likely to be powerfully affected by whether or not we, with I hope the United States, are able to put up a counter plan in the economic field to Hitler's.[45]

In the same month that onslaught on Chamberlainite Conservatism, *Guilty Men*, was published by Gollancz and immediately had enormous sales. All these were not merely straws in the wind. They were products of the end of Chamberlain's government and the

---

[43] See below, 125–6.
[44] *The Times*, 1 July 1940. The leader was written by E. H. Carr.
[45] Quoted in Addison, *Road to 1945*, 122.

formation of Churchill's coalition on 10 May 1940. My own view is that Labour would have won any election held after July 1940—a consequence, *ex hypothesi*, of the swift conversion of many voters from Conservative to Labour. The only other interpretation warranted by the evidence is that there was indeed a very rapid fall in support for the Conservative Party but 'what counted was the way opinion moved progressively from a generalized discontent to a focusing of that discontent on the Tories and then a crystallizing of opinion in favour of Labour' via Labour proxies.[46] That is possible. But (I would argue) the electoral truce concealed the movement to Labour, and in a partisan two-party system (which it effectively now was and largely had been since 1931) only Labour could be the beneficiary of the Tory decline once it began and whenever the election was held.

What caused this rapid radicalization? Hitherto foreign policy has largely been absent from the discussion. That is because, though influential in a number of elections (especially 1918 and 1935), it did not shape the electorate's fundamental judgements until the military crisis of May–June 1940. Equally, appeasement was never an issue at a general election, though it was an issue at several by-elections. These suggest that appeasement was popular or else that the electorate was indifferent to foreign affairs and voted on other grounds. Certainly those anti-appeasers who made it an issue did not do well. But after the occupation of Czechoslovakia (March 1939) most people seem to have steeled themselves to a likely war. Until April–May 1940, however, what people expected and what actually happened were quite different. Although Britain was technically at war and had been since 3 September 1939, there was no real war. Appeasement was not seen to 'fail' until the invasion of Norway in April 1940: it was not until then that its consequences, military and political, became manifest. The trouble with appeasement, both as policy and rhetoric, was that it could not partly fail. If it failed it failed absolutely. And with its failure it brought down the reputation of its

---

[46] Sibley, 'Swing to Labour', 28–9.

makers. The German occupation of Denmark, the Norway campaign (the occasion for the fall of Chamberlain) and the invasion of the Low Countries and France represented (rightly or wrongly) absolute failure. Olivia Cockett recorded in her diary the reaction at work to the occupation of Denmark, the least of the disasters: 'A good deal of adverse comment about the Way We Run the War. All topped up with "Well it will be all right tonight—[Chamberlain is] going to speak" with much derision.'[47] There is evidence that people were aware of the significance of the debate in the House of Commons on 7–8 May. That most famous of Mass-Observation diarists, Nella Last, noted on 5 May 1940 that at the WVS centre at which she worked 'for the first time there was talk of war everywhere—and what would happen in Parliament. Some thought it would mean the resignation of Mr Chamberlain.' Though the majority took the bulldog British view that Norway had brought it upon itself by being 'too neutral', one realist said: ' "It's quite *true*—it is the end of *everything*." '[48] Also telling is the feeling, especially on the Chamberlainite wing of the Conservative Party, that the formation of Churchill's coalition, if not the end of everything, meant the end of the Tory Party as people had known it. That they believed this shows how many Conservative eggs were in one basket; what a colossal gamble appeasement had been. When appeasement failed, therefore, so almost inevitably did the political system which gave it birth.

The fall of Chamberlain was due to a crisis within the political elite both about the way the war was to be fought and (possibly) whether it was to be fought at all.[49] How many within the Conservative Party would have been prepared to negotiate with Hitler—if indeed there were any—we do not know, but Churchill's seizure of the premiership (for that in effect is what it was) decided the issue. It

[47] R. Malcolmson (ed.), *Love and War in London: A Woman's Diary, 1939–1942* (Waterloo, Ont., 2005), 69.

[48] R. Broad and S. Fleming (eds.), *Nella Last's War, 1939–1945* (London, 1981), 53–4.

[49] For the fall of Chamberlain and the formation of the Churchill government see Addison, *Road to 1945*, 93–102.

meant the war would be fought to the end. It also meant that Labour would enter the government. All knew, not least Churchill, that a war to the end could not be fought without the labour movement and its political agent, the Labour Party. This was said specifically by some Conservative MPs immediately after the debate which brought down Chamberlain and even before Churchill had succeeded him. Supporting a parliamentary recess P. C. Loftus, Conservative MP for Lowestoft, said:

> Surely, the best method, now that we all realize there has to be a complete change of Government, that there have to be new members from all parties and members from outside, men such as Sir Walter Citrine and Mr Ernest Bevin in the Government, would be to have this recess of 10 or 12 days in which daily consultations could take place . . .[50]

Sir H. Morris-Jones, the MP for Denbigh,[51] also argued for a recess: 'great events are pending in the country at the present time, and not a small event will be the meeting next week of representatives of the working classes of the country'—he meant the annual conference of the Labour Party. No government backbencher would have said that six months earlier since it constituted an admission that the Conservative Party could no longer legitimately claim to be the representative of the working classes, once an essential component of its rhetoric.[52] The issue of the moment, he continued, was 'whether organized Labour is to participate in the Government of the State'. Churchill himself, in winding up the debate for the government, during which he had had a couple of sharp passages with Labour backbenchers, in an aside whose meaning could hardly be clearer, said: 'Well, the question [about the Norway campaign] was asked by a very influential person, not a member of the House, Mr Bevin—who is a friend of mine, working hard for the public cause, and a man who has much gift to help [Churchillian for much

---

[50] *HCD* 5s, 360, clmn 1444 (9 May 1940).

[51] He was actually a Simonite Liberal; but of course a supporter of the government.

[52] *HCD* 5s, 360, clmn 1439 (9 May 1940). The implication of this comment was grasped by the Conservative MP for Stone, Sir Joseph Lamb, who interjected: 'Who are the representatives of the working class in this country?'

to give].'[53] It is difficult on reading this to not to conclude that Churchill intended to offer Bevin the ministry of labour in a government he had not yet been asked to form.[54] The speed with which opinion abandoned Conservatism was thus a result of a 'high political' crisis which overthrew, or at least immensely weakened, suddenly and unpredicted, the predominant Conservatism of the 1930s.[55]

The second reason for the speed of change was the movement of working-class opinion. In 1939 the Conservative Party's largest single constituency by some way was working class: a mass of working-class voters whose 'objective' class position probably differed little from working-class Labour voters. It was therefore essential to the Tory Party that working-class Tories continued to believe the Labour Party was 'unfit' to govern—that familiar phrase of the interwar years—even though many were attracted to the individual policies for which Labour stood. Throughout the 1930s, with a good deal of help from the Labour Party itself, the Conservatives had been very successful at doing this. They had marginalized Labour by denying it legitimacy. So entrenched had they become that such legitimacy was theirs to give or deny. In May 1940 all this disappeared. The price Labour demanded for entering a coalition was the resignation as prime minister of Chamberlain—the personification with Baldwin of the Toryism of the 1930s; and if anything its harsher side.

[53] *HCD* 5s, 360, clmn 1351 (8 May 1940).

[54] David Reynolds has suggested that not all Tory members of Churchill's cabinet, including Churchill himself, favoured war to the end. Rather they hoped for a war sufficiently successful to negotiate a 'decent' peace with Germany. The problem for the 'decent' peace is that Hitler would never have accepted its conditions (which included his own elimination), and that is why no one seriously proposed it. On the contrary, Britain's attitude to Germany steadily hardened—as the German resistance was to find. As an estimate of the minds of the elites, Reynolds's suggestion, therefore, has probably little actual significance. (D. Reynolds, 'The "Decision" to Fight on in 1940: Right Policy, Wrong Reasons', in *From World War to Cold War: Churchill, Roosevelt and the International History of the 1940s* (Oxford, 2006), 78–9.)

[55] This was not without international comparison. Much the same happened in Australia and for much the same reason. In 1941 a crisis within the conservative parties over the conduct of the war—indeed whether they could conduct it—and the defection of crucial elements of their parliamentary support brought the Labor Party to power. That led to a huge and almost immediate swing to the left which was manifested in the general election less than two years later. (P. Hasluck, *The Government and the People, 1939–1941* (Canberra, 1952), 491–523.)

The entry of Labour into Churchill's coalition, and its entry as indispensable prop, immediately gave it legitimacy as a governing party. More than that, legitimacy was bestowed by the Conservative Party itself. In circumstances of possible national defeat—the debate on 7 May began as a debate about Norway and ended as a debate about Britain—the Tories were obliged to call upon Labour to save the nation. This was to undo at a stroke the work of twenty years. There could scarcely have been a clearer signal to that rather passive working-class electorate used to taking its cue from the Conservative Party—especially to younger voters who might in other circumstances have voted Tory but whose political habits were not yet fixed. The Labour leadership was quick to see the implications of this and how strong their position had become. In urging the Labour Party to accept office in Churchill's coalition Attlee said that Labour was determined that the world which emerged from this war must be a world 'attuned to our ideals', and there is little doubt he meant it. His deputy, Arthur Greenwood, said that to refuse office would be to miss the opportunity of a lifetime: the kind of opportunity Labour had sought fruitlessly since 1931.[56] Greenwood was right: once the decision to fight the war to the end had been made Labour could be the only beneficiary.

Much of the electorate, therefore, had been radicalized very fast; had, that is to say, changed their mind about the Conservative Party and its right to govern. What constituted this radicalization? Did those who voted Labour have any clear idea of what they were doing? Was radicalization confined only to those who voted Labour? We should try to answer these questions. One interpretation of what happened is a social–solidaristic one. The constitution of wartime radicalism, it argues, was a new form of collective action, a kind of social reciprocity, which derived from popular experience of the first evacuation (1939–40) and the blitz (*c*.1940–1). Such reciprocity did not necessarily eliminate social hostility, might indeed have inflamed it, but it did force the pre-war elites to acknowledge hitherto

---

[56] S. Brooke, *Labour's War* (Oxford, 1992), 52–3.

unacknowledged degrees of social inequality and the propriety of attempts to diminish it. The evacuation, by exposing the life and conditions of the poor to the not-poor (or the less poor), also exposed the real imperfections of British democracy and the failures of policy in the 1930s. Such failures were understood to be systemic: evacuation was, in Runciman's words, the *crise révélatrice* of British society[57] and undoubtedly came as a shock to some: social guilt was followed by a determination to make amends. The effect of the evacuation, therefore, was to broaden the definition of democratic citizenship and widen the scope of social solidarity. 'Perhaps more than any other event', Sonya Rose has written, '. . . the evacuation was represented in public discussions in ways that challenged the idea that British national identity was unitary' precisely because it occurred before 'fair shares' and the 'people's war' gave the war itself a democratic purpose.[58]

The blitz, it has been argued, did the same. It broke up the narrow social relationships of pre-war England and introduced new forms of social reciprocity—'all in it together'. Like the evacuation and what it revealed, the blitz, in Field's words, 'illustrated graphically the inadequacy of civil defense [*sic*] preparations'. The raids 'helped build a sense of the nation as an authentic democratic community rather than a remote set of structures'.[59] It was, therefore, to a considerable extent upon the experience of the evacuation and the blitz that the edifice of wartime radicalism was built, partly because it completed the transformation of social relationships and social reference groups which Runciman, in what remains the neatest piece of Second World War sociology, argued underlay the radicalization of much of the working class. The war, by the actions of the state and by a military and industrial mobility enforced by the demands of war, upset the boundaries within which political judgements had

[57] Runciman, *Social Theory*, III, 270.

[58] S. Rose, *Which People's War: National Identity and Citizenship in Britain, 1939–1945* (Oxford, 2003), 62.

[59] G. Field, 'Social Patriotism and the British Working Class: Appearance and Disappearance of a Tradition,' *International Labour and Working-Class History* 42 (Fall 1992), 23–4.

hitherto been made. What was accepted as tolerable in the 1930s, because everyone appeared to be in the same boat, in retrospect became intolerable with the discovery that in reality they weren't. The awareness, Runciman writes, 'of the actual situation of others was enormously heightened by the simple fact of physical movement and broader social contacts'.[60]

Although Runciman's argument still has support—and is, it seems to me, difficult to refute—the view that the evacuation and the blitz had a particular role in radicalization no longer does. Few would now agree that the evacuation led to a 'rearrangement of values'. John Macnicol has argued that, on the contrary, both Whitehall and the voluntary services held to entrenched attitudes to the working class. To them the seemingly appalling behaviour of so many evacuee children, not to speak of their mothers, was a result of working-class *mores*, not the social conditions in which they lived. The Whitehall view, he notes, was held in 'a much more robust form' by much of the middle class. 'In short, the social debate on evacuation probably served to *reinforce* existing analyses of working-class poverty rather than to change them.'[61] Evidence is there to support him. As one student of the evacuation noted: 'from every quarter came rumours and reports of distress and disillusion. The town was ill at ease in the country. The country was shocked at the manners and morals of the town.'[62] One mass-observer, Muriel Green, wrote of rural Norfolk: 'the village people objected to the evacuees chiefly because of the dirtiness of their habits and clothes. Also because of their reputed drinking and bad language. It is exceptional to hear women swear in this village or for them to enter a public house. The villagers used to watch them come out of the pubs with horror.'[63] Nor is evidence absent from the House of Commons. In a debate on evacuation (which was to become notorious) on 14 September 1939 the Liberal

[60] W. G. Runciman, *Relative Deprivation and Social Justice: A Study of Attitudes to Social Inequality in Twentieth-Century England* (Pelican edn, Harmondsworth, 1972), 92.

[61] J. Macnicol, 'The Evacuation of Schoolchildren', in Smith (ed.), *War and Social Change*, 24–7.

[62] S. Isaacs, *The Cambridge Evacuation Survey* (London, 1941), 2.

[63] Sheridan (ed.), *Wartime Women*, 58 (29 Oct. 1939).

National (i.e. government) MP Sir Henry Fildes said: 'here we have the Minister [of Health] getting up and without a word of apology to the community for the dreadful scourge that he had placed upon the homes of Britain . . . I do not think that the Minister appreciates at this moment the bitter feeling that there is against his Department on the matter.'[64] Evelyn Waugh's novel *Put Out More Flags* captures this particular anguish very well.

The radicalizing effect of the blitz also now tends to be discounted—largely on the basis of Mass-Observation evidence. Tom Harrisson, after he re-worked the Mass-Observation material on the blitz years later, decided that much popular memory of it was mythical. Although he conceded that the blitz played a part in realizing some social-democratic expectations 'mainly as one impetus towards equal sharing of war's burdens' the real change came later 'influenced largely by the length of war and the great numbers of people eventually involved in it'. And though he thought there had been an increase in general self-confidence 'it cannot be over-emphasized that nearly everyone tended to attribute this feeling to their own personal practically unaided efforts. There was little to justify increased confidence in the political system, national or local . . . Living through the blitz had no more long-term effect on political thinking than on social habits. It was not that *sort* of experience.'[65] If anything the Mass-Observation material points to social breakdown and civil dislocation as characteristic of the blitz.

Mass-Observation plays an important part in this story. Its huge archive has in the last few years or so become an increasingly important resource for historians. The blitz and the evacuation are no exception.[66] Mass-Observation provides us with a sense of the period—of individual and collective voices caught off-guard—which we can

---

[64] *HCD* 5s, 351, clmns. 885–6 (14 Sept. 1939). See also the exchange between Campbell Stephen, ILP MP for Glasgow Camlachie and C. N. Thornton-Kemsley, Conservative MP for Kincardine.

[65] T. Harrisson, *Living through the Blitz* (Penguin edn, Harmondsworth, 1990), 313.

[66] On the evacuation Tom Harrisson and Charles Madge drew upon Mass-Observation evidence in their contemporary study *War Begins at Home* (London, 1940). Ruth Inglis has also drawn upon Mass-Observation in *The Children's War: Evacuation 1939–1945* (London, 1989).

find almost nowhere else. As a form of social anthropology or human ethnography it is a mixture of the fragmentary and the diffuse—odd conversations recorded in a pub or at work—or the curiously pedantic: *exactly* how many couples were making love on Brighton beach on a summer's night. Much depended on the quirks and preconceptions of individual observers and the quirkiness of the evidence is part of its charm. It is, however, difficult evidence to 'read' and easy to 'misread', something true also of equivalent forms of social observation. Mass-Observation, for instance, in what was published as *War Factory* (1943), gave an account of women war workers as almost wholly divorced from the war and their work, which in fact is very partial and often inaccurate.[67] The mass-observers themselves could have very rigorous views of what constituted the political. One clerk in the ATS noted of her colleagues' comments on the coming election in 1945: 'The notions that some of our girls hold are astounding. They have absolutely no idea of what the parties stand for and transcribe everything into terms of their own position in the Forces . . . I expected apathy, but apparently most of the girls intend to use their votes; this is even more disturbing.'[68] There is obviously a problem here of which the observer seems unaware. That 'most of the girls intend to use their votes' in a country where voting is not compulsory is presumably the important phrase.

Material drawn from Mass-Observation is among the kind of evidence that has led Fielding, Thompson, and Tiratsoo—leaders of what James Hinton has called the 'apathy school'[69]—to conclude that the evacuation, the blitz, strikes or debates about reconstruction did little to radicalize the population.[70] In fact, they (and especially Fielding) doubt that anything coherent happened at all. Fielding does concede that the Beveridge Report was important as a criterion:

[67] Mass-Observation, *War Factory: A Report* (London, 1943). For a more balanced view see P. Summerfield, *Reconstructing Women's Wartime Lives* (London, 1998).

[68] Sheridan (ed.), *Wartime Women*, 236–7.

[69] J. Hinton, '1945 and the Apathy School', in *History Workshop Journal* 43 (Spring 1997), 268–71.

[70] S. Fielding, P. Thompson, and N. Tiratsoo, *England Arise! The Labour Party and Popular Politics in 1940s Britain* (Manchester, 1995), 19–39.

parties and politicians were often judged by their attitude to it.[71]
He also admits that the desire for change represented more than just
'frustration'. But popular opinions, nonetheless, were 'vague; they
were barely coherent; they were unrealistic; they were impossible to
organize'.[72] The 1945 election was like other elections: it 'forced an
unconvinced public to decide between two parties. As a consequence
instead of popular partisanship and expectant idealism the election,
like others before or since, generated widespread disengagement and
pre-emptive cynicism.' People did not vote Labour with conviction.
'If the anti-Conservative vote went to Labour', he writes, 'rather
than the divided Liberal Party it was perhaps more due to a disbelief
in the latter's ability to win or the absence of a candidate than
any strong feeling that Labour was preferable.'[73] Non-voting 'was
simply the most extreme symptom of a prevalent popular confusion,
apathy and cynicism about the political system that survived the
war'.[74]

In reaching this conclusion Fielding draws heavily upon Mass-
Observation and similar material and sometimes stretches it further
than it will go. He cites, for instance, as an example of the typical
apolitical fundamentally uninterested voter a man interviewed by
Mass-Observation. The interviewee said: 'I don't feel all that interested [in the 1945 election], but I'm going to vote all the same,
Labour of course.'[75] What matters in that quotation, however, is not
'I don't feel all that interested', but 'Labour of course'. That points to
a whole new set of assumptions people feel to be so fundamental they
do not need repeating. Again, Fielding and his colleagues adduce as
another instance of popular cynicism a record of three conversations
overheard by Bernard Newman, a journalist who was attached to the

[71] S. Fielding, 'What Did "The People" Want? The Meaning of the 1945 General
Election', *Historical Journal* 35, 3 (1992), 633–4.

[72] S. Fielding, 'The Second World War and Popular Radicalism: The Significance of
the "Movement away from Party"', *History* 80, 259 (June, 1995), 55.

[73] Fielding, 'What Did "The People" Want?', 630.

[74] S. Fielding, '"Don't Know and Don't Care": Popular Political Attitudes in Labour
Britain, 1945–51', in N. Tiratsoo (ed.), *The Attlee Years* (London, 1991), 107.

[75] Ibid. 108.

ministry of information, and recorded in his *British Journey* (1945), a combination of state of the nation and slice of life written towards the end of the war. He wrote:

One day in May, 1944 I was involved in several conversations—one in a roadside café for lorry drivers, one with women in a queue for cakes, and a third in a fish-and-chip shop. I noted down the principal topics of conversation: post-war housing, the Bevin boys,[76] strikes, one-man businesses, the second-hand furniture ramp, equal pay for equal work, income tax, the cut in the cheese ration, poor quality of corsets, holidays away from home, overcrowding in trams and buses, wasting petrol, shortage of matches, high wages for boys and girls, and the bad distribution of fish.

Of these conversations, Newman concluded that 'we are indeed parochial in our outlook: "selfish" is perhaps a better word'.[77] Why these conversations, however, should be thought especially parochial or selfish or unpolitical is very puzzling. By my count five of the topics are strictly political and the others are exactly what we would expect of conversations in wartime.[78] Like the ATS clerk who was appalled that her colleagues were going to vote, those who wish to deny the particularity of wartime radicalism and assert the apoliticism and cynicism of the whole business, adopt an exceptional standard of politicization and misunderstand the nature of most people's politics. Thus Fielding seems surprised that people could be more interested in the result of a football match than voting or prefer non-political films to political. But that's life and the non-political does not have to exclude the political. Hardly anyone leads a purely 'political' existence, and those who do are usually dangerous.

---

[76] These were young men conscripted by the ministry of labour to work in the mines. Thus Bevin boys, after the minister of labour, Ernest Bevin.

[77] Fielding, Thompson, and Tiratsoo, *England Arise!*, 39.

[78] I am not alone in objecting to Newman or the use made of him. See also Hinton, '1945 and the Apathy School', 268: 'According to whom, one wonders, were these issues trivial. And why should evidence that most people were primarily concerned with such issues be construed as a lack of interest in politics?'; J. Marriott, 'Labour and the Popular', *History Workshop Journal* 43 (Spring 1997), 262: Were these issues trivial or parochial? 'Not so (as the Tories are instinctively only too well aware). People's lives were framed by such anxieties; the fortunes of the Labour Party and popular politics in the period have to be understood in relation to these concerns and attempts of people to deal with them.'

Furthermore, the fact that people had real grievances is more significant than that grievances were 'vague'. Characteristic of the war years is how open and strongly felt these grievances were and how soon they were expressed, as much in Mass-Observation as anywhere else, particularly after the fall of Chamberlain's government opened the floodgates. In June 1940, immediately after the formation of Churchill's coalition, Olivia Cockett noted that the male clerks at work, in talking about the 'situation', were 'full of grievances against the rich and the government'.[79] Grievance could be found in unexpected places. The social psychologists, Elizabeth Slater and Mark Woodside, who were actually studying working-class attitudes to marriage, 'were immediately made aware [among their sample] of that swing towards Socialism that subsequently surprised the country at the general election of 1945'.[80] The reader is indeed surprised by the depth of grievance in that book and the aggression with which it could be expressed. Grievance also underlay the widely noticed popular contempt for the heroes of the 1930s, especially Baldwin. 'If any Tory wants a shaking', Tom Harrisson wrote, 'go and see the film "Guess What" and hear what happens when Baldwin appears.'[81]

In fact, it cannot be doubted that there was a marked radicalization of opinion, however unformed (something Fielding himself concedes),[82] and that it occurred rapidly after the fall of Chamberlain. It is then that the 'myth' of the evacuation occurs—that it had a socially solidaristic effect, itself part of the movement to the left. That such an effect was rarely observable during the first evacuation is true; but that evacuation, not merely the first but the largest, was half over by May 1940: over 80 per cent of those mothers and children who had left their homes in September 1939 had returned by January 1940.[83] Its partial end coincided with the fall of Chamberlain and the German invasion of the Low Countries and France. But what

[79] Cockett in Malcolmson (ed.), *Love and War in London*, 94.
[80] E. Slater and M. Woodside, *Patterns of Marriage: A Study of Marriage Relationships in the Urban Working Classes* (London, 1951), 82–3.
[81] Harrisson, 'Who'll Win?', 32
[82] Fielding, 'What Did "The People" Want?', 633.
[83] Children unaccompanied by mothers were more likely to stay.

people came to think of the evacuation after May 1940 was not entirely unanticipated. Harold Nicolson thought that one effect of the evacuation, which he conceded was a 'perplexing social event', 'will be to demonstrate to people how deplorable is the standard of life and civilization among the urban proletariat'.[84] In December 1939 an evacuated London teacher, who otherwise had no illusions, suggested that nonetheless 'perhaps evacuation has done good in that it has revealed those conditions under which many of our children have been reared. May great improvements be the outcome of these revelations.'[85] It was also recognized—no doubt too late—that although as a physical and logistic exercise the evacuation worked well its failures in human terms were many—largely, Margaret Cole wrote, because it was designed by 'minds that were military, male and middle class'.[86] If the 'authorities' had planned for the social and educational problems of evacuation, Susan Isaacs argued, 'with a tithe of the labour and intelligence which we put into questions of transport, if human nature had been taken into equal account with geography and railway timetables, there would in all likelihood not have been so serious a drift back to the danger areas'.[87] But the first evacuation and the immediate response to it were a product of *pre-war* social relationships and a public social culture that was profoundly modified after May 1940. As I have suggested earlier, what was freely, and without embarrassment, said in September 1939 could not be said (certainly without embarrassment) after May 1940. It is then that the idea of the evacuation as an exercise in social solidarity takes hold as a kind of reworked memory; and it is possible that such reworking was responsible for the 'myth' of the blitz a little later in the war.[88] It is also then that the relationship between

[84] Nicolson, *Diary with Letters, 1939–1945*, 33.

[85] Sheridan (ed.), *Wartime Women*, 68.

[86] Padley and Cole (eds.), *Evacuation Survey*, 4. For further criticism of this male and middle-class evacuation see D. Morgan and M. Evans, *The Battle for Britain: Citizenship and Ideology in the Second World War* (London and New York, 1993), 72–5.

[87] Isaacs (ed.), *Cambridge Evacuation Survey*, 4.

[88] Travis Crosby has suggested—somewhat in the same way as W. G. Runciman—that the real effect of the evacuation was to radicalize the evacuees by showing

the population and the state becomes more reciprocal.[89] Until May 1940 the 'people' were fairly passive: not much was demanded of the state by them and little was given. The fall of Chamberlain was, as I have argued,[90] a crisis of the political elite during which the population were largely observers; though not necessarily ignorant observers. From that moment, however, in part because the crisis coincided with the transformation of the war, attitudes changed. In the weeks following Dunkirk Home Intelligence reported strong support generally for state direction and intervention, if only to guarantee equality of sacrifice.[91]

Radicalization of opinion was more than just the expression of grievance, even if grievance were an important element of it. People seemed to have had a reasonable idea of what the war might do and what they wanted from it. Tom Harrisson, who, as we have seen,

---

them how the other half lived. 'The evacuation revealed to many of the urban poor—a natural Labour constituency—the realities of class and privilege in Britain.' (T. Crosby, *The Impact of Civilian Evacuation on the Second World War* (London, 1986), 146.) This is a nice argument but difficult to evaluate. To many evacuees it exposed them not so much to class privilege as to the respectable culture of the rural poor or semi-poor, with whom they were disproportionately billeted. But no doubt many were also exposed to the social attitudes of the provincial middle class, which could hardly have failed to radicalize.

It has sometimes been suggested that the well-known study *Our Towns: A Close-Up* (London, 1943), written by members of the Women's Group on Public Welfare (which had informal connections to the National Federation of Women's Institutes) is an example of the survival of this plain-speaking tradition. *Our Towns* was a response to the first evacuation and what it was thought to reveal—and did reveal—of the culture of the urban poor. The study began in 1939 and was unsurprisingly in the spirit of its time. While, however, it accepted that the complaints about the behaviour of many of the evacuees were justified much of the evidence on which it drew was actually pre-war and familiar to contemporary social investigators. Furthermore, the study itself largely adopted an 'environmental' explanation for such behaviour. It especially blamed housing and the educational system, and thus pre-war social policy. To this extent it was, I would argue, in the genre of wartime social reform. (For a detailed analysis of *Our Towns*, see J. Welshman, 'Evacuation, Hygiene and Social Policy: the *Our Towns* Report of 1943, *Historical Journal* 42, 3 (1991), 781–807. The Report, Welshman concludes, 'echoed interwar debates about behaviour and citizenship but also reflected the ideas that would shape the welfare state in the post-war years' (786)—which seems to me right.)

[89] We might also conclude that, whatever happened at a popular level, the evacuation did encourage the state to be innovative in social policy. (J. Welshman, 'Evacuation and Social Policy during the Second World War: Myth and Reality', *Twentieth Century British History* 9, 1 (1998), 28–53.)

[90] See above, 120–2.   [91] S. Brooke, *Labour's War*, 55.

doubted that the blitz did much to radicalize opinion, nonetheless concluded that people had 'radical' expectations of the war: less class distinction, more state control, education reforms, levelling of incomes and increased social services were thought the most likely outcomes.[92] As Field has pointed out, most contemporary surveys of opinion detected four fundamental themes: support for the expansion of social services; a conviction that the state could and should maintain full employment; a growing faith in 'planning' (partly a result of admiration for the Soviet Union); the development of a language of social citizenship.[93] The extraordinary support for Beveridge must be seen in terms of these expectations: it seemed to embody all of them. Those who doubt that the war was about anything much must explain how within a fortnight of its publication 95 per cent of the population had heard of the Report and most had a fair idea of its contents. It spoke to a population ready to listen, which is one reason why it was so widely publicized. They need also to explain the success of certain dissident left-wing candidates in the 1945 elections. In North Hammersmith D. N. Pritt, elected as the Labour MP in 1935, expelled from the Party in 1940 because of his opposition to Labour's policy towards the Russo-Finnish War, and by 1945 thought to be as close to being a Communist as you could get without actually being one, polled 18,845 votes to the Labour candidate's 3,165. In Mile End, the Communist candidate Phil Piratin defeated the sitting Labour member and elsewhere Communist candidates won respectable votes. Nor should we overlook the eccentric Alexander Hancock, a Northamptonshire farmer who stood against Churchill as an independent (in reality a proxy Labour candidate in the absence of one) and who won 10,488 votes, 'much to everyone's surprise'.[94] Pritt and Piratin

---

[92] Harrisson, *Living through the Blitz*, 312. There were, however, a significant number who apparently also expected dictatorship or 'fascism'.

[93] Field, 'Social Patriotism and the British Working Class', 29–30. But he also rightly notes that the position of women within these themes was more problematic.

[94] *The Times House of Commons 1945*, 27. In his manifesto Hancock advocated one hour's productive work a day (six days a week leisure) and the development of a 'philosophic community'.

almost certainly owed their victories to their association with the Soviet Union, then at its most admired, but that was part of the radical mix. Hancock owed his relative success to the fact that large numbers of people were not going to vote Conservative, whoever the Conservative was.

Not only did the war restore the social and economic integrity of the great working-class communities of the North—with London the bedrock of the labour movement—it tended to universalize a 'Labour' political culture among the working class as a whole, something deliberately promoted by those Labour members of the coalition government disproportionately represented in its domestic portfolios; the significance of which did not escape Churchill. In November 1944 he wrote to Attlee (a letter never sent) that he 'felt very much the domination of these [reconstruction Committees] by the force and power of your representatives, when those members who come out of the Conservative quota are largely non-Party or have little experience or Party views'.[95] The result of such universalizing was to sweep into the Labour Party much of the working class that had hitherto stood outside it, most notably in the West Midlands. A striking example of this is provided by a comparison of Coventry and Blackburn and how they voted in 1945. In July 1940 Mass-Observation, working both for the government and the National Institute of Economic Research, visited Coventry and Blackburn. In Coventry the war factories were at full blast—'men lurching home unshaven with eyes black-circled from lack of sleep'. In cafés, cinemas, and public houses 'five pound notes were common currency'. They remembered 'the café of the Rex Cinema, whose soft music mixed with the twitter of live birds, flitting behind glass along the length of two walls, with a painted back-scene of sea and sand, and a painted signpost marked "Le Touquet": here sat well-paid young fitters and their sweethearts'. In Blackburn, on the other hand, even war did not bring prosperity. 'It was a ruin of its former self.'[96] In 1935 the Conservatives won both Blackburn and

[95] Quoted in Brooke, *Labour's War*, 168.
[96] Madge, *War-Time Pattern of Saving and Spending*, 112–13.

Coventry by almost exactly the same margins. In 1945 Labour won both; but Coventry—epitome of pre-war prosperity—by a much bigger majority on a significantly larger swing.[97] There were, of course, probably local reasons for Coventry's marked swing to the left. There was continued migration to the town from the North which could further have radicalized the workforce, as it did elsewhere in the South and the Midlands. During the war Coventry also became a highly unionized motor town but with often acrimonious relations between the employers and the two main unions, the Transport and General Workers Union and the Amalgamated Society of Engineers. But there were other influences as pervasive, if not more so. After May 1940 Coventry was subject to the same radicalizing influences as the rest of the country.[98] But it was also subject to the state and a scale of intervention almost inconceivable in 1939. This overrode such particular advantages as Coventry might have had before the outbreak of war. And with the state came the Labour Party.

The war itself significantly modified structures of deference within England. It was not just the much-advertised 'rudeness' of working-class persons (and shopkeepers)[99] but the way in which the working class saw itself and was seen by others. The best way of observing this is by comparing the 'tone' in which royal commissions treated working-class issues before and after the Second World War and the conclusions they reached. To compare, for instance, the minutes and reports of the royal commission on betting of 1932–3 with those of the royal commission of 1949–51 is to compare different worlds. This was not wholly a social transformation, but it was of real significance and worked strongly to Labour's benefit.[100]

---

[97] Blackburn (a double member seat) in 1935: Cons. 37,932, Lab. 34,571; in 1945 Lab. 35,182, Cons. 26,325. Coventry in 1935: Cons. 37,313, Lab. 34,841; in 1945 (now two seats) Lab. 72,618, Cons. 38,866, Comm. 3,986, Lib. 2,820.

[98] The centre of Coventry was, of course, subject to heavy bombing in 1940, though how far that had an extra radicalizing effect is difficult to say. My guess is not much.

[99] See below 169–71.

[100] Though in the case of betting much of the Labour Party, not altogether paradoxically, did not participate in such transformation as there was. (G. McClymont, 'The Labour Party's Attitude to Gambling, 1918–1970', unpublished Oxford D.Phil. thesis (2006), 231–47.)

It is also likely that radicalization occurred across the spectrum: that the locus of English politics simply shifted left. Nella Last, whose party political allegiance (Tory) never showed any sign of movement and who seems to have believed Churchill's contention that a Labour government would mean some kind of Gestapo,[101] is a good example. She noted of Beveridge's radio broadcast of 2 December 1942:

Never since I first listened to a speaker on the air have I felt as interested as I was tonight by Sir William Beveridge. I'll feel a bit more hopeful about the 'brave new world' now, and begin to feel a *real* effort will be made to grasp the different angles of the many problems. His scheme will appeal even more to women than men, for it is they who bear the real burden of unemployment, sickness, childbearing and rearing—the ones who, up to now, have come off worst. There *should* be some all-in scheme.[102]

She welcomed what was to become the 1944 Education Act; especially the provision for free secondary education. She regretted how many of her sons' bright friends were denied a full secondary education because their parents, unlike the Lasts, could not afford it.[103] It is probable that many of those who voted Conservative in 1945 favoured the Beveridge Report in some form—indeed if the BIPO polls are even reasonably accurate that must be the case; a conclusion the Conservatives themselves reached. Even the willingness to talk about politics or express grievance publicly was a change. In a country where there were so many taboos against speaking openly about politics this itself was a radical departure. Labour benefited because its association with such radicalization was more complete than the other parties.

Furthermore, the war, if only temporarily, redefined English patriotism and the idea of England in such a way as to incorporate an

---

[101] Giving reasons for voting Conservative in 1945 she said she disliked 'co-ops and combines. I hate controls . . . and heaven save any Nosey Parkers who intruded into my domestic life with any "Gestapo" methods.' (Fleming and Broad (eds.), *Nella Last's War*, 287–8 (10 June 1945).) She was referring to Churchill's notorious speech of 4 June 1945 in which he suggested that a Labour government would be driven to use something like a Gestapo to enforce its policies.

[102] Ibid. 219.   [103] Ibid. 248.

essentially social-democratic interpretation. That Labour was lucky here, and that a Tory interpretation was still vigorous (in part rescued by Churchill) is undeniable, but in 1945 Labour for once did not have to prove its patriotism.

In the election itself Labour won 393 seats and its allies a few more: a gain of almost 240 seats.[104] As ever, the electoral system exaggerated the victory. Labour won many small inner-city seats, and the scattering of Labour voters via evacuation, war work or military service meant that it won many seats it would not have done had the elections been held a few months later when people had started to return home.[105] Labour also benefited from a big decline in the business vote as a result of a change in the electoral law.[106] On the other hand, it suffered from electoral 'bunching'—the piling up of huge majorities in a comparatively small number of seats—which was to do it much damage in the 1950 and 1951 elections.[107] Labour gained everywhere, but the swing was greatest in England, where it had most to gain. For the first time ever Labour polled better in England than in Scotland; though, of course, nowhere near as well as it did in Wales.[108] Within England the swings were greatest in those areas where Labour had lost ground most in the 1930s—Birmingham and the West Midlands and the North East. In other words 'working-class' England (even Liverpool, where Labour won eight of the eleven seats), regardless of previous differentials, behaved pretty uniformly for the reasons I have suggested.

What can we conclude therefore? First, that the movement to the left—however we describe it—occurred very rapidly, in May–July

[104] The results of the election in England were: Labour 331, Conservatives and allies 167, Liberals 5, Communist 1, Common Wealth 1, Independents 5. Labour won 48.5 per cent of the vote, the Conservatives and allies 40.2 per cent, Liberal 9.4 per cent.

[105] Abrams, 'The Labour Vote in the General Election', 26.

[106] Before 1945 a business voter was automatically put on the electoral register. In 1945 the business vote had to be claimed. (P. G. Richards, 'The Labour Victory', *Political Quarterly*, Oct. 1945, 351.) Even so, the Tories won a number of seats as a result of the remaining business vote.

[107] See below, 172–3.

[108] In Scotland Labour won 47.6 per cent. Though if to that figure is added the ILP and Communist vote the 'left' did slightly better in Scotland than in England. In Wales Labour got 58.5 per cent of the vote.

1940, and was primarily the result of a change in the way much of the working class (and some of the middle class) saw the Conservative Party and their own relations with English society. It was, in other words, an ideological change; a shift in perception rather than a 'structural' shift. This shift, however, was the result of a political crisis largely confined to the political elite but which, once resolved, had the almost inevitable effect of radicalizing much of the population. The only conceivable political beneficiary of this was the Labour Party. Second, radicalization was genuine; people were not apolitical or cynical. Nor did they vote Labour because they could think of nothing else to do. The suggestion that they would as willingly have voted Liberal had circumstances allowed is to misunderstand the Liberal Party and everything that had happened since 1918. That grievances were often inarticulate does not alter the fact that they were grievances and sometimes strongly held. In any case, people seem to have had a reasonable idea of what they wanted, and the Beveridge Report gave that idea coherence. Hence its popularity. To call this 'socialism', however, is probably going too far. 'Socialism was the key [1945] election issue', Ina Zweiniger-Bargielowska has argued.[109] Whatever it was for the leadership, socialism as such was not the key issue for the electorate. Labour won because it was identified with Beveridge and because it was the beneficiary of a widespread but imprecise hostility to the old order.

Much of this was felt throughout Great Britain. But there was a particular English reason for the Labour victory. The Conservative Party, for all its attachment to the Union, was above all the party of England—a status which drew upon its identification with the English nation and a conception of England the Tory Party was thought to embody. The crisis of May–June 1940 was probably one of the few occasions in modern English history in which Tory claims to this status were unconvincing. There is no doubt that many in the Tory Party and the English electorate, rightly or wrongly, felt

---

[109] I. Zweiniger-Bargielowska, *Austerity in Britain: Rationing, Controls, and Consumption 1939–1955* (Oxford, 2000), 211.

the course of 1939–40 to be a humiliation which robbed the Party of its old authenticity and permitted Labour, to its own surprise, to stand for the English nation.[110] This was the point of Leo Amery's celebrated instruction to Arthur Greenwood, the deputy leader of the Labour Party, in the House of Commons on 2 September 1939: 'Speak for England'. *Guilty Men* accused the Conservative Party of many things, but what gave it real force was the accusation that the guilty men were not just incompetent but in some way traitors.

[110] Ward has argued reasonably enough that the Labour Party prepared itself for this moment by defining 'British socialism' before the war as the socialism of the ordinary Briton: a doctrine 'integral to the parliamentary history of the nation'. Labour was not rendered unpatriotic 'by the mood of a red decade but had been preparing for the people's war for a number of years'. (P. Ward, 'Preparing for the People's War: Labour and Patriotism in the 1930s', *Labour History Review* 67, 2 (August 2002), 181.) Labour could not, however, choose the circumstances in which this patriotic socialism could be actualized. What it could do was to exploit the moment when it came.

5

The English Road to Socialism

The Party victorious in 1945 had, of course, a pre-history. The programme that the Labour Party presented to the electorate in 1945 was not developed overnight and was a product of more than just the Second World War. Indeed, to a large degree it had been formulated even before the outbreak of war. In this chapter I wish to discuss the evolution of that programme and consider the ways in which, and with what success, it was implemented by the Attlee government. To do so, we need to go back a little, to look at the Labour Party's reaction to the disaster of 1931 and its further electoral defeat in 1935. That is when the story of the Attlee government begins.

I have suggested that the events of 1931 largely destroyed a form of ethical socialism associated particularly with MacDonald and Snowden, but not only with them.[1] One of the consequences is that in the 1930s, Ben Jackson has argued, 'economic theory' largely drove 'fellowship' out of the Labour Party. Fellowship, he suggests, was missing from the writings of Dalton, Gaitskell, Durbin, or Jay in the 1930s. 'The substitution of economic theory for idealist philosophy or evolutionary imagery precipitated a shift from an organicist understanding of the social unit to a more individualist analysis.'[2] The argument for equality was now grounded in an economical–theoretical interpretation: 'Keynes was not an egalitarian, but the important point was that his most influential

---

[1] See above, 81–5.
[2] B. Jackson, *Equality and the British Left: A Study in Progressive Political Thought 1900–1964* (Manchester, 2007), 228. Hugh Dalton, though Keynes's pupil, was not of course a Keynesian, but the principle holds true of him as well.

disciples were.'[3] Since these men were evermore influential in the evolution of Labour policy, doctrines of fellowship were increasingly missing from the Labour Party itself. Although this argument perhaps underrates the continued importance of 'physical planning' in Labour thinking, it is, I think, largely right.[4] But the change was, of course, not just intellectual. It was a result of a change in the social origins of the Labour leadership. With the exception of Ernest Bevin, who is a rule-proving exception (and who had been converted to a quasi-Keynesian economics by Keynes himself), Herbert Morrison (the son of a policeman and thus only on the border of the working class) and Aneurin Bevan, every significant member of Attlee's government was of middle or upper-middle-class origin. The decay of the autodidact tradition accompanied the process by which the leadership of the Labour Party passed from the working to the educated middle class.

That process, however, reflected changes in the educational and social composition of the Parliamentary Labour Party as a whole. J. F. S. Ross once suggested that the Conservative Party was the party of the public school, the Liberal Party the party of the secondary school and Labour the party of the elementary school.[5] After 1945 that was true only to the extent that Labour had more MPs with just an elementary education than any other party. It is also the case that trade union sponsored MPs—more likely to have had only an elementary education—had safer seats; thus more likely to be in parliament. If, however, we look at the educational backgrounds of Labour's parliamentary candidates in the 1950 election we find a profile very different from that of the country as a whole and from the Labour Party of 1931. In the Labour Party, as in the Conservative Party, a higher proportion of public school candidates were elected than non-public school; and one-fifth of Labour's

---

[3] Ibid. 213.

[4] R. Toye, 'Keynes, the Labour Movement and "How to Pay for the War"', *Twentieth Century British History* 10, 3 (1999), 259.

[5] J. F. S. Ross, 'The New House of Commons', *Pilot Papers: Social Essays and Documents* 2, 1 (March 1947), 32.

candidates had been educated in public schools or 'privately'. The professions contributed the largest proportion of candidates; and of these 'teachers' were the highest number (111). But there were also seventy-eight lawyers and thirty-two journalists. In other words, the Labour Party was now as much a party of the educated (and educating) middle class as the working class.[6]

The 1931 election also demonstrated that Labour could not expect to fight an election on its 'maximal' programme and win. In that year, in an understandable reaction to what happened and in an attempt to blame 'capitalism' and 'the bankers' for the crisis, Labour came closer to fighting an election on the basis of clause IV than it had ever done.[7] It was the last throw of the old Labour Party: a party characterized by caution which momentarily concluded that caution had got it nowhere. By 1934 some caution had returned; and not merely for electoral reasons. The dominant elements in Party policy-making—which included the unions, even at local level[8]—were sceptical of the economic efficacy of the 'maximal' programme as well as nervous of the electorate's reactions. The programme which emerged in 1934, *For Socialism and Peace*, was therefore more coherent and less ambitious: a mix of public ownership, social welfare and 'planning'. It was much less coherent in foreign policy, on which the Party was unquestionably divided, but that in 1934 mattered less.[9] It was basically on this programme that Labour fought the 1945 election, though in 1937, partly in reaction to Labour's defeat in 1935, there was some further refinement. *Labour's Immediate Programme* (which G. D. H. Cole thought had at least 'the great merit of precision')[10] closely approximated the victorious programme of 1945. The NEC described it as a combination of 'Socialism and Social Amelioration': a revealing distinction. There was to be extensive public ownership—coal, rail, and all the utilities—and the Bank of

---

[6] H. G. Nicholas, *The British General Election of 1950* (London, 1951), 45–6.

[7] For that programme, see Thorpe, *The British General Election of 1931*, 159–62.

[8] Worley (ed.), *Labour's Grass Roots*, 107. R. M. Martin, *TUC: The Growth of a Pressure Group 1868–1976* (Oxford, 1980), 213–18.

[9] For the electoral significance of foreign policy in the 1930s, see below, 192–3.

[10] G. D. H. Cole, *A History of the Labour Party from 1914* (London, 1948), 346.

England was to become a public corporation. (The private banks, unlike 1931, were, however, dropped from the list.) There was to be no return to the gold standard and a National Investment Board was to direct investment more profitably and in the social interest. The state was to be much more active in the distribution of industry and in the 'special areas'—areas of the country which the National government could not bring itself to call depressed. Social welfare was to be extended. Labour also promised—a triumph of hope over experience—'social' utilization of the land and a living wage for agricultural workers.[11] And it took its stand on parliamentary democracy which, despite some imperfections, it thought the only political basis for such a programme. Foreign affairs again received pretty scant treatment—partly because the Party was still divided over foreign policy; partly because foreign policy was thought not to be central to the average elector's concerns. *Labour's Immediate Programme* was designed for an election that was never held—an election Labour was very unlikely to win. But, barring some important details, it was the programme on which Labour fought the 1945 election.[12]

The war itself did not add much to this programme. The vexed issue of family allowances was settled when the TUC finally accepted them; but it was the coalition government which actually introduced them in 1945. Labour's policies for health—what became the NHS—were filled out (and, of course, further modified under the Attlee government) but the principle of a universal, non-contributory health system had been accepted before the war.[13] Although the particular association of the Labour Party with the Beveridge Report was to be of great electoral significance, the Party had adopted similar proposals at its annual conference shortly before the Report's

[11] Though in practice Labour was increasingly standing for the revival of 'agriculture' as an interest and trying to turn itself into the party of the farmers. (Griffiths, *Labour and the Countryside*, 217–315.)

[12] Brooke, *Labour's War*, 30–2.

[13] C. Webster, 'Labour and the Origins of the National Health Service', in N. A. Rupke (ed.), *Science, Politics and the Public Good* (London, 1988); J. Stewart, *'The Battle for Health': A Political History of the Socialist Medical Association, 1930–1951* (Aldershot, 1999).

publication—but without Beveridge's unexpectedly dramatic flair.[14] If the war did little to shape Labour's policies, it did, as we have seen in the last chapter, provide Labour with indispensable opportunities. Above all it legitimated a Labour view of the world and how it should be organized; it also legitimated the state as a social and economic actor, even if it did not entirely eliminate the Labour movement's ambivalence towards that actor. The huge increase in the scope of the state familiarized the electorate with it, and encouraged, if anything, an overoptimistic belief in its efficacy. The Labour Party was, rightly or wrongly, in the public mind thought to be the party of the state *par excellence* and it was, as I have suggested, the inevitable beneficiary of this optimism.

These, and the radicalization of the electorate during the war, liberated the Labour Party. Yet in considering the Attlee government's programme and its implementation we should remember that the war was not only a liberating agent. In some ways it shackled the Party. For one thing it turned an outsiders' party into an insiders' party; and that was as much inhibiting as emancipating. Before 1939 Labour was never seriously critical of England's political arrangements or what passes for its constitution, or at any rate was ambivalent, but it stood in oblique relation to them. As Nick Owen has pointed out Labour, though not uncomfortable with parliament or its rituals, was uncomfortable in the old social milieu. Labour MPs, with the predictable exceptions of MacDonald, Snowden, and Thomas, hardly ever went into 'society' and 'society' rarely went after them. Labour MPs in London, Owen writes, led a 'somewhat lonely, *déclassé* existence'.[15] Although MacDonald was aware of the importance of the honours system as a means of patronage and reward, he hardly ever honoured working-class people. As a rule of thumb peerages went to those without male heirs. (MacDonald

---

[14] Aneurin Bevan wrote of this: 'And if it be asked how it happens that a reformer so sedate has been able to fashion a weapon so sharp, and how a government so timid should have presented materials for its fashioning, we must answer in the famous words of Karl Marx, "that war is the locomotive of history"' (*Tribune*, 4 Dec. 1942).

[15] N. Owen, 'MacDonald's Parties: The Labour Party and the "Aristocratic Embrace", 1922–31', *Twentieth Century British History* 18, 1 (2007), 34.

himself refused a peerage.) Arthur Henderson refused to sign the majority report of the royal commission on the honours system (1922) on the ground that the system was so flawed it should be swept away.[16] There was not universal approval when Harry Snell accepted a peerage (in 1931) and Walter Citrine (secretary of the TUC) and Arthur Pugh (of the Iron and Steel Trades Confederation) knighthoods in 1935. Snell, who was unmarried, in fact went to the Lords in order for Labour to fill its ministerial quota in the upper house when he became Under-Secretary for India. 'Attendance at Labour meetings', he later wrote, 'became for the first time an unpleasant experience, and on more than one occasion I was cut, or snubbed, by old associates, regardless of the fact that I had gone to the Lords, not for personal reasons, but to satisfy party as well as constitutional requirements.'[17]

Owen has suggested that the Second World War resolved the social tensions which arose from Labour's uneasy attitude to honours and the insiders' world. The war removed 'temptation' by shutting down 'society', by abolishing court dress (on grounds of austerity), which had always caused difficulties for Labour,[18] and by making the honours system seem class neutral rather than a signifier of class privilege. In general he is right; but the argument needs some modifying. Even before 1914 Labour was not entirely hostile to the honours system;[19] and in the 1930s was inching its way towards a more open accommodation. In 1936, at the request of the 1935 annual conference, the national executive reported on the honours system and for several reasons, legal and social, concluded that Labour should accept it pretty much as it stood. Although that

---

[16] Although Henderson, who had two male heirs, pressed MacDonald for a peerage in 1930 so, he said, as to free him from constituency and party duties. He was offered and refused one in 1931, after the fall of the Labour government, when he could hardly have done anything else.

[17] Snell, *Men, Movements, and Myself,* 249.

[18] According to the ILP'er John Paton, photos of members of the first Labour government in formal wear drew the comment that 'it's a lum [top] hat government like a' the rest' (J. Paton, *Left Turn! The Autobiography of John Paton* (London, 1936), 168).

[19] McKibbin, 'Why was there no Marxism in Great Britain?', in *Ideologies of Class*, 19.

report was referred back nothing further was done and members of the Party were free to do as they wished.[20] Certainly there was never any attempt to repudiate the system as such. In any case how far did 'temptation' disappear? Arguably, 'society' now had, probably for the first time, a real interest in embracing Labour. If anything 'duchessing' was literally stepped up. That social gadabout 'Chips' Channon, Conservative MP for Southend, recorded one amusing incident (1943) at his *petit palais* in Belgravia:

Within a few minutes, on the dot of 5.30, Herbert Morrison walked in, escorted by three Home Office henchmen: Socialists never really know how to behave, but before too long, he was surrounded by fashionable ladies, and seemed to enjoy their company. I led up 'Kakoo' [duchess of] Rutland and Mollie [duchess of] Buccleuch, and his one eye roved at them with approval.[21]

The ideological character of the war, the apparent democratic solidarity, the seeming success of 'fair shares', and, of course, victory further legitimated both the state and the constitution in the eyes of the labour movement. In addition, the war undermined a formal party politics based upon class conflict or class tension, even though class tension was now common in the country at large. In 1943, for instance, Harold Laski, a man on the left of the Labour Party, wrote that 'during the summer and autumn of 1940 there was something that is not difficult to describe as a regeneration of British democracy. The character of the struggle was defined in terms which made the identities between citizens a hundred times more vital than the differences which had divided them.'[22] As Stephen Brooke has noted, throughout the war 'the question of class versus community was resolved forcefully in favour of the latter'.[23] Had Britain been successfully invaded, on the other hand, there might have been well-placed quislings. But it was not, and however much it was doubted in the 1930s or by those writing about the 1930s and

---

[20] For this, see Cole, *History of the Labour Party*, 344.

[21] R. Rhodes James (ed.), *Chips: The Diaries of Sir Henry Channon* (London, 1967), 351.

[22] Quoted in Brooke, *Labour's War*, 272.   [23] Ibid. 273.

the 'guilty men', the patriotism of no class was officially impugned during the war itself.[24]

The war and the cold war also changed significantly the character of the Labour Party as an international social-democratic party. The old leadership of the Party, especially Henderson and MacDonald, were very conscious of the Party's role in the international socialist movement and the importance of that movement.[25] As much as any Marxist party, Labour believed that the future of the British working class was inextricable from that of the international working class. Labour had joined the International before 1914 and its leaders assiduously attended its meetings: they were much more familiar with the continental socialist parties than any of their successors in 1940s or 1950s. The British labour movement, as the most numerous, least divided and richest in Europe, had been instrumental in rescuing the non-Bolshevik parties in the old Second International and in the construction of its successor, the Labour and Socialist International, after the First World War. Together with support for the League of Nations and (usually) collective security in the 1930s that represented an internationalism which largely disappeared after 1945. The Bolshevik revolution, then Nazism, then the cold war had, of course, done much to wreck the international labour movement anyway, but that the British Labour Party alone of the major European socialist parties survived the war intact reinforced its parochialism, its Britishness, its slight contempt for those socialist parties that had gone under, and its increasing reluctance to believe that the political and constitutional practices of continental socialism had anything to offer it. Indeed, Labour now saw itself, if anything, as a patron of European socialism; a stance encouraged by the anti-communism of the cold war and by Britain's dependence on America. The Labour Party not so much learnt from the European

---

[24] It is worth noting that it was Herbert Morrison as home secretary and minister of home security who released Oswald Mosley from internment in 1944: not without controversy.

[25] The best study of this is D. J. Newton, *British Labour, European Socialism and the Struggle for Peace* (Oxford, 1985).

socialist parties as rescued them. Its role was not that of student but of saviour.[26] As Martin Francis has pointed out, with the exception of Sweden, 'there was universal acceptance that Labour had little to learn from the internal economies of other Western European states'.[27] The Second World War, R. K. Middlemas notes, 'encouraged a somewhat complacent and very insular belief in the value of British institutions and traditions, especially when these were compared with those of other European nations'.[28] From this complacency the labour movement was not exempt.

Furthermore, the emergence of Christian democracy in Europe, a movement which in Labour eyes was the product of many doubtful and conceivably clerical-fascist influences, further made continental models suspect.[29] European federalism, often associated with Christian democracy, was also suspect at a moment when Labour felt it at last was able to discharge its programme without interference. In the longer term such suspicion was to blind the Labour Party to the extent to which extensive welfare provision, forms of social solidarity, and (on the whole) democratic institutions were characteristics of continental Western European political systems after 1945.

The war thus left Labour with a mixed inheritance, some of it unhelpful. Nonetheless, the Party fought the 1945 election on the basis of a programme, *Let Us Face The Future*, devised during the war, and by 1950 had achieved more or less everything it promised. The programme, as we have seen, differed little except in detail from the last pre-war programme and presented the same mixture of public ownership, public housing, welfare provision, industrial modernization, planning and land reform. Some of this, given the circumstances, almost inevitably fell by the wayside; but two forms of legislation, nationalization and what contemporaries had begun to call the welfare state, were much more enduring. Public ownership

---

[26] For a full discussion of this see P. Weiler, *British Labour and the Cold War* (Stanford, 1988).

[27] M. Francis, *Ideas and Policies under Labour 1945–1951* (Manchester, 1997), 229.

[28] R. K. Middlemas, *Power, Competition and the State*, I (London, 1986), 114.

[29] Francis, *Ideas and Policies under Labour*, 229.

became central to Labour because it always seemed appropriate to a socialist programme. As an objective, to be embodied in the famous clause IV, the nationalization of the means of production and distribution (exchange came later) was inserted in the 1918 constitution of the Party without debate: uncontested even by people who in fact were sceptical or opposed. But since it represented a moral critique of capitalism, as much as a practical proposal, it was difficult to oppose.

Labour was to give four further justifications for nationalization.[30] The first was as a form of social humanitarianism: public ownership would protect industry from the brutality of the trade cycle and 'unplanned' capitalism. The miners, especially and understandably, favoured such a policy. The second was that public ownership constituted a form of economic redistribution: from the shareholder to the workforce on one side and from the producer to the consumer on the other. The third was as an exercise in industrial democracy; the transference of managerial authority, in whole or in part, to the workforce. The final one was efficiency and modernization: public ownership was simply more efficient and responsive than private ownership. Nationalization, furthermore, an argument which was rather developed *post hoc*, would give the state strategic control of the economy even if technically it did not own it.

In practice, few of these justifications had much substance. Public ownership was not responsible for any significant redistribution of income. The shareholders of the nationalized industries were (notoriously) generously compensated. Indeed, given the degree to which pre-war dividend payments were maintained at the expense of necessary investment, almost certainly overcompensated. By 1945 most of those industries to be nationalized were hardly viable in the private sector. Coal and railways demanded heavy re-equipment costs after six years of wear-and-tear and underinvestment, and both

---

[30] The best, though undervalued, study of nationalization remains E. Eldon Barry's *Nationalisation in British Politics* (London, 1965).

were losing their monopoly—coal to oil and rail to the roads. Most
shareholders understandably thought this was a good time to get out,
to offload the costs of new investment on to the taxpayer. Nor did
nationalization lead to any obvious empowerment of the workforce.
As is well known, the model adopted for the nationalized industries
was that of Herbert Morrison's London Passenger Transport Board
(LPTB).[31] Morrison always favoured a technocratic, non-political,
business-minded form of industrial government; just as he wished to
win for Labour the professional and managerial middle classes—one
of the reasons why in 1945 he gave up his Hackney seat to fight East
Lewisham. Morrison did not even favour appointing trade unionists
to the boards of nationalized industries; possibly the origin of his
long feud with Ernest Bevin who, as secretary of the Transport and
General Workers Union, did.

But the unions themselves, whatever Bevin wanted, were either indifferent to worker participation in management or actually opposed.
Their leaderships were nervous of anything that might increase the
authority of the shop-floor at their expense: one possible consequence
of worker-participation. Nor did they want to become bosses, which
any form of worker-participation in management might have en-
tailed. In their eyes there was already enough shop-floor suspicion of
the union leadership. As Eldon Barry has argued:

In this reorganization of industries the only role reserved by trade union
leaders for themselves was the traditional one of safeguarding the interests
of their members; and for this purpose 'recognition' and a medium for
joint discussion with the management were needed. But responsibility for
industrial production was to be avoided.[32]

Nor, as a result, were they prepared to abandon collective bargaining;
in their view, as we have already observed, the immovable foundation
of the British system of industrial relations. Their conception of
a nationalized industry, therefore, was like Morrison's: a private

---

[31] For the evolution of the London Passenger Transport Board, see B. Donoghue and
G. W. Jones, *Herbert Morrison: Portrait of a Politician* (London, 1973), 141–50.
[32] Barry, *Nationalisation in British Politics*, 324–5.

corporation whose shares all happened to be owned by the state, and where the ordinary rules of collective bargaining continued to operate. The result was that labour relations in the nationalized industries were no better (though usually no worse) than they had been before public ownership. Of the nationalized coal industry, for instance, it was said:

Scores of examples could be given of the prevailing idea among workers that any suggestion emanating from management, since it is designed for greater profit, is likely to be some underhand attack. It will benefit one side or the other; coincidence of interests is unthinkable and they cannot conceive of the boss being philanthropic.[33]

Since the existing management tended to be confirmed in place—they were, after all, the professionals—this is hardly surprising. Preservation of the existing management (in this case Lord Cobbold) was true even of the Bank of England, also nationalized by the government. Although a trade union representative was appointed to the Court of Directors, the Court continued to be dominated by the City merchant banks, as it always had been. The bad relations between the Bank and Harold Wilson's 1964 government were a telling commentary on this form of public ownership.

Nor can it be argued that the state achieved any kind of strategic direction of the economy via nationalization. The government never had a clear idea of what the relationship between the nationalized industries and the rest of the economy should be. Those industries were expected to behave 'commercially' and follow ordinary business practices. As Alec Cairncross (who believed there was no economic or technical rationale for nationalization) wrote, there was a 'dilemma which greatly troubled the Labour government, between leaving the boards to "get on with the job" and persuading, or directing them, to pay regard to the wider objectives of the government'.[34] As is the way with dilemmas there was no solution. Had (for example)

[33] N. Dennis et al., *Coal is Our Life* (London, 1956), 33.
[34] A. Cairncross, *Years of Recovery: British Economic Policy 1945–51* (London, 1945), 494.

the automotive and chemical industries and the high street banks
been nationalized, overall direction of the economy might have been
possible. But they weren't and could not have been. Since many
of these firms were actually international it would have been very
difficult to have nationalized them even if the government had
possessed a clear idea of the function of public ownership in the first
place. As a result, the state was left with industries, some declining
and unprofitable, which were still essential but which the private
sector on the whole was glad to be rid of.[35]

Nevertheless, as Cairncross admitted, nationalization was 'a response to strongly held political and moral convictions and from that
point of view was largely inevitable'.[36] In the case of coal and the
railways these political pressures were decisive: the unions believed
state ownership was in the interest of their members because the
state would shelter their members from the market and manage
decline, if decline there were, more generously. There was also a
belief, strong on the left of the Party, that 'bigness' and centralized
control were synonymous with efficiency, and that the state could
manage bigness more efficiently. Even among those who believed
in bigness, however, like Harold Wilson, there were doubts: hence
Wilson's sour comment that the left wanted to make Marks and
Spencer as efficient as the Co-op.

Yet the political imperative remained strong: a belief that public
ownership was socialism—its irreducible minimum—and that a
commitment to public ownership was a confirmation of the Party's
socialism. The Attlee government nationalized coal, the railways,
parts of road transport,[37] iron and steel (very controversially) and
carried through to full nationalization the electricity system and civil
aviation, which the Conservatives had in effect brought into public
ownership (as they had mining royalties) in the 1930s. But there

---

[35] Though that was not necessarily true of some of them, like electricity or aviation,
which, nonetheless the private sector showed little sign of wanting to recover.

[36] Cairncross, *Years of Recovery*, 494.

[37] The original proposal to nationalize all road haulage had to be abandoned in
face of the well-supported opposition of the smaller road hauliers (Pelling, *The Labour
Governments*, 81–2).

was a further 'shopping list', a second wave, which was even harder to justify on economic grounds than the first. These included the industrial assurance societies and sugar. Both of these were very risky. The great industrial societies, like the Prudential or the Royal Liver, had through their agents immediate access to working-class households; to take them on was something even Lloyd George declined to do in 1911.[38] The government weakened its draft legislation on the insurance companies; but it was not brought to parliament before Labour left office in 1951. The threat to sugar was defeated by a determined campaign directed by Lord Lyle, creator of Mr Cube, Tate and Lyle's jaunty champion of free enterprise. That the government was prepared to take nationalization this far gives us some sense of its significance to Labour's definition of socialism.

In the creation (or completion) of the welfare state, Labour did what it promised, and much of what it did was in the tradition of British welfare legislation—that is, was based upon the principle of insurance. Pensions, unemployment benefit and other similar payments were technically 'earned' by the payment of National Insurance contributions. The department which administered welfare, so that no one would misunderstand, was called the Ministry of National Insurance (an innovation of the wartime coalition). A strategy adopted by Lloyd George to make the National Insurance Act (1911) acceptable to those who disliked 'handouts'—by likening the Act to an insurance policy and thus to provident behaviour—was, via Beveridge, built into the system. There were two important differences, however, between Attlee's welfare system and the Edwardian one. Before 1914 pensions were paid on a non-contributory basis—they were not an insurance policy. After 1945 pension benefits were accumulated by the payment of National Insurance contributions.[39]

---

[38] The agents collected the weekly contributions towards life and funeral policies which people purchased from the industrial societies. Lloyd George had originally excluded the societies from the 1911 National Insurance Act, but caved in partly for fear of what the agents might do to the Liberal Party. (For this episode, see Bentley B. Gilbert, *The Evolution of National Insurance in Great Britain* (London, 1973), 360–2.)

[39] Though this was a development begun by Churchill in 1925 when he tied widows' and orphans' pensions to National Insurance contributions.

The other was that Attlee's welfare state was universal. Under Attlee everyone was entitled to pensions, family allowances and unemployment insurance. Before 1914 the middle class was excluded from all such benefits. There were strong arguments for universality. Everything suggests that a highly discriminatory system, one based strictly upon perceived 'need'—like the contemporary American one—ends up treating the needy as badly as everyone else.[40] The only system that 'works' is one in which the middle classes have a material interest. They felt strongly their exclusion from the pre-war system, one of the reasons why the dole, seemingly perpetual and unearned, was so politically contentious,[41] and the Attlee government had no intention of alienating them yet again. There was also the argument from social solidarity: that a common entitlement, indeed the doctrine of fair shares itself, was a social bond which both protected the welfare state and class-unity by a kind of mutuality. It was, however, an ungenerous system. Not deliberately, but as a result of the tradition of social policy in which it was created. As the years went by, therefore, it had to be propped up by increasingly complicated additional payments.[42]

Universality also characterized the National Health Service (NHS)—unlike the pre-1939 system. The NHS was probably the Attlee government's only social legislation ideologically acceptable to more or less everyone, and it, as much as full employment, tied the working class to the Labour Party.[43] The argument for universality in health services was as politically persuasive as it was for the payment of 'insurance' benefits. In this case the middle classes, at any rate the well-to-do middle classes, had it both ways. As part of the bargain the minister of health, Aneurin Bevan, was forced to make with the

[40] For an important discussion of this in both the British and international context see P. Baldwin, *The Politics of Social Solidarity: Class Bases of the European Welfare State* (Cambridge, 1990), 1–54, 107–34.

[41] See above, 102.

[42] This was a consequence largely, though not entirely, of the niggardly state pension which was never adequate.

[43] For the introduction of the NHS, see C. Webster, *Problems of Health Care: the National Health Service before 1957* (HMSO, 1988); *The National Health Service: A Political History* (second edn, Oxford, 2002).

consultants private medicine and 'pay' beds in NHS hospitals were preserved, as were the private insurers. The NHS was (and is), despite its ideological significance to the Labour Party, therefore unlike the modern Canadian system, for example, where private insurance is simply excluded from the federal health service. It was (and is) a hybrid which favours those who can afford private healthcare but guarantees everyone free healthcare.

The third element in the Labour government's policies was 'planning'. Although no previous Labour government had tried it, planning, like public ownership, was part of Labour's tradition. It proceeded from an assumption that capitalism was not only unfair, but also inefficient and wasteful. Planning was 'rational'; a product of human intelligence not of an erratic and unpredictable market.[44] Furthermore, the war itself seemed to legitimate planning as an economic mechanism and the remarkable military performance of the Soviet Union probably reinforced its legitimacy. Although most of Labour's younger economists were sceptical of planning as policy even in the late 1930s, this was not true of an Edwardian Fabian like Hugh Dalton, Attlee's first chancellor of the exchequer. However sceptical some might have been Labour fought the 1945 election as a 'planning' party, and unquestionably many MPs and Party members thought planning both practicable and morally superior to market capitalism. But equally many had only a vague conception of planning. For some, including Dalton, it represented a repudiation of the policies of the 1920s and of the apparent capitulation to the bondholder. In defending his policy of 'cheap money', for example, Hugh Dalton told the House of Commons in April 1947 that 'so long as the National Debt endures—and that may be for a long time yet—the Chancellor of the Exchequer must be on the side of the active producer as against the passive *rentier*'.[45] To others it meant rationing, since rationing, like planning, implied a partial or complete

---

[44] The best overall study of this is R. Toye, *The Labour Party and the Planned Economy, 1931–1951* (Woodbridge: RHS/Boydell Press, 2003). For the Attlee government specifically, Cairncross, *Years of Recovery*, 299–353.

[45] Quoted in B. Pimlott, *Hugh Dalton* (London, 1985), 462.

repudiation of the price mechanism. What is not clear is how far planning and rationing were deliberate policies or simply forced on the government by the circumstances of the 1940s. Political conditions did not permit the abandonment of rationing if only because of memories of what happened in 1919–20 when the Lloyd George government, under strong pressure, abolished rationing as soon as it could. To repeat that after 1945 would have undermined the notion of 'fair shares' which was essential to the political strategy of the Attlee government and to the social equipoise on which it balanced. Control of demand, especially for dollar denominated imports, and controls on capital and exchange transactions were in the circumstances inescapable. Most people declared a belief in 'fair shares', even those who were not always its beneficiaries, and in these circumstances 'fair shares' was impossible without rationing. Planning in the strict sense, to the extent that it had ever been practised, was, however, largely abandoned by 1947. Physical planning in an economy which was always, despite nationalization, going to be predominantly private, whatever the Labour Party might have wished, was never really workable, as Labour ministers soon discovered. Even if it were, the unions undermined it by their refusal to suspend collective bargaining. They indeed agreed to wage restraint from 1948 to 1950, though with increasing reluctance and only on the understanding that free collective bargaining as the basis of wage-setting should remain 'unimpaired'.[46] A planned economy with a free market in wages was simply oxymoronic. Nor would direction of labour, which might, for instance, have alleviated the coal crisis (caused partly by a shortage of labour in the mines), have been any more acceptable, either to the unions or anyone else in the labour movement.

The Labour Party was inclined to argue at the time that these policies were a unique social revolution: a model to the world, if only because it was non-violent. At the time such a view was shared by some outsiders. The French economist and journalist

---

[46] Morgan, *Labour in Power*, 133, 371–3; Pelling, *The Labour Governments*, 265.

Bertrand de Jouvenel wrote of England (he meant Britain) in the late 1940s:

Because England has been spared the neuroses which come from occupation; because there are no political trials going on in any forum, either of the Court or public opinion or of conscience; because men's minds are not given over to informing against others or defending themselves, are not embittered by either impunity or injustice; because of this inestimable advantage, the attention and intelligence of Britain are available alike for considering the problems of the future and broaching the questions which confront not only herself, but the whole of Europe.

For this reason England is today a sort of look-out man for the rest of Europe, and it is in this respect that I have considered her.[47]

Britain was certainly politically favoured. Neither invaded nor occupied, nor possessed of a *vichyiste* political elite, Britain could perhaps act as look-out man. But we can equally well argue that Britain did between 1945 and 1950 what all European states were doing, or which some states, like Sweden or New Zealand, had done before the war. All western societies (with the partial exception of the United States) created welfare states or something like them, and all did for the same political and social reasons. All, for example, were driven by a desire to encourage social solidarity and diminish class tension. They differed in some details—most, for instance, had insurance-based health systems—but not in type. The most obvious difference was that the continental systems became more generous than the British though the conditions under which they were developed were much more difficult. In all countries rationing was severe after the war, and for the same reasons. Furthermore, in most, as I have suggested, Christian democracy rather than social democracy was predominant. This is to argue, in other words, that there were 'objective' pressures for the construction of welfare states which operated everywhere in post-1945 Europe, Britain included.

In the British case socialism, we might argue, was actually a form of modernization: not looking-out but catching-up. This was

---

[47] B. de Jouvenel, *Problems of Socialist England* (London, 1949), xiv.

a justification that Labour sometimes gave for nationalization. As Tomlinson points out, Labour shared a widely held view of what had gone wrong with British industry between the wars. 'Hence Labour's policies on nationalization could be seen as aimed at rationalization by new means, giving a "socialist" twist to a well-established consensual agenda.'[48] In 1945, for example, Britain's railways were decrepit, not just because of wartime wear-and-tear but because they were privately owned. The case for state ownership of the railways was almost unanswerable and had been at least since the end of the First World War. A failure of nerve by Lloyd George left them in the private sector, there to become, as Eldon Barry argued, a millstone around the neck of the British economy.[49] Britain's were the only ones in Europe in private ownership (apart from a handful of small private lines) which is why the case for public ownership in Britain on grounds of 'efficiency'—which meant modernization—always seemed one of the more convincing. And, if pressed, defenders of public ownership could and did argue that 'modernization' and 'socialism' went hand in hand. Nonetheless, modernization was not the same as 'fair shares' or democratic participation; could indeed be antithetical to them. That, in turn, was to land later Labour governments in real difficulty as modernization seemed more necessary than fair shares.

However mixed the motives and whatever the results, the social and economic policies of the Attlee government did significantly modify the British economy and British social policy. Conspicuously absent, on the other hand, from the government's programme was any serious reform of the country's electoral-constitutional system or its status hierarchy. The country's ancient form of voting was, despite the Edwardian Labour Party's commitment to electoral reform, untouched and most thought it should be left that way. Separate university representation was abolished as was separate representation of the City of London—both inevitable although

[48] J. Tomlinson, *Democratic Socialism and Economic Policy: The Attlee Years, 1945–1951* (Cambridge, 1997), 99.
[49] Barry, *Nationalisation in British Politics*, 238.

the end of the university seats meant the end of a system which had produced two of the most useful MPs of the interwar years, Eleanor Rathbone (English Universities) and A. P. Herbert (Oxford University). The business vote—weakened in 1918—disappeared and the House of Lords 'veto' was reduced from two years to one. The last, however, was not the result of a considered policy but of the government's difficulties with the legislation to nationalize iron and steel.[50] And that was it. Even the status quo in Northern Ireland was confirmed, though everyone knew what it was—gerrymandered constituencies and a system of patronage that entrenched Protestant Unionism and discriminated openly against the Roman Catholic minority with fateful long-term results. While the social democratic parties of the continent were all engaged in refounding or reforming the political institutions in which they operated the Labour Party made no attempt to do the same, or even to think about it. Those demobbed in the later 1940s found a political and electoral system scarcely any different from the ones returning tommies found in 1919.

Why was this? One reason was the Labour Party's semi-withdrawal from the international socialist movement, to which I have referred. Here the assumptions of political and moral superiority were important. They divorced Labour from alternative and less institutionally conservative forms of social democracy. Another was purely instrumental. A House of Lords with a limited veto was perhaps as close to a unicameral legislature as Britain was likely to get, and Labour inclined to unicameralism. An unreformed and undemocratic voting arrangement, it was argued, produced strong majoritarian government and that, together with a House of Commons dominated by the executive and the whips' office, ensured the more or less unfettered enactment of a government's programme. It also meant (all being well) no coalitions and no negotiations, particularly with the Liberal Party—a comment on the fraught character of Labour–Liberal relations since 1900. There was a third, more secret reason, one that

[50] Pelling, *The Labour Governments*, 85–6.

Labour MPs rarely admitted to themselves: that strictly proportional representation would in ordinary circumstances probably return an anti-socialist majority to the House of Commons. That is, the democratic electorate was undependable. As Harold Laski, reflecting on the 1931 election result, put it:

Mr MacDonald's victory is so disproportionate to the votes cast for him in the country, that the claims of proportional representation have been urged with added vigour since the election . . . [Such] a change in the system of election would assume the proportions of a serious disaster. For it would perpetuate the dangers which would attend upon minority Government not only maintaining in being the three-party system, but quite probably encouraging further fission. Thereby, it would weaken the executive power at a time when only strength and coherency can make for honest and straightforward government . . . Our system has, of course, its limitations; but, worked with goodwill and common sense, these do not seem likely to destroy the purpose at which it aims.[51]

This was after an election in which Labour polled almost one-third of the votes in England but won exactly twenty-nine seats (and even fewer in the rest of Britain); and after a crisis during which the system was obviously not worked with goodwill. On the contrary, it was worked remorselessly to the disadvantage of the Labour Party.

There was obviously more than just instrumentalism to all this. More even than the argument often proposed that the electorate was entirely uninterested in constitutional or electoral reform. The fact is that the Labour Party, on the whole, had absorbed uncritically the ideological and institutional defences of the British political system: that it was class- and party-neutral; that it made for 'strong' government; that it had been legitimated by a unique and victorious national history. In moving an address of congratulations to the king at the end of the war with Japan Attlee told the house of Commons:

However well and skilfully constitutions may be framed they depend in the last resort on the willingness and ability of human beings to make them work. Our British Constitution, in war and peace, works because

[51] H. Laski, *The Crisis and the Constitution: 1931 and After* (London, 1932), 44.

the people understood it and know by long experience how to operate it. A constitutional monarchy depends for its success to a great extent on the understanding heart of the monarch. In this country we are blessed with a King who . . . combines with an intense love of our country and all his people, a thorough appreciation of our Parliament and democratic Constitution. In the difficult times ahead I believe that the harmonious working of our Constitution, in which the people's will is expressed by King and Parliament, will be an example of stability in a disordered world.[52]

Even allowing for the conventions of such an occasion this is a remarkable statement—a eulogy of a perfect constitution guaranteed by a people-loving monarch. But these sentiments were not confined to Attlee. In 1947 Herbert Morrison told the Liberal leader Clement Davies that, rather than reform the House of Lords 'we should try to maintain continuity and not set up something new and different from the past',[53] a comment which anticipated Morrison's own highly conservative interpretation of the British constitution in his book *Government and Parliament: A Survey from the Inside* (1954). It is hard to imagine a continental social democrat in 1947 defending an upper chamber of parliament whose membership was drawn almost exclusively from the hereditary peerage. Miles Taylor's argument, therefore, that the Labour Party was a serious party of constitutional reform flies in the face of historical fact, especially as he himself admits that for the 1945 government 'the test of legislative efficiency was the ultimate consideration in constitutional reform'[54]—a very feeble measure of constitutional propriety.

The House of Lords was not alone in escaping reform. The 1945 government did not consider reform of the public schools or even worry much about their relationship to society, although Churchill and Butler wondered whether they could or should survive the war. This is an important instance because in an ideal world their reform (or disappearance) was probably necessary to any form of democratic

---

[52] *HCD*, 413, clmn 59 (15 August 1945).
[53] Quoted in Morgan, *Labour in Power*, 85.
[54] M. Taylor, 'Labour and the Constitution', in D. Tanner, P. Thane, and N. Tiratsoo (eds.), *Labour's First Century* (Cambridge, 2000), 166.

socialism as defined by the Labour Party, and was understood to be so—if only because of the influence of R. H.Tawney. His book *Equality* (1931), which, if not the bible of the labour movement had almost biblical status, had described the public schools as giving unearned access to the peaks of English state and society to a small number of people whose only common qualification was that they had attended one of the better public schools. 'There is a public education', he later wrote, 'for the great majority of children, and a private education system for the select minority, whose fathers were distinguished by the possession of larger bank accounts.'[55] The issue was not really whether the public schools provided a superior education. In fact, it was unlikely that their teaching was any better than that in the grammar schools despite what their defenders said. It was their role in apparently perpetuating a self-recruited governing elite that was the issue. This was widely known in the Labour Party and repeated often enough during the Second World War. Yet Chuter Ede, co-author of the 1944 Education Act and a former teacher, thought a state monopoly of education would be wrong,[56] while in 1946 Attlee told the boys at his old school (Haileybury) that he thought the 'great tradition would carry on'.[57] This was fraught with consequence. As Martin Francis has pointed out, once the decision had been made in effect to preserve the public schools (though preservation or non-preservation was never an actual issue) it became even more difficult to abolish the grammar schools should Labour wish to do that: it would have been hardly fair—and when Labour did set about the abolition of the grammar schools in 1965 was hardly fair—to deny the non-well-to-do a superior education while permitting the well-to-do to buy one.[58] In this way the doctrine of 'fair shares' propped up the status quo.

The fact is that anything strongly defended ideologically, whether it be public schools or the sugar industry, was left alone by the

---

[55] In the introduction to G. C.Leybourne and K. White, *Education and the Birth-Rate* (London, 1940), 9.
[56] Brooke, *Labour's War*, 190.   [57] Francis, *Ideas and Policies under Labour*, 163.
[58] Ibid. 203.

Attlee government. As a kind of index: not one of those ideological supports of Conservatism identified by Frank Parkin and to which I have previously referred, was touched. Not the monarchy, the aristocracy, the Church, the 'ancient universities', the armed forces (whose patterns of recruitment, promotion and hierarchy were a continuing scandal),[59] the public schools, the structure of industrial management or inherited social hierarchies more generally. Nor is that an exhaustive list. Peter Hennessy has argued that

> it would be absurd to have expected the Attlee government beset by the basic, fundamental problems of scarcity and supply, the need to convert the war economy to a peacetime one and the imperatives imposed by the overriding requirement to hoist exports and restore the external balance of the British economy, to tackle such citadels of 'class' privilege as the public schools or the ancient universities or those great professional standing armies such as the law. The real mystery remains the unwillingness to modernize those institutions whose high performance was central to the Government's performance such as the Civil Service.[60]

At one level that is fair comment. The government was so buffeted by almost daily crises that any long-term or 'structural' planning was obviously difficult. Furthermore, unlike the situation in so many European states in 1945, Labour was faced with a powerful established social and status system which was very much intact and confident in its own defence. Yet at another level his is a very problematic conclusion. If it is the case, for example, that the civil service needed 'modernizing' then that surely is because it was a product of precisely those citadels of class privilege—the public schools and the ancient universities whose patterns of recruitment were no more open than the army's—that Hennessy thinks the Attlee

---

[59] C. B. Otley, 'The Educational Background of British Army Officers', *Sociology* 7 (1973), 200–1.

[60] P. Hennessy, *Never Again: Britain 1945–51* (London, Penguin edn, 2006), 434. This is a difficult issue and the extent to which the civil service has 'failed' has been continually debated since 1945. My own view is that it has not really failed; indeed when given good political leadership has performed pretty well, quite as well as the civil service of other comparable countries. If it has failed, however, it has failed because the whole political system of which it is a part has 'failed'. The failure of the former cannot be distinguished from the failure of the latter.

government could not have been expected to reform. To modernize one, however, you must modernize the other. Furthermore, there is an implication in his comment that if the government had had the time and the tranquillity it would have tackled the citadels of class privilege. But there is no evidence they had any such plans before they left office in 1951. The argument that the Labour government made 'no attempt to challenge entrenched systems of deference and preferment, or the privileged institutions they maintained' might be exaggerated, but not by much.[61]

How far the Attlee government's programme was 'socialist' is an almost pointless question. There is little agreement about what constitutes socialism or the criteria by which we can judge it. But those who implemented the programme *thought* it was socialist, that it represented both a social transformation and a system of values superior to any alternative. Yet it was a peculiar form of socialism; the socialism of a particular generation, one which drew a clear distinction between the economy and social policy on the one hand, and Britain's status and class system on the other. This was a kind of compartmentalized socialism in which political institutions and social structures, and the ideologies which supported them, either differed from or mattered much less than 'policy'. Once the first wave of the Attlee government's reforms had beached itself and then ebbed this distinction landed Labour in an almost inescapable *impasse*.

Nonetheless, by 1950 the Labour Party had largely done what it said it would and the Conservative and Liberal Parties had to adjust themselves to that; as they had to the 'judgement' of the 1945 election. More recently historians have tended to emphasize the extent the Conservative Party's adjustment lay not in a comparatively calm acceptance of what Labour had done, but in an aggressive redefinition of 'socialism'—which was now bureaucracy, red tape, taxation and, above all, a vindictive austerity. Ewen Green suggested that the Conservatives fought the 1950 and 1951 elections not on the slogan

---

[61] D. Morgan and M. Evans, 'The Road to Nineteen Eighty-Four', in B. Brivati and H. Jones, *What Difference did the War Make?* (Leicester, 1993), 60.

'the welfare state and the mixed economy are safe in our hands' but 'set the people free'.[62] Ina Zweiniger-Bargielowska has strongly argued that the Conservative revival was based upon a new form of electoral mobilization: consumption against production and women against men: 'There was little common ground on the issue of consumption and living standards between Labour and the Conservatives during the late 1940s and early 1950s. This debate was highly ideological and conducted in terms of competing philosophies, namely socialism versus capitalism and positive versus negative notions of freedom.'[63] In this revival gender is more important than class. It represented a revolt of women against the 'collectivist, productionist agenda' of the Labour Party in favour of the Conservative Party's consumptionism. The 'female Conservative preference in 1951 goes a long way towards explaining the Conservative victory'.[64] This argument has some truth but also two possible flaws. It underrates the extent to which the Conservative Party did adjust itself to the welfare state, and thought it had to; and it overrates the extent to which the Tory Party had to devise new forms of mobilization (indeed how far the Tory Party changed much at all) and the significance of 'austerity' in its recovery.

How far Conservative 'adjustments' were cosmetic and how far real matters less than the fact that they were made. Many in the Tory Party were genuinely radicalized by the events of 1940 or else recognized they had to appear radicalized. Butler could be depicted as either, but in his case the distinction probably has little meaning. For whatever reason he was radicalized. Although Churchill did his best to exclude major reconstruction 'issues' during the war itself he also knew there was no going back to 1939—and his memory of the 1920s and his own chancellorship made him a poor defender of the status quo. He told the House of Commons in August 1945, for instance, that the 'national ownership' of the Bank of

---

[62] E. H. H. Green, *Ideologies of Conservatism* (Oxford, 2002), 220.

[63] I. Zweiniger-Bargielowska, *Austerity in Britain: Rationing, Controls, and Consumption* (Oxford, 2000), 206.

[64] Ibid. 252–62. For a fuller discussion of the women's vote in the 1940s see below, 173–4, 187–9.

England did not 'raise any issue of principle'[65] and neither he, nor any other leading Tory, seriously opposed the nationalization of coal, the railways, and the utilities. (Though they were, of course, opposed to the nationalization of steel and the 'second wave'. But so were many in the labour movement.) Although the NHS was not as the Conservatives would have designed it, it was, especially after Bevan's concessions to the doctors, bearable. Indeed, as Helen Mercer argues, Labour's programme of public ownership differed little from Harold Macmillan's in *The Middle Way*.[66] In 1942 that old grouch, Sir Cuthbert Headlam, Tory MP for North Newcastle, who was constitutionally opposed to progress, expressed his astonishment that even the most old-fashioned Tory and Liberal MPs now believe in 'the State'.[67] Churchill's designated successor, Anthony Eden, was personally hostile to individualist liberalism and thought the Party should be as well. In 1946 he wrote to Ralph Assheton, the Party's chairman, of a draft pamphlet, seeking more detail on 'industrial' questions:

This is after all the biggest issue of the day and I do not think it is just enough to say we believe in freedom and free enterprise. What is our conception of the function of the state in relation to our industry? I tried to set this out—not very well I frankly admit—in my Hull speech. What is our industrial policy?[68]

In Eden's case pre-war memories also counted for much. When told that Samuel Hoare, his predecessor as foreign secretary in

[65] *HCD* 5s, 413, clmn 94 (16 Aug. 1945.) The journalist Collin Brooks records an amusing incident in 1940. At a dinner for General Sikorski (Polish prime minister in exile) he found himself on one side of Churchill with Ernest Bevin on the other. 'The talk was general, although Bevin and I rather rudely talked over the Premier's knee about the Macmillan Committee and Winston's folly in 1925 in countenancing deflation.' He does not record Churchill's reaction. (N. J. Crowson (ed.), *Fleet Street, Press Barons and Politics: The Journals of Collin Brooks, 1932–1940* (Cambridge, 1998), 273 (17 Sept. 1940).)

[66] H. Mercer, 'The Labour Governments of 1945–51 and Private Industry', in N. Tiratsoo (ed.), *The Attlee Years* (London, 1991), 71. For *The Middle Way* see above 106–8.

[67] S. Ball (ed.), *Parliament and Politics in the Age of Churchill and Attlee: The Headlam Diaries* (Cambridge, 1999), 335 (28 Sept. 1942).

[68] Ramsden, *Age of Churchill and Eden*, 241; and Ramsden, ' "A Party for Owners or a Party for Earners". How far did the Conservative Party change after 1945?', *Transactions of the Royal Historical Society* 5s, 37 (1987), 60.

1936 and an arch-appeaser, was proposed for the shadow cabinet, he said: 'There is no hope for the Tory party unless we can clear these disastrous old men out, and some of the middle-aged ones too!'[69] Furthermore, the *Industrial Charter* (1947), the Party's gesture of peace to the industrial working class, was seriously meant despite its obvious cosmetic implications. Macmillan and Butler, its progenitors, certainly took it seriously. Ramsden's conclusion that the Party largely accepted Macmillan's position on the *Charter* and that in any case it was broadly in line with 'the philosophy that had been emerging since 1931' is surely correct.[70] In my view the Conservatives fought the elections of 1950 and 1951 on two slogans: the welfare state is safe in our hands *and* we will set the people free.

Thus the Tories, for whatever reason, clearly thought 1945 demanded 'positive' policies rather than just reaffirmations of individualism or hostility to bureaucracy. But did the Conservative Party have to change much in order to do this? As Schwarz has pointed out, even before the 1945 election it was a coalition of all 'moderate' anti-socialist forces, and here 'moderate' is as important as 'anti-socialist'.[71] The Baldwin and Chamberlain governments were not reactionary: their bias was deflationary in the 1920s and towards business in the 1930s but in neither decade were they dominated by traditional elites. Furthermore, the gestures towards inclusion demanded by the National government further weakened old-school Toryism. The infusion of Simonite Liberals, like Leslie Burgin or Leslie Hore-Belisha (who both became cabinet ministers, and one of whom, Hore-Belisha, was removed from the War Office by a coup—the last—engineered by the traditional elites)[72] reinforced its moderation.

The post-war Conservatives followed Baldwin's rule—that an anti-socialist front depended for its success on the absorption of

---

[69] Ramsden, *Age of Churchill and Eden*, 100.   [70] Ibid. 152–3.

[71] Bill Schwarz, 'The Tide of History. The Reconstruction of Conservatism', in Tiratsoo (ed.), *The Attlee Years*, 153.

[72] In 1940. He was forced out by an alliance of the officer corps and Buckingham Palace, but was restored to office as Minister of National Insurance in Churchill's reconstructed National government in 1945. He then lost his seat.

the Liberal electorate, and that, as in the 1930s, acted as a check on the animal spirits of traditional Toryism. The Liberals fought the 1945 and 1950 elections seriously: they put up 306 candidates in 1945 and 475 in 1950. Both elections were disappointing. They won twelve seats in 1945 and nine in 1950. Much of the old Liberal electorate had already gone Tory,[73] and it continued to slip disproportionately in their direction. The Tories concluded (partly as a result of polling) that the swinging vote was like the Liberal vote and that in wooing the second they would win the first. One way of appropriating the Liberal vote was to appropriate the name Liberal. The Woolton–Teviot agreement of April 1947 had allowed the Party to fuse with the Simonite Liberals (now called the National Liberals)[74] and the fused associations bore the name Liberal as well as Conservative. In 1950 fifty-three Conservative candidates stood as some form of Liberal, and seventeen were elected including the celebrated 'radio doctor' Charles Hill, who won Luton from Labour as a 'Liberal and Conservative'. Those now most likely to vote Conservative, small businessmen, professionals and managers, were once the heart of the old Liberal vote. And of the actively religious, nonconformists appear to have been the most hostile to the Attlee government.[75] This neo-Baldwinian strategy was largely successful. The Liberals put up only 109 candidates in the 1951 election and most of these lost their deposits. Only six were elected, five without Conservative opposition. The bulk of the former Liberals voted Conservative, thus beginning a decade when England had a genuine two-party system. In 1951, 97.6 per cent of English electors voted either Labour or Conservative. The Liberal Party which was to emerge in England in the later 1950s was detached from most of the social foundations of the old Liberalism and, unlike the Labour and Conservative Parties, was divorced from strong class, age, or religious ties. It

---

[73] See above, 91–4.

[74] For the details of this agreement, see Ramsden, *Age of Churchill and Eden*, 200.

[75] Admittedly on the basis of narrow evidence. See Benney et al., *How People Vote*, 111.

became a 'residual' party representing, however, an increasingly large residuum.[76]

The social character of Conservative candidates at the 1950 election also looks very similar indeed to the interwar years. One hundred and ninety eight were senior businessmen (either owners, directors or managers); twenty-five were in 'business-finance'. Three hundred and eight candidates were from the professions, of whom the dominant elements were lawyers and (this being the Conservative Party) former members of the armed forces.[77] The forces gave the Party its particular character, as they always had done. Observers of the 1950 election were struck by the military atmosphere at Tory constituency offices. Someone was 'O/C Transport', someone else 'O/C Loudspeakers'.[78] There is no evidence that the Conservative party in 1950 was more open or 'democratic' than in the 1920s or 1930s. On the contrary, it was less so. In 1918 only 10 per cent of Conservative MPs had been to Eton. In 1950 that figure was 23 per cent. In the interwar years one-quarter of Conservative ministers had been to grammar schools. Thereafter there was a 'resurgence' in the number of those who had been to Eton and Harrow. It is clear, W. L. Guttsman wrote, that the '"silent social revolution" of the past half century has largely by-passed the leadership of the Conservative Party'.[79]

Having 'positive' policies does not, of course, preclude more negative ones. That attacks on austerity and bullying bureaucracy were part of the Tory armoury goes without saying. Churchill led the way and himself coined the word 'queuetopia' in January 1951. How much electoral success the Conservatives achieved by these attacks is, however, questionable. That rationing and queueing were unpopular with many women we know and their unpopularity was increasingly well-organized by bodies like the Housewives' League and the Mothers' League. They made their

[76] This was incipient even in 1950. See Nicholas, *The British General Election of 1950*, 55–60; Bealey et al., *Constituency Politics*, 272.

[77] Nicholas, *The British General Election of 1950*, 52.   [78] Ibid. 245.

[79] W. L. Guttsman, *The British Political Elite* (London, 1965), 96, 291–4.

presence felt. In March 1947 Cuthbert Headlam noted wearily that he was always getting postcards from women demanding that Shinwell (minister of fuel and power) and Strachey (minister of food) should be dismissed. 'There is a body called the League of Housewives (or some such name).'[80] Furthermore, the general greyness of life and absence of things much of the middle class took for granted alienated even those once sympathetic. The reaction of Gilbert Murray, Barbara Hammond, and Mary Stocks, epitomes of the old progressive class, to the Labour government is one of the more *triste* vignettes in Peter Clarke's study of them. Murray voted Conservative in 1950 and 1951 ('the sufferings of the world weigh upon us less than the absence of servants'); Barbara Hammond would have done in 1951 had she not had flu; Mary Stocks did not have flu and voted Conservative. Only trade unionists, Murray thought, could now afford holidays.[81] It affected some almost irrationally. John Jewkes, the economist, in an introduction to his book *Ordeal by Planning*, which was almost a bestseller, wrote:

I have written this book reluctantly. I know that it will offend some of my friends and I fear it may hurt some of those with whom I worked in friendly co-operation during the war. But I had no option. For I believe that the recent melancholy decline of Great Britain is largely of our own making. The fall in our standard of living to a level which excites the pity and evokes the charity of many richer countries, the progressive restrictions on individual liberties, the ever widening disrespect for law, the steady sapping of our instinct for tolerance and compromise, the sharpening of class distinctions, our growing incapacity to play a rightful part in world affairs—these sad changes are not due to something that happened in the remote past. They are due to something that has happened in the last two years.[82]

---

[80] Ball (ed.), *Parliament and Politics*, 492 (7 March 1947). In May Headlam went to a meeting organized by the Housewives' League, which was addressed by its leading light, Dorothy Crisp. He was interestingly not impressed; especially not impressed by Crisp 'of whose oratory I have heard so much' (ibid. 507–8, 30 May 1947).

[81] P. F. Clarke, *Liberals and Social Democrats* (Cambridge, 1978), 285–9.

[82] J. Jewkes, *Ordeal by Planning* (London, 1949), vii. The introduction was written in November, 1947.

How far, nonetheless, the consumers' revolt damaged Labour is questionable. It was, as Morgan notes (and as contemporaries realized), primarily a middle-class women's revolt.[83] It was directed at the Labour government certainly; but also at shopkeepers (themselves now usually Conservatives) who were not thought to show a proper deference. This had been an issue in the First World War and was again in the second. Nella Last, tired of queues and rationing, recorded her unexpected experience with one shopkeeper in surprisingly trenchant terms: 'I got really beautiful fish . . . and the shopkeeper, a bitch of a woman who has insulted people terribly in the war, was so polite I felt embarrassed . . . Nasty wretch. When things are plentiful I bet she doesn't get much custom.'[84] But despite that comment Mrs Last, who before the war had chaired a Conservative ward association and whose individualism was as strong as ever, declined to chair one in January 1947 because she could not oppose Labour wholeheartedly. And that has significance. It suggests that there were limits to the housewives' revolt, or at least a high degree of ambivalence.[85]

In arguing the case for 'austerity' as a significant factor in the Conservative revival we can overinterpret or misinterpret the 1950 election result. The Labour majority in the House of Commons did indeed disappear: from nearly 150 to six. And in parts of the country, especially in the suburban ring around greater London, there was a significant swing to the Conservatives. But the overall swing to the Conservatives was less than 3 per cent and the great majority of those who voted Labour in 1945 did so in 1950. One of the main reasons for the fall in the Labour majority was, in fact, technical: the electoral redistribution of 1948. The extent to which the 1945 boundaries favoured Labour is easily underestimated. The striking

---

[83] J. Morgan, 'Queuing Up in Post-War Britain', *Twentieth Century British History* 16, 3 (2005), 288. See also D. Kynaston, *Austerity Britain, 1945–51* (London, 2007), 118.

[84] P. and R. Malcolmson (eds.), *Nella Last's Peace* (London, 2008), 19. Also J. Hinton, 'Militant Housewives: the British Housewives League and the Attlee Government', *History Workshop Journal* 38 (Autumn, 1994), 139.

[85] Ibid. 141–2.

feature of that election was not Labour's lead over the Conservatives (which at 8% was not huge) but the size of the swing to Labour compared with 1935—in other words 1945 was a measure of how badly Labour had done in 1935. If the 1950 election had been fought on the old boundaries Labour would have had a majority of about sixty. Redistribution counted for about one-quarter to one-half of Labour's losses.[86] The 1948 boundaries, by 'bunching' the Labour vote, undoubtedly further disfavoured Labour; something the government knew but did little to correct.[87] The result was that of the sixty largest majorities, fifty were Labour. Had the proportions of the vote been reversed—had the Conservatives won 46.1 per cent of the votes and Labour 43.5 per cent—the Tories would have had a majority of between sixty-five and seventy.

Other indices also need to be treated with scepticism. Some have argued that the huge turnout in 1950—84 per cent—was a result of the Tories getting to the polls people who had not voted in 1945 and now wished to vote Conservative. But the highest median turnout was in Labour seats—in those forty-eight seats where Labour's majority was at least 40 per cent of the total. Many of those were mining seats: a tribute both to the solidarity of the mining communities and to the nature of their ties to the Labour Party. Even the huge rise in the membership of the Tory Party can be misleading. Ramsden notes the increases in those outer London constituencies where the Conservatives did well in 1950. In terms of increase in membership the 'winning constituencies' in 1947–8 were Uxbridge, Wembley North, and West Woolwich.[88] But although the Conservatives did well in Wembley and Woolwich, they failed to win Uxbridge, either in 1950 or 1951, although it was very marginal. Frank Bealey and

[86] These calculations are drawn from Nicholas, *The British General Election of 1950*, 4–5. Nicholas also suggests that the Tories won about 10 seats as a result of the postal vote which they clearly organized more efficiently than Labour.

[87] The home secretary, Chuter Ede, only late in the day realized what the boundary commissioners were doing. They had proposed to reduce the size of the House of Commons to 608 by abolishing a large number of city seats in England. The Attlee government then legislated for the creation of 17 extra seats for England. Without that Labour would probably have lost the election altogether despite its lead in votes.

[88] Ramsden, *Age of Churchill and Eden*, 111–12.

his colleagues point out that while in Newcastle-under-Lyme there was a big increase in the membership of the Conservative Party after 1947, it had no discernible effect on the Conservative vote in 1950.[89] Nor is it likely that the 1950 result was in a special sense determined by gender: that the Conservative gains were due to the preferences of 'females'. Zweiniger-Bargielowska has argued that the Conservatives won women's votes, not because women were sociologically or inherently disposed to vote Conservative, but because the Tories presented themselves specifically as a woman's party whereas Labour's propaganda 'was based on the assumption that women's interests could be conflated with those of their men folk'.[90] At one level this argument is unexceptionable. As I suggested of the 1930s, the Conservative Party clearly stood for a version of social reality that seemed to many women true to life. But there are also problems with such an argument. For one thing the polling Zweiniger-Bargielowska uses is not wholly reliable[91] and in any case it does not support her argument. The gender 'gap'—the difference between the way men and women voted—is actually much smaller in 1950 (when hypothetically it should have been much larger) than it was in 1945. Furthermore, it is a fair bet that most members of the Housewives' League and similar bodies, if they voted in 1945 voted Conservative. It is, anyway, only arguing a distinction without a difference. A gender 'gap' in the 1940s dependent upon 'consumptionism' (Conservative) and 'productionism (Labour) fits the traditional explanation of the 'gap'—that women inhabited

---

[89] Bealey et al., *Constituency Politics*, 115. Membership rose to 5,000, over twice that of the local Labour Party.

[90] 'Explaining the Gender Gap: The Conservative party and the Women's Vote, 1945–1964', in M. Francis and I. Zweiniger-Bargielowska, *The Conservatives and British Society* (Cardiff, 1996), 196.

[91] Her figures are not those of actual elections, but are based upon people's recollections of how they voted and these lead to apparent inaccuracies. In 1951, for example, the polls suggest that 51 per cent of men and only 42 per cent of women voted Labour. Since Labour got 49 per cent of the votes in the election for those figures to be right many more men than women would have had to vote—which is possible but unlikely. The figures also suggest that in 1950 46 per cent of men and 43 per cent of women voted Labour. But since Labour actually got 46.1 per cent of the votes either or both these figures have to be wrong.

the private sphere and men the public—rather well. Women had *always* disproportionately supported the Conservative Party and probably did so in much larger numbers before 1939 than in 1950.[92]

The more important question is why, given the real hardships of life under Attlee, hardships which many thought unnecessary, Labour did so well in the 1950 election. The first reason is that the cohort radicalized by the war on the whole stayed radicalized; and the feeling among them that Labour was 'their' party and best represented their interests remained strong. Mark Benney and his colleagues, when they studied the constituency of Greenwich (which Labour won from the Conservatives in 1945), found that Labour voters 'wholeheartedly accepted the view that the Labour Party represents the working class'.[93] The Labour Party was, above all, the party of full employment and the NHS. It had taken time for Labour to become the party of full employment but by 1950 the electorate accepted that claim, which is possibly why the old 'depressed areas' remained so loyal to Labour.[94] As for the NHS, it probably did more to tie the electorate ideologically to Labour than almost anything else. The second reason is that in working-class seats controls and rationing appear not to have been important issues, whatever they were in middle-class constituencies.[95] For much of the working class, after all, life was better under Attlee. For them the comparative poverty of the interwar years was a type of rationing more stringent than anything experienced in the late 1940s. The result was that in much of working-class England (and Wales) there was virtually no swing to the Conservatives in 1950; and in some parts of the north east Labour actually gained.

---

[92] For a fuller treatment of this argument, see P. Norris, 'Gender: A Gender Generation Gap', in G. Evans and P. Norris (eds.), *Critical Elections: British Parties and Voters in Long-term Perspective* (London, 1999), 162 and *passim*.

[93] Benney et al., *How People Vote*, 122.

[94] Nicholas, *The British General Election of 1950*, 297–8. Nicholas also notes that the swing to the Conservatives was highest in areas of lowest unemployment in the 1930s. There is, of course, a class factor here and 'classness' as much as levels of employment might be the significant variable.

[95] Benney et al., *How People Vote*, 148.

And yet within less than two years Labour was out of office. In October 1951 there was a second general election which Labour narrowly lost—though once again winning more votes than the Tories. The election itself is a puzzle. Although the government's majority was only small it had not been under much pressure. Attlee announced his intention to have another election to a cabinet with only seven ministers present: an election Labour expected to lose. Attlee cited the convenience of the king, who was about to make a trip to Australia and New Zealand. A revealing explanation, whether true or not. Few other socialist parties would cite the convenience of the sovereign as a justification for risking the loss of office. It is unlikely, however, that that was the real explanation. Possibly Attlee thought the demands of the election might restore discipline to the Party after the major disputes over rearmament and the subsequent resignations of Aneurin Bevan and Harold Wilson.[96] The real reason, however, is that the narrowness of Labour's politics, its refusal to think seriously about the institutions of a social-democratic or socialist state, however defined, had left the Party with nowhere to go. The electorate was obviously either indifferent or opposed to any further nationalization but it was public ownership almost more than anything else which held the Party together, politically and ideologically. While people could believe in public ownership they could believe in themselves as socialists, however much they might differ on other issues. Once they doubted either the efficacy or popularity of public ownership there could be no agreement on socialism. That is why someone like Hugh Dalton continued to insist on the political importance of nationalization even though, to judge by his more despairing comments, he doubted its efficacy.[97] The ideological cul-de-sac in which Labour found itself helps to explain the passivity with which it fought and lost the 1951 election.

[96] For the details of this, see Pelling, *The Labour Governments*, 242–59.

[97] Out of office and fearing a German revival, he said: 'Free economy Germany will be forging ahead; with their gifts of efficiency displayed to the full. And we, in our mismanaged mixed economy overpopulated little island, shall become a second-rate power, with no influence and continuing "crisis"' (quoted in Pimlott, *Hugh Dalton*, 611).

That was the party of 1931 rather than the party which seized its moment in 1940. Nor did anyone conclude that the electoral system which had given the Conservatives largely an unearned victory was in any way defective. Furthermore, the abandonment of office in 1951 meant that the Party could never exploit the comparative prosperity of the 1950s which might have provided it with a way out of its cul-de-sac.

The Conservatives had fewer problems. They had a view of England which was ideological and social elites and institutions to protect; but they were not committed to any particular way of doing this. And since what they regarded as fundamental was simply assumed, they did not need to define or find legitimating ideologies, as Labour did. They merely adopted the popular bits of Labour's programme and abandoned the rest. Nor was Churchill now the man to take on the labour movement or risk alienating his own working-class vote, as the appointments of the emollient R. A. Butler as chancellor and the equally emollient Walter Monckton as minister of labour made plain. Given the unspoken nature of their ideological assumptions and the role of the state in supporting such assumptions,[98] to the Conservatives the attaining and holding of office was what mattered. In 1951 the Labour leadership mistakenly took the opposite view.

[98] For them see below, 194–8.

6

England: Social Change, Historical Accident, and Democracy

In this chapter I would like to bring together the argument, and particularly its three principal themes, all interrelated: the relationship between structure and contingency, that is, the extent to which party politics was determined by fundamental social changes on the one hand, and by contingency, historical accident, on the other; the sociology of the English electorate—why people voted as they did; and the relationship between these two and the kind of democracy which had emerged in England by 1951.

In any explanation of the evolution of political culture the historian is faced with the old problem of the autonomy of ideological allegiances and constructs. Do ideologies emerge functionally from social structures or do they have their own life? How far do political ideas and behaviour exist independently of the world in which men live and have their being? In this case the question revolves around the two pivotal dates in our period, 1931 and 1940. The first finally established the electoral hegemony of the Conservatives after the false starts of the 1920s; the second unexpectedly ended it. These are actually difficult questions to answer. We can argue that the politics of these years followed their own logic, largely divorced from society except when economics (like the 1931 crisis) or external events (like the fall of the Chamberlain government) intervened. Or that even then a kind of autonomous political narrative determined how men and women reacted to such interventions.

The years 1931 and 1940, however, demand different kinds of explanations. There was certainly a political crisis in 1931, which had its own logic, but which ended forms of politics whose foundations were very much in society. Although the Conservatives and their allies did not plan what happened in 1931 the Conservatism which emerged in the 1930s was closely tied to the social evolution of the English middle classes.[1] Throughout much of the 1920s the English middle class was recognizably Edwardian. At the top it was led by the old free professions: law, medicine, the church, the military, the senior civil service, the colonial and Indian civil services, and the self-employed practitioners of the traditional technical professions like architecture. It was their members who set the tone, more even than the business–financial middle class. On occasion, they also spoke for the large clerical–commercial lower-middle class characteristic of Edwardian England. It was they who suffered most from that re-ordering of wealth which occurred during and after the First World War and who most resented the apparently undeserved good fortune of the profiteers and the seemingly truculent and selfish behaviour of the trade unions. They were still well represented in the upper echelons of the local Conservative associations and it was they who were most opposed to the continuation of Lloyd George's coalition. The particular nature of post-war anti-socialism was also shaped by them, as was the rather apocalyptic view of socialism as a species of Bolshevism and a threat not only to them but to civilization as such.

From the late 1920s onwards, however, the structure of the middle class altered. Not only did it grow at an accelerating rate but its composition changed. It became more technical, scientific, and commercial. The occupations that grew fastest were scientific–technical–commercial; something true at all levels of the middle class. There was, furthermore, a steady growth in the 'public' middle class—teachers, librarians, technicians, and what were increasingly called social workers. The older free professions either stagnated in numbers or grew only slowly. The number of middle-class self-employed also fell rapidly. Increasingly lawyers and architects, for example, worked for others. The Conservative Party successfully

---

[1] I have argued this in more detail in *Classes and Cultures*, 46–9.

rearranged itself around this expanded middle class and its society; or at least made itself acceptable to them. It rebalanced itself, so to speak, from the old middle class (if we can call it that) towards this newer, larger, more diverse middle class. It was Stanley Baldwin's achievement to guide and personify this change: that is his significance as Conservative leader. The change in the social composition of the middle class and the manner by which the Conservatives adjusted to it had a marked effect on the political tone of the 1930s. The extreme class tension of the 1920s was absent; social relationships were more relaxed and the Conservative Party was less inclined to mobilize its vote via overt anti-socialism and anti-trade unionism. Both were still there, of course, but socialism increasingly became identified with incompetence rather than malice. What socialists wanted might even be deemed worthy, simply impossible. An obvious reason for this relaxation is that Labour's defeat in 1931 was so overwhelming and the trade unions so weakened by depression that socialism seemed that much less threatening. Another, though more doubtful, is that as members of the middle class themselves became employees they became less ready to identify automatically with the interests of employers.

It would be imprudent to argue that the 1931 crisis was responsible for all this: social change does not come so fast and usually has more complicated origins. But it made possible the political and ideological regrouping that shaped politics in the 1930s. I suggested in an earlier chapter that by 1939 Conservative political predominance seemed unchallengeable; that, unlike the 1920s, the party system was now stable and anything but provisional. I also argued that there were three more 'logical' ways of organizing politics than the 1920s managed to do. After 1931 those three ways were all adopted. Fusion between Conservatives and Liberals occurred *de facto* under the umbrella of the National government and largely on terms set by the Conservatives. Although an unattached Liberal Party just survived it was only a shadow of the party of 1914. In practice, there was now only one anti-Labour Party. Free trade was abandoned in 1931–2 as were the monetary policies of the 1920s, to the benefit of business and some of the unemployed. Finally, while the National government was not really a 'producers'' government, it was not a rentiers' government either. The adoption of protection and the limiting of capital exports weakened the City of London and the international money market, while debt conversion—the lowering of interest rates charged to the national debt—the neglect of the sinking fund and a policy of 'cheap money' (keeping bank rate at 2%), which reversed the 1920s policy of keeping bank rate high to protect London's international position, all worked against the interests of the rentier.

There was no doubt a contingent event in 1931, but it both accelerated and symbolized structural change. That is not true of 1940—the second pivotal date of our period. The political revolution of that year had no social-evolutionary origins, nor did Labour's victory in the 1945 election. England's social structure no more favoured Labour in 1945 than it did in 1939; and favoured it less than 1918. If an external agency mattered it was not social change but the state. The rapid growth of its activity during the war both legitimated a 'Labour' view of how society should be organized and tended to bring within a 'Labour' political culture many working men and women, especially within the skilled working class, hitherto outside it. But 1940 was pivotal because in that year many people simply changed their minds as to how the world should be run and who should run it. They did so because the premises upon which they based their political judgements were suddenly falsified, or appeared to be falsified, by the events of May 1940: the fall of Chamberlain and the rise of Churchill, whose rise also meant the rise of Labour.

The politics of the late 1940s and the return to office of the Conservatives in 1951 equally had little to do with social-structural change. The middle class continued to grow at the expense of the working class, but much of that growth occurred within the 'public' middle class, many of whose members were sympathetic to Labour. Furthermore the manual working class still constituted about two-thirds of the working population. Labour's problem was that the number of sympathetic middle-class voters was significantly smaller than the number of working men and women sympathetic to the Conservatives. Nonetheless, most of the gains made by Labour in 1945 were permanent. The movement against Labour in 1950 and 1951 was comparatively small, and it is possible, as I have argued,[2] to exaggerate the extent to which the Conservative recovery was a result of the mobilization of a new anti-socialist majority based upon the voter as consumer. Anti-socialism was, of course, still a weapon in the armoury of the Conservatives. Socialism stood, as it always had, for red tape, vengeful taxation, unwanted extensions of public ownership and fanciful, if virtuous, hopes, and in the context of the cold war it could be associated with an increasingly unpopular Soviet Union. But socialism was now officially understood to exclude from its scope working men and the trade unions as such: an extension, in fact, of Baldwin's policy in the 1930s. This narrower definition was a recognition of the new power of the Labour-voting working class. Those parts of the welfare state understood to have widespread support, like the NHS, were not defined as socialism, but red tape and high taxes were. This was an ecumenical anti-socialism with which few voters, even Labour ones, could in practice disagree.

Much of what I have described in this book was the result of movements deeply grounded in English society and social experience: the assumption, ever more widely held, that politics was about class and that class relationships were usually antagonistic; the tendency for the social organizations which underlay politics to become bound by class; the increasing secularization of politics (in the sense in which I have used the word secularization); the developing power and range of the state, even if such development was irregular and controversial. All these pointed to the emergence of a politics based largely on two parties, Labour and Conservative, which represented the two most important classes—middle and working, broadly defined.

But the historical evolution of this political system was not inevitable. As a political model it was never flawless. Many, even if they thought of themselves as middle or working class, did not believe

[2] See above, 171–4.

that their class position should decide their political allegiance, and so deviated from a presumed norm. Furthermore, the two-party system which had emerged by 1951 was as almost as much the result of contingency as inevitability. Although the Liberal Party's supports were creaking in 1914 it still required an unprecedented event, the First World War, to bring them down. And even then some still stood. Equally, in 1939 the Conservative Party's political predominance was unthreatened and it took the exceptional political–military crisis of 1940 to overturn it. The Second World War actualized something that was always possible—a politics primarily determined by class—but never more than always possible. These historical accidents also helped shape the kind of democracy England was to be. Had the Liberal Party survived as one of the major parties of the state we can envisage a democracy rather different from that which was in place by 1951; one less attached to the English state and its values. Had the Conservative Party's hegemony not been overthrown in 1940 then a quasi-American individualist democracy could eventually have been enthroned based upon a middle-class associationalism much of which had American origins.[3] Neither happened. The Liberal Party did not survive as one of the major parties of the state and the Conservative hegemony was overturned.

Why did people vote the way they did and why did so many deviate from a presumed norm? The electors of England in these years did not vote randomly nor were their political allegiances unchanging, but they were influenced by a number of sometimes incompatible forces. Of these, the most important was social class, but for the years before 1940 it was, despite its significance, a weak determinant which became weaker as we descend the social scale. Much the largest element in the English electorate was the manual working class; throughout this period about 70 per cent of the total. Until the Second World War, however, its vote was fundamentally divided. In 1918 the majority of working-class electors who did vote opted for the Lloyd George government, which meant Conservative

---

[3] I have discussed this in more detail in *Classes and Cultures*, 96.

or Coalition Liberal. In the election of 1922 a higher proportion, though still a minority, voted Labour. In 1924 that minority rose a little, partly because much of the old Liberal working-class vote went Labour. Thereafter, with the exception of the 1931 election, when the clear majority supported the National government, almost half the working class voted Labour. The other half increasingly voted Conservative. Taking the interwar years as a whole we are justified in concluding that the majority of working men and women did not vote Labour, and although we would expect on sociological grounds each cohort of new voters to vote Labour disproportionately, at some point in the 1930s they appear to have stopped doing so. From 1945 onwards, however, the majority of the working class did vote Labour; and it is from then that observers assumed class was the main reason why people voted as they did.

The working-class vote, somewhat waywardly, and with major deviations in 1931, when it lurched right, and 1945, when it lurched left, thus moved semi-continuously to Labour. The majority of the middle-class vote was always anti-Labour, even though a significant proportion voted Labour in the 1940s. Only among the elite of the upper middle class was support for Labour negligible. But although always anti-Labour it was not unanimously pro-Conservative. In the 1920s, particularly, it strayed. In 1923 much of the northern middle class voted Liberal, and in 1929 much of the rural community and the provincial middle class. Only after 1931 did the great majority of the middle class consistently vote Conservative, and only after then that most of the countryside became unhesitatingly Tory.

Why did people vote either Labour or Conservative in such increasing numbers? If asked, people rarely said it was self-interest.[4] Nor did they have an overtly punitive view of politics: they believed, no doubt with some deliberate self-deception, that their party served the best interests of everyone. Middle-class Tory voters voted Conservative (they said) because the Conservative Party stood for education, competence, respectability, fairness, good humour, free

---

[4] Benney et al., *How People Vote*, 122.

enterprise and (unlike Labour) did not politicize everything. Conservative politics was apolitical politics. But their Conservatism was not always uncritical. When observers began to undertake serious surveys of political attitudes in the 1940s they were surprised at the extent to which 'ordinary' middle-class Conservatives thought the Conservative Party in practice the party of the rich, the 'upper class', and not necessarily of them.[5] Sometimes, as in the early 1920s, these views got the Conservatives into trouble. Nonetheless, it was thought the party most likely to defend the middle class from socialism, however socialism was defined, though hostility to socialism was often expressed in 'neutral' (for instance constitutional) terms.

The typical Labour voter was usually not driven by strong passions, nor by any marked dislike of the Conservative Party, nor, for the most part, by any serious objection to the overall structure of English society. Nor was he or she interested in Labour's ideological debates. But, however much they thought Labour stood for everyone, Labour voters had a generally conflictual view of society and were more open about admitting it—though Labour's women voters held such a view less strongly and less publicly. Labour voters, even those who thought Labour could govern in everyone's interest, doubted whether that was possible in practice. They tended to assume that one man's gain was another man's loss—usually their loss.[6] Trade unions, however moderate, could not but help encourage this view, which was implicit in the business of collective bargaining and was why members of trade unions, whatever their occupation, were readier to vote Labour than anyone else. Trade unions, however, were more likely to recruit in places where conflict was sociologically inherent—large factories, for example, with complicated managerial structures. How far the unions encouraged conflictual views is, therefore, a more open question. Many of their members held such views before they joined a union, which is probably one reason why they became trade unionists. After 1945, as we have seen, there was a strong feeling among Labour voters, both men and women, that

---

[5] Benney et al., *How People Vote*, 122.   [6] See above, 103–4.

Labour was 'their' party, and full employment and the NHS were often cited as proof of that.[7] But it was a reputation hard-earned.

The extent to which class had become the dominant variable can be measured by comparing the political behaviour of England and Scotland in this period. In the Edwardian years England and Scotland moved in opposite directions. In 1910 the Conservatives recovered strongly from their defeat in 1906 in England, but made no net gains at all in Scotland. After 1918, however, England and Scotland nearly always moved in tandem; the Conservatives always doing better in England than in Scotland but not significantly so. Between 1945 and 1959 England and Scotland voted exactly the same way. In 1955, *mirabile dictu*, the Tories got over 50 per cent of the votes cast in Scotland—the same proportion (50.3 per cent) as in England. In a modified way the same is true of Wales. At no point in this period did the Conservatives and their allies win a majority of the Welsh seats; but they polled much more strongly than before 1914. Between 1931 and 1945, for instance, they won all three Cardiff seats.

Any political generalization about England as a whole in these years is likely, therefore, to be true of Scotland. And vice versa, because as a determining variable class had become more important than nationality or religion and acted to suppress the political manifestations of religion, nationality or even region. The 1931 crisis thus had the same effect in Scotland as in England and the flight of so much Scottish Liberalism into the Tory camp hastened the process by which Scottish politics became assimilated to English politics. That both class-parties, Conservative and Labour, were strongly unionist was to some extent accidental but the significance of class was to encourage a uniformity of political allegiance and a unionist sentiment unusual in the modern history of the United Kingdom.

Yet even if class-based voting increasingly became the norm there were many in this period who departed from it. There were

---

7 See above, 174.

those who voted against their apparent class interest. Of them, the most numerous were working-class Tories: in 1950 the largest single voting bloc in the Conservative family. When asked why they voted Tory they gave answers similar to those of middle-class Conservatives: the Conservatives were better educated[8] and so more fitted to govern. Working-class Tories also respected wealth, the possession of which was, like education, thought a sign of fitness to govern. They were less likely to belong to trade unions, who were held to cause needless conflict, and less likely to work in places where unions might be found. Working-class Tories were also suspicious of politically ambitious working-class men and women. The politically ambitious were thought to be merely out for themselves. To this degree working-class Tories tended to defer to local social elites. Working-class Conservatism was thus very much a product of environment. There is a clear relationship between Conservative-voting and social heterogeneity. The more middle class a constituency the more working men and women voted Conservative; and it did not require much of a middle class to do this. Mining constituencies in Durham and Yorkshire or seats in the East End of London became so strongly Labour partly because they were overwhelmingly working-class communities with little intermediating middle class.

There were, of course, those who went the other way. Labour, as we have seen, always had significant middle-class support.[9] In 1945 almost 30 per cent of those in middle-class occupations voted Labour; about the same proportion of working men and women that voted Conservative. Even in 1950 perhaps a quarter of 'lower professionals' and one third of those in 'lower white-collar' occupations voted Labour.[10] About the Labour-voting middle classes we can probably make two generalizations. The first is that many were employed by local or national government: in other words, though their work

---

[8] Though this could work against the Conservatives. The late Henry Pelling told me that when he asked his army driver in 1945 how he was going to vote, he replied he would vote Labour because Mr Attlee was a much more educated man. He had discovered from the *Daily Mirror* that Attlee had been to Oxford but Churchill had not been to university at all.

[9] See above, 141–2.   [10] Bonham, *Middle Class Vote*, 129.

might not have differed much from those in the private sector, their employer was the state and they had, therefore, an interest in its expansion, and an attachment to Labour as the party of the state. Employees of the state, furthermore, were more likely to belong to trade unions than those in the private sector and so readier to vote Labour for that reason. The second is that white-collar Labour voters were in notoriously discontented and marginal occupations. The two-thirds of employees in what contemporaries called 'black-coated' occupations who voted Conservative were among those most hostile to the Labour Party, while their colleagues who voted Labour were among those most fed up with their jobs and its routines, and most alienated from dominant social values.[11] We must remember, however, that Labour's middle-class vote never approximated the Conservatives' working-class vote. In 1950 about two million members of the middle class voted Labour; but about 6.5 million members of the working class voted Tory. In the history of England's modern political parties that difference is crucial.

There were also marked gender-deviations from the presumed norm. A striking characteristic of English electoral patterns in the last twenty years has been the tendency for gender-based differences in voting behaviour to weaken or disappear. Broadly speaking, since the late 1980s men and women have voted very much the same way: if anything, women have been more inclined to vote Labour than men. This is a result of profound social changes not confined to England and a real departure from the way the sexes voted in our period. Between 1918 and 1951 women in all social classes were more likely to vote Conservative than men. Even in 1945 the differences could be surprisingly wide. Whereas about 65 per cent of working-class men voted Labour only about 53 per cent of working-class women did so. This tendency could produce amazing Conservative majorities. In 1931, admittedly an extreme case, between 70 per cent and 75 per cent of women electors must have voted for the Conservatives

---

[11] I have discussed this elsewhere. McKibbin, *The Ideologies of Class*, 149–59.

and their allies.[12] In the third chapter I suggested various reasons for
this: that women tended to acquire political knowledge at second
hand and so were less familiar with political change; that the Labour
Party's politics, despite the degree to which it tried to make itself
acceptable to women, was too 'masculine', too tied to the trade
unions and social conflict; that the Conservative 'programme', such
as it was, seemed closer to life as it was lived.

Why middle-class women voted Conservative is fairly self-evident.
But why working-class women voted Labour *at all*—and the majority did in 1945 and probably in 1950—is not. That Labour
was the party of the NHS and full employment is almost certainly
one explanation. Nella Last, as we have seen, hoped that women
would support the Beveridge Report since it was they who had to
bear the burden of unemployment and poverty.[13] The expansion of
the welfare state during and after the war—particularly in its role
as a family supporting institution—probably led many women to
support the Labour Party as the party of the welfare state. But this
is very much a product of the later twentieth century. Before 1939
the welfare state was too narrow in scope to command that kind of
loyalty, and Labour's self-description as the women's party was never
convincing, especially after its failures in office before the war.

Yet women's 'class experience' (in the widest sense) was broadly
similar to that of men and we would expect many of them to
respond in the same way. Family dynamics also played a part. Where
men and women openly shared a political culture they were likely
to vote the same way—not necessarily Labour, but more often
Labour. In homes where politics was simply never discussed that
was less likely. Furthermore, though it is often rightly argued that

---

[12] This is to some extent guesswork and is based upon an extrapolation from what we
know of post-1945 voting patterns. In 1931 the National Government got 69 per cent
of the votes in England. If we assume that there was, as after the Second World War,
a clear tendency for women to vote Tory in higher numbers than men, then a figure
of 70–75 per cent seems reasonable. Some of these women, of course, reverted to the
independent Liberals in 1935. Others returned to the Labour Party.

[13] Nella Last, of course, remained a Tory after 1945, but a less full-blooded one than
before the war. See above, 171.

women in work—especially young women before marriage—had different workplace politics from men, we should not exaggerate the difference. In certain circumstances, particularly where women were working full-time and expected to continue working full-time, women's attitudes did not in practice differ much from men's; another way in which their class experience was broadly similar.[14]

These two deviations from presumed norms account in large part for the Conservative Party's relative electoral success in this period. Which deviation—the disproportionately large number of working-class men and women who voted Tory or the disproportionately large number of women of all classes who voted Tory—was the more significant is rather a toss-up. Both in fact are 'true'; but the first, since it is the more comprehensive explanation, is 'truer'.

Such norms were also undermined by religious or national-ethnic allegiance. These were almost the last years in English history when the vast majority of the English were by colour homogenous. But they were not by religion or ethnicity homogenous; and that heterogeneity was a major, though declining, determinant of political affiliation. Throughout these years there was an obvious relationship between active Anglicanism and Conservative-voting. There was also, however, a (weakening) relationship between nonconformity and Liberal-voting, and a very weak one between nonconformity and Labour-voting. This was more divisive on the whole within the middle classes since they were more likely to be actively religious. As I have suggested, this division tended to heal as the nonconformist middle class was absorbed into the Conservative family.[15] There was, however, a sectarian religious division, a product of ethnicity as much as religion, which mostly benefited the Tories. The most obvious is 'Protestant' hostility to Irish Catholics, to be found wherever there were Irish Catholics but notoriously on Merseyside. The Conservative Party in Liverpool was a genuinely working-class institution and Liverpool was probably the only part of the

[14] I have discussed this elsewhere (*Classes and Cultures*, 135–7) and above, 99–100.
[15] See above, 91–4.

country where it was. Its sectarianism was unconcealed, though the Conservative leadership in London was adept at looking the other way, and it turned Liverpool into a Conservative city for most of this period. Although Labour did win a majority of Liverpool's seats in 1945 (the only time), in 1950 Liverpool was the one city in England where the Conservatives won a majority of the parliamentary seats. The political effects of such sectarianism lasted until the 1960s, when Labour finally came into its own, a result partly of social and cultural change and partly of rehousing, which broke up the religious–ethnic ghettos. At the turn of the twenty-first century it was (at least in parliament) the most proletarian and 'Labour' city in the country. The Liverpool Conservative Party no longer exists.

Hostility to the Irish was a complicated phenomenon. It was religious, ethnic-national and economic. Calculating the relative importance of each is very difficult and probably not worth trying. On the other hand, though this represented a loss to Labour it was only a net loss. The Irish-Catholic vote increased steadily throughout the period and was strongly Labour.[16] It was Labour because most Irish voters were working class and often very working class, and because both their religion and nationality alienated them more than anyone else from the country's dominant institutions and values. Labour's working classness, its growing detachment from the Protestant religions, and its long history of supporting Home Rule made it the obvious political home for the English Irish.

Before 1914 hostility to 'aliens', that is to Jewish immigrants, especially in the East End of London, also, it has been argued, benefited the Conservatives.[17] More recently, however, this view has been disputed. Brodie has suggested that anti-alienism did not significantly benefit the Tories despite the fact that the leading East End 'anti-alien', Major Evans-Gordon, was Conservative MP for Stepney. He points out that much of the more established Jewish

---

[16] In Liverpool this guaranteed Labour at least one seat. Labour inherited Liverpool Scotland from the Irish Nationalists in 1929 and thereafter never lost it. The Conservatives did not bother to contest it even in 1931.

[17] Particularly by Henry Pelling, See *Social Geography of British Elections*, 42–7.

community supported the Conservatives and that, anyway, the highly diverse microcultures of the East End make generalizations difficult.[18] Much of his evidence supports this conclusion. It is possible, of course, as he notes, that the Tories had it both ways: the support of the established Jewish community and the support of non-Jewish indigenes who were hostile to the Jewish migration of the late nineteenth and early twentieth century. That would be analogous to the Conservatives' attitude to Roman Catholicism: it was the Party of an often reactionary recusant Catholicism as well as the party of working-class anti-Catholicism. Given that the Tory Party rarely missed an opportunity to stir xenophobic pots I incline to that view. Even if 'anti-alienism' yielded the Conservatives fewer votes than was once believed, it was not for want of their trying.

After 1918, however, and especially after 1922, whatever was the case before the war, anti-alienism rapidly ceased to earn the Tories electoral dividends. That was due largely to the huge increase in enfranchisement in the East End (many of the new voters being 'non-established' Jews who had been off the electoral registers before 1914), which clearly favoured Labour. Social anti-semitism did not disappear from English life—on the contrary, it was pervasive—but electorally it largely lost whatever salience it had. Indeed for Labour the enfranchisement of so many Jewish voters in 1918 probably represented a net gain—they outnumbered the die-hard political anti-semites. To the extent, however, that there was a Jewish voting bloc, it fragmented after the Second World War as class allegiance began to override religion and ethnicity.[19]

How far the electorate was moved to vote one way or the other by individual policies, by the 'issues', is a difficult question to answer. The evidence is mixed. After 1931 protection was probably popular in parts of the country, though how many actually voted for it

---

[18] M. Brodie, *The Politics of the Poor: The East End of London, 1885–1914* (Oxford, 2004), *passim* and 185–93 especially. See also the treatment of this question in D. Feldman, *Englishmen and Jews: Social Relations and Political Culture, 1840–1941* (London and New Haven, 1994).

[19] G. Alderman, *Modern British Jewry* (Oxford, 1992), 335–45.

in 1931—since it technically was not the National government's official policy—is hard to say. (That the Conservatives would introduce it in some form, however, was an open secret.) 'Beveridge' was clearly popular in 1945 and many voted for it. But only a few were persuaded by the Report to vote Labour. The decisive shift in opinion had already taken place. What Beveridge did was to give opinion something around which to organize and a new political mood coherence and detail. In 1950 'full employment' and 'nationalization' were clearly issues and both mattered to the voters, but as issues they usually tended to reinforce existing allegiances rather than encourage conversion.[20]

Foreign policy was always in my view electorally marginal, though foreign policy questions were not absent. In 1918 many politicians certainly hoped that hostility to Germany would bring them votes, and Lloyd George's policy towards Turkey—the 'Chanak crisis'—played its part in his government's fall in 1922, if not necessarily in the subsequent election. In 1924 the Labour government's policies towards Russia were thought by the Conservatives to be electorally unpopular and 'anti-Bolshevism' surely contributed to the size of the Conservative victory. The timing of the 1935 election was influenced by the Abyssinian crisis and all parties, not least the Tories, thought that supporting the League of Nations, or to be seen to do so, was politically advisable.[21] The mid-1930s also represented the high-point of the League of Nations Union, an organization which had much in common with traditional Liberalism, had a very large membership and formidable mobilizing powers, and which neither the national Conservative Party nor local Conservative Associations were anxious to alienate.[22] It is possible that Tory losses in the 1935 election would have been greater had Baldwin not placated

---

[20] Milne and Mackenzie, *Straight Fight*, 132.

[21] For the 1935 election see T. Stannage, *Baldwin Thwarts the Opposition: The British General Election of 1935* (Oxford, 1980).

[22] For the League of Nations Union, see M. Ceadel, *Semi-Detached Idealists: The British Peace Movement and International Relations, 1854–1945* (Oxford, 2000), chs. 8–10. For an example of the strength of the League's political and organizational authority, the 'Peace Ballot', see Ceadel, 'The First British Referendum: The Peace Ballot, 1934–5', *English Historical Review* 95 (1980), 810–39.

them. How much greater we don't know. On the other hand, had Hitler delayed his war for a year, foreign policy could hardly fail to have been a significant issue, possibly *the* issue, in the 1940 election. But Hitler didn't and that election, of course, was never held.

As to the comparative importance or unimportance of individual issues the best evidence we have is probably the opinion polls of the late 1930s—to which I have referred—when policies associated with the Labour Party were shown to be popular, but few of those who did not already vote Labour were ready to change their vote in order to attain them. What primarily determined political allegiance was ideological–sociological identification: a sense among voters that their party stood for the world as they understood it and wished it to be. Usually these identifications are very durable and require exceptional disruptions to expunge them. Such a disruption occurred, in my view, in 1940.

In these years England and the other nations of the Union experienced an unprecedented economic depression and went to war twice. Britain alone of the major powers fought in both world wars from beginning to end and per capita spent more on both than anyone. Yet at the end of these sometimes heroic forty years, which destroyed the political structures of much of the rest of the world, England was recognizably the same country. Its political and ideological institutions had scarcely changed, and its social hierarchies were largely intact. The way people looked at the world had changed, but not as much as it might have. At the same time, however, the party system was very different. The Liberal Party, in office in 1914, had only a shadowy existence in 1951. The scope of the state had been greatly extended as had the size of the active electorate; and all without violence. This apparently harmonious marriage of stability and democracy gave birth to a good deal of self-satisfaction. In a famous article in the *Sociological Review* (1953) the sociologists Edward Shils and Michael Young wrote of popular behaviour at the time of the present Queen's coronation:

Over the past century, British society, despite distinctions of nationality and social status, has attained a degree of moral unity equalled by no other large national state. The assimilation of the working class into the moral consensus of British society, though certainly far from complete, has gone further in Great Britain than anywhere else, and its transformation from one of the most unruly and violent into one of the most orderly and law-abiding [nations] is one of the great collective achievements of modern times.[23]

To anyone observing the post-1945 wreckage of those European states brought to ruin largely because they could not assimilate their working class into a moral consensus that must indeed have seemed a great collective achievement. But on whose terms was this moral consensus established?

There were four reasons for the stability of the British political system in our period. The first was its possession of a high degree of legitimacy *before* the First World War, unlike, for example, even relatively stable states like France, Germany, or Italy, where there were always some either hostile to their regimes or who felt excluded by them. In 1914, with the important exception of many Irish, rightly or wrongly few in Britain were hostile to or felt excluded by its political arrangements. The second is that Britain was victorious in the First World War. That war was won at a shocking human and physical cost, and a significant weakening of Britain's international standing (though also, paradoxically, there was an increase in her imperial and quasi-imperial obligations), but it was won and the legitimacy of Britain's political and social system confirmed. The third was that throughout the interwar years the middle classes were always on the winning side, and, though not exactly on the winning side in 1945, they were not exactly on the losing side either. The final reason is that in Britain (and especially in England) a large proportion of the industrial working class supported a party of the right—as they had in 1914—and in hardly any other country was this so. Even in 1945, as we have seen, about one-third of the working class voted Conservative, which is why the middle class was usually

---

[23] E. Shils and M. Young, 'The Meaning of the Coronation', *Sociological Review* 1 (1953).

on the winning side and why it was never radicalized as much of the continental middle class was. In the political history of England in this period the survival of the Conservative Party intact is the crucial datum: in 1914 it was the largest political party in England, as it was in 1951, despite war, depression and that huge expansion of the electorate. And it was led by a man, Churchill, who had first stood as a Conservative candidate in 1899, fifty-two years before, and who was first elected as a Conservative MP fifty-one years before. Stability and legitimacy combined to preserve almost untouched England's political system and its ideological supports. They also emerged unscathed from the Second World War and the Attlee government, both of which might have overturned them. Their preservation in turn supported stability and legitimacy in a kind of circular process. What developed was a political–constitutional system whose largely unwritten conventions were observed by most people even though they favoured some much more than others.

After the First World War people increasingly spoke of England as a democracy, something many would not have done before 1914. They did so largely on the strength of the franchise legislation of 1918 and 1928—a tacit recognition of how limited the Edwardian franchises were. The Conservatives, despite the fact that it had done them no harm, were nervous of democracy and thought it had to prove itself. Labour was officially optimistic, and had to be, but privately had real doubts. As to how far England had 'democratized' between the wars, the evidence differs. In part, of course, the answer depends upon what criteria we choose. The outward and ceremonial forms of the English state were still semi-feudal; a social hierarchy which preserved most types of cultural privilege stood firm, and, as a result, the majority of the population never had anything like equal claims on society. Large numbers of people, furthermore, freely abdicated any active political role or judgement in favour of elites who were still largely Edwardian. The country's principal political institutions were entirely unreformed. On the other hand, the franchise, though not unblemished, was by 1928 effectively universal and, partly in consequence, the acknowledged social rights

of the working class were widened. Income distribution was less
extreme than before 1914 and the well-to-do undoubtedly paid
more tax. There was some democratization of social attitudes. A
good instance of this can be found in a comparison of Seebohm
Rowntree's 'poverty line' of 1901 with his 'poverty line' of the
1930s.[24] In constructing a poverty line Rowntree attempted to find
a wage-level below which people, no matter how provident they
were, could not live anything like a civilized life. The 1901 poverty
line was a simple subsistence one; in fact drawn so narrowly as to
be actually unhelpful for social policy. The 1930s line, however,
was more generous: a recognition that there was now more to life
than just food and rent, and that surely represented some kind of
democratization. As did the fact that the second study had much
more on styles of life—for example, leisure activities—than the
first.[25] The conclusion we draw in face of this evidence, therefore,
is fine. Nevertheless, on balance, I think the hope many expressed
at the end of the First World War that a democratic society based
upon democratic political institutions would evolve in England was
not fulfilled.

The Second World War, both in practice and potential, unquestionably encouraged renewed expectations of such a society. It
resulted in what I have called elsewhere a redistribution of social

[24] For his 'poverty lines' see B. S. Rowntree, *Poverty: A Study of Town Life* (London,
1901), 85–115; Rowntree, *Poverty and Progress: A Second Social Survey of York* (London,
1941), 11–33. The difference was the inclusion in the 1936 minimum of 'personal
sundries' which were rigorously excluded in 1901.

[25] Rowntree had already devised a significantly more generous definition of a
working-class standard of life in the first edition of *The Human Needs of Labour*
(London, 1918) and defined it even more generously in the second edition (1937).
In 1918, for instance, he concluded that a minimum requirement for a working-
class family was a three-bedroom house with a 'scullery-kitchen preferably with a
bath in it' (*Human Needs of Labour*, 126). In 1937 he thought a scullery-kitchen
'and a bathroom' was the minimum (1937 edn, 115). The extent to which he had
moved beyond a narrowly constructed poverty line can be seen in his comments on
the necessary elements of a single woman's wage: 'A girl's prospects for making a
satisfactory match depend to a considerable extent upon her ability to dress attractively.
She needs not only respectable clothes but clothes for evenings and Sundays.' (This
sentence in both editions.) We might also note that both editions are prefaced by
a quotation from Mr Justice Higgins—he of the famous Harvester Judgment. See
above, 19.

esteem.[26] That of coalminers and bank clerks was thought by contemporaries to be the benchmark here: after 1940 the one up and
the other down. The war, as we have seen, released grievances people
often did not know they had. Many of the old elites also thought
the game was up and did so from the moment Churchill's coalition
was formed. Shortly after that government was formed, Lord Salisbury, on being asked by Harold Nicolson at a casual meeting what
he was doing, replied that he was trying to save the Conservative
Party.[27] In 1942, as we have noted in the second chapter, Churchill
and Butler were almost resigned to the extinction of the public
schools, something inconceivable three years before. Furthermore,
the 1945 election result was undoubtedly a consequence of the
radicalization of opinion: to deny that is to ignore the reality of
the war.

The question is: could that 'reality' have been preserved after
1945? We can argue that such reality is easily exaggerated: the
Labour victory in 1945 was not, after all, as decisive as it appeared
on first sight. Equally, some historians have argued that preservation
was unlikely simply because the mood of the war was passing,
dependent on unique and so unrepeatable events.[28] Indeed, that in
failing to recognize this, they would argue, the Labour government
got itself into serious difficulties. It is, however, equally easy to
exaggerate the electoral decline of the Labour Party in 1950 and
to make too much of the singularity of wartime experience. Many
of the war's effects did, after all, turn out to be permanent. There
was an autonomous and lasting, if incomplete, democratization of
life, one of whose beneficiaries was the Labour Party itself. That
some at least of the radicalism of the war was dissipated under
the Attlee government, partly because of circumstance (more or
less permanent economic crisis), but partly by choice seems in fact

---

[26] McKibbin, *Ideologies of Class*, 291.

[27] 'Yesterday in the Ministry [of Information] I observed Lord Salisbury in a top hat
and frock-coat coming down the stairs. I said, "What are you doing here?" "Trying to
save the Conservative Party." ' (Nicolson, *Diaries, 1939–1945*, 94, 6 June 1940.)

[28] Jackson, *Equality and the British Left*, 237.

undeniable. The Attlee government left in place political and social institutions which systematically worked against the Labour Party at the one moment they might have been reformed. The result was that Labour's crucial post-war electoral base, though much larger than in 1939, was not a broad-based democracy but one over-reliant on trade union membership, 'heavy' manufacture and mining, and council housing, a base which, with the exception of council housing, was shrinking even in the 1940s. This also had indirect consequences for the Conservative Party. Throughout this period whatever political strategies the Conservatives adopted were a response to the Labour Party. Even when it was at its weakest Labour's mere existence shaped the Conservative Party's behaviour. Once the Conservatives had made the necessary adjustments to 1945, however, the narrowness of Labour's policies meant that they were under little pressure to further democratize the Party. As a result, as I have argued, the Conservative Party was hardly any more open than it was in the 1930s. Fundamentally, the Conservative and Labour Parties agreed on the political, ceremonial, and emotional forms of the English state: even the Conservative argument that it was the party of local democracy and Labour the party of the bureaucratic state was largely rhetorical—as Poplar's Poor Law guardians had reason to know.[29] In the first chapter I suggested that the decline of the Liberals vitiated England's political culture. The Liberals, as the party of nonconformity and Celtic Britain, to some extent stood outside the hierarchies of the English state and eyed them in a rather jaundiced way. This was much less true of Labour. The Conservatives and Labour disagreed about the economic function of the state, not about the state and its institutions as such. The Labour Party's definition of the state was largely Tory, a paradoxical result of Labour's increasing detachment from Liberalism and political

[29] 'Poplarism' was the name given to attempts by boards of guardians to give more generous scales of relief than their rate returns permitted. The new scales were paid from borrowing and were first practised by the Poplar guardians. In 1926, Baldwin's government took powers to remove such guardians and replace them with others appointed by the ministry of health.

nonconformity; a result also of its socialism, a doctrine which drew a clear distinction between 'capitalism' and 'society'. It was thought possible to reform one without the other; as it was thought possible to create a democratic state by redistributing wealth but not social or political authority.

Two possible forms of democracy might have developed in England in this period, though neither did.[30] The first was an individualist, rather Americanized democracy based upon the rapidly growing social organizations of the English middle class, many of which, as I have suggested, were, like Rotary, American in origin or spirit. They laid the ground for a new kind of social relationship which could have disrupted existing hierarchies and political structures. How far this might have happened but for the Second World War is hard to say. But it did not happen. The effects of the war and its unexpected political outcome turned the middle classes inwards, made them more defensive, and they were once again mobilized by the Conservatives, now as the party of free enterprise. How far the Conservative Party could actually have been an agent for an Americanized politics is debatable. It was never a wholly middle-class party. It was an alliance of an older political and social elite and a newer middle class. That elite had little interest in an Americanized system, nor in a politically active membership which would have seemed the corollary. The 'retinue' structure of the local Conservative Associations with their passive membership and essentially social function was not conducive to democratic politics. And they were given little encouragement to practise it.

The second alternative—one the Second World War could easily have thrown up—though not wholly antithetical to the first, was nonetheless very different: an English social democracy based upon economic redistribution on the one hand and democratized political and social institutions on the other. The Labour Party went some way towards the former, but hardly any way towards

---

[30] See also McKibbin, *Classes and Cultures*, 533–6.

the latter. In doing (or not doing) this there was probably a tactical element. Economic reforms arguably could be made more acceptable to those likely to be hostile if they were implemented within the old social system: monarchic socialism was less alarming than republican socialism. But this cannot be anything like a complete explanation. In the 1940s, rather, the Labour Party was led by a generation that thought serious institutional reform was incidental or of little interest to its electorate, and who were too ideologically and personally attached to the institutional status quo anyway.

Unlike the leadership of the Conservative Party, the social character of Labour's leadership changed markedly between 1914 and 1951. Although aristocractic and 'territorial' influences had declined in the interwar years the Conservative Party's leadership remained aristocratic-gentry-upper middle class: that was the tone of the Party throughout. Labour's leadership, however, as we have seen, was predominantly working class at the beginning of the period but predominantly educated middle class at its end. Had the Party's leadership remained working class would it have made any difference? Perhaps; but those working-class leaders were themselves very divided in their attitudes to the institutional status quo. They were, it is true, suspicious of the old hierarchies and disliked many of their manifestations. But they were also in awe of them and Britain's parliamentary constitutionalism, and freely accepted the existence of a 'non-political' public sphere whose rules were usually devised by others. Those who were critical, if they lived long enough, usually came to terms with tradition, especially after the Second World War. David Kirkwood, once a Clydeside incendiary, in due course accepted his peerage. Furthermore, history held them in its firm embrace. The late-Victorian and Edwardian political and social systems had in practice strongly favoured the organized working class in Britain—almost more than in any other comparable country—and, like the autodidacts they often were, many of its leaders found it difficult to imagine a different one.[31] The succeeding middle-class leadership, however, was also ambivalent. Many, like Attlee, had no quarrel with the country's status system; and that was true of most of Attlee's cabinet. A later generation, from the less well-established middle class, were more sceptical. But their scepticism was often economic rather than political. Like the young Harold Wilson they were inclined to think that the old system was 'inefficient' and a cause of Britain's apparent international uncompetitiveness. This criticism was to grow stronger in the later 1950s. But, like Attlee's 'generation', they also were nervous of attacking anything strongly defended. In the 1960s, Anthony Crosland, in theory a strong egalitarian, was happy to abolish the grammar schools, but would not touch the public schools nor forbid the direct-grant schools from becoming public schools.

The moral consensus celebrated by Shils and Young two years after Labour had weakly surrendered office was thus a consensus largely constructed by Labour's opponents—though not without concessions. As the 1930s failed to produce a functioning individualist democracy, so the 1940s failed to produce a functioning social democracy. What emerged was an awkward compromise based upon a tacit agreement between the Conservative and Labour Parties: a semi-democratic quasi-constitutionalism which had accommodated significant social and political change and whose legitimacy derived from the stability it seemed to guarantee. But as a system it came under increasing stress when it found itself unable any longer to accommodate such change. Indeed, it was more likely to obstruct it. English society became, so to speak, more democratic of its own accord. The social hierarchies and conventions which once underpinned it decayed, but did so within formal social and political institutions that remained largely unreformed. The two—social

---

[31] I have argued this elsewhere. McKibbin, *Ideologies of Class*, 16–23. See also above, 81–2.

change and institutional rigidity—worked against each other. This in turn meant that these institutions could no longer guarantee the stability which was their legitimating function. Such was the legacy of the 1940s to the later twentieth century: a society with powerful democratic impulses but political structures and habits of mind which could not adequately contain them. It was an unresolved tension which was to dog England for the rest of the century.

Index

Abrams, M. 110–11
Addison, C. 26, 39, 84 n
Addison, P. 114
Amalgamated Society of Engineers
	(ASE), 135
Amery, L. 139
Anglicanism, Anglicans 39,91; *see also*
	Conservative Party
Anti-Waste 48–9
Army Bureau of Current Affairs
	(ABCA) 113
Asquith, H.H. 22, 23, 25, 27, 29, 38,
	61
Assheton, R. 166
Attlee government 110, 143, 144, 152,
	153, 158, 163, 197–8, 201
Attlee, C.R. 123, 134, 160, 164, 174,
	201
Australia 19, 57, 79
autodidactic tradition 84, 104, 200

Balderston, T. 56
Baldwin, S. 37, 41, 42, 54, 55, 61, 64,
	65, 85, 91, 95, 101, 130, 167, 179
Balfour, A. 4
Barlow Commission (Royal
	Commission on the Distribution
	of the Industrial
	Population, 1937), 107
Barry, E. 150, 158
Bates, J. 38
Bealey, F. 172
Beaverbrook, Lord 55
Bevan, A. 141, 144 n, 154, 175
Beveridge Report 127, 133, 136, 138,
	143, 144, 188, 192
Bevin, E. 75, 81, 84, 86, 121, 150
Blake, R. 14
blitz 123, 124–5, 126, 127, 133
Bonar Law, A. 14, 34, 37, 54
Bowley, A.L. 42
British Institute of Public Opinion
	(BIPO) polls 114, 117; *see also*
	Gallup polls
British Journey 129

British Legion 94
Brodie, M. 190
Brooke, S. 146
Burgin, L. 167
Butler, R.A. 161, 165, 167, 176, 197

Cairncross, A. 151–2
Cairo 'parliament' 113–4
capital levy 45, 50–2
Carson, E. 22
Chamberlain A. 34, 37, 40, 45
Chamberlain government 104, 118,
	130, 177
Chamberlain, J. 19, 54, 55, 91
Chamberlain, N. 65, 89, 107, 114,
	115, 117, 120, 132, 180
Chamberlainite Conservatism 118
Channon, H. ('Chips') 146
Christian democracy 148, 157
Churchill coalition 119
Churchill, W.S. 21, 26, 38, 45, 62,
	116, 119, 121, 134, 161, 165,
	176, 180, 195
Citadel, The 107
Clynes, J.H. 83, 86
Cockett, O. 120, 130
Cole, G.D.H. 142
Cole, M. 82 n, 131
Conservative Party and
	Anglicanism 13, 96, 189
	and anti-alienism 190–1
	and anti-Catholicism 189–90
	and anti-socialism 14, 61, 65–6,
		101, 181
	and democracy 182, 199
	and Liberal land campaign 11
	and middle class 177–8, 199
	and nonconformity 24, 91–2, 168
	and Representation of the People Act
		(1918), 28
	and Taff Vale Judgment 4
	and social background of
		parliamentary candidates 38,
		169
	and tariff reform 12, 54–5, 88